Management
for a
Small Planet

Management for a Small Planet

Third Edition

Jean Garner Stead and W. Edward Stead

M.E.Sharpe
Armonk, New York
London, England

Library of Congress Cataloging-in-Publication Data

Stead, Jean Garner.
Management for a small planet / by Jean Garner Stead and W. Edward Stead—3rd ed.
p. cm.
Previous ed. entered under: Stead, W. Edward.
Includes bibliographical references and index.
ISBN 978-0-7656-2308-9 (cloth : alk. paper)
1. Economic development—Environmental aspects. 2. Natural resources—Management.
3. Strategic planning. 4. Industrial management—Environmental aspects. I. Stead,
W. Edward. II. Stead, W. Edward. Management for a small planet. III. Title.

HD75.6.S74 2009
333.7—dc22   2009002560

Printed in the United States of America

This book is printed with soy ink on recycled paper

The paper used in this publication meets the minimum requirements of
American National Standard for Information Sciences
Permanence of Paper for Printed Library Materials,
ANSI Z 39.48-1984.

CW (c)   10   9   8   7   6   5   4   3   2   1

Dedicated to:
Garner Lee and Mike
and
"The Cousins"
You are our family, and we love you all

Contents

Preface

We began our journey toward this third edition of *Management for a Small Planet* at Western Illinois University in 1977. Jean was teaching economics and working on her MBA at the time, and Ed was teaching organizational development, organizational behavior, and organizational theory. While doing research for an MBA paper, Jean was introduced to the works of Herman Daly on steady state economics. It was a paradigm-shifting moment for her. Daly challenged everything she had learned while earning her undergraduate and master's degrees in economics, and it didn't take long for her to bring Ed into the fold. She passionately introduced him to the works of Daly, E.F. Schumacher, and others who were systematically debunking the unlimited-growth-is-possible-and-desirable-forever myth fostered in mainstream economics. We pursued our newfound interests with intensity over the next couple of years, all the while preparing many of our meals from Frances Moore Lappe's *Diet for a Small Planet*. In 1979 we decided to write a book for managers that expressed our passion, and it didn't take much of a creative juxtaposition for the title to reveal itself to us: *Management for a Small Planet*. Four years later Jean earned her PhD at Louisiana State University, having the opportunity to study under both Herman Daly and corporate social responsibility pioneer Edmund Gray. From that point forward we read, studied, and developed our ideas and frameworks, and in 1992 the first edition of *Management for a Small Planet* was published.

The publication of that book opened the door to a very rewarding academic career for us, including the publication of the second edition of *Management for a Small Planet* in 1996 and the publication of *Sustainable Strategic Management* in 2004. In addition to having the opportunity to publish our ideas, one of the most rewarding aspects of our career has been our associations with our colleagues in the Organizations and the Natural Environment Division and the Social Issues in Management Division of the Academy of Management. These fine people have worked tirelessly over the years to ensure that the greater social system and ecosystem in which business organizations are embedded are given their just due in management education and research. It has been and continues to be a real privilege for us to count these dedicated people among our colleagues and friends.

Parallel with our academic journey over the past 30 years has been our family journey. Our daughter, Garner Lee, was born in 1980. From the moment she arrived, she was the heart and soul of our spiritual and emotional motivation to contribute to the preservation of the human habitat. With her came the sudden realization that this planet does not belong to us. It belongs to our children and our children's children. During the early years of her life, Garner Lee taught us that we are all links in the chain of human existence and that it is our responsibility to keep the chain strong for generations to come. Garner Lee was 12 years old when the first edition of this book was published and she is 29 now. She has earned her undergraduate and master's degrees, she is married to a wonderful young man named Mike Green, and they both have established solid careers in New York City—hers in education and his in financial management. They are planning to have their own children soon, and there is a good chance that their children and grandchildren will be around to usher in the twenty-second century on January 1, 2100. Seeing our own family chain stretch out before us in this way gives us more resolve than ever to be a viable part of the sustainability revolution going on in the world today.

There are many people who have contributed their time and effort to making this book as good as it can be. As with all of our other books, we must begin by thanking our M.E. Sharpe editor, Harry Briggs. We've been working with Harry since we sent him three sample chapters from the first edition of *Management for a Small Planet* in late 1990. He has been in our corner ever since. No one works harder than Harry to ensure that we have a quality book, and no one works harder than Harry to promote our work in the marketplace. As we've said in all four of our book prefaces, you are the best, Harry.

Our most special thanks go to Mark Cordano of Ithaca College for all of his invaluable assistance with this book. He encouraged us to write this new edition of *Management for a Small Planet* long before we ever considered doing it, and he walked with us every step of the way as we completed it. He spent many hours in open discussion with us, he read and edited every chapter for us, and he gave us very valuable feedback on our ideas and the ways that we presented them. Mark's diligent input improved both what we said and how we said it. He epitomizes the true meaning of the words—colleague and friend—and we are forever in his debt for all that he did to help us with this book.

Our special thanks also go to Jim Powell, founder and CEO of the Powell Companies, and to the James and Sandy Powell Foundation for funding Jean's 2007–8 academic leave from East Tennessee State University (ETSU). Because of this kind support from Jim and the foundation, Jean was able to take a year away from teaching in order to bring this book to completion. In this same vein we would like to thank Phil Miller, chairperson of ETSU's Management and Marketing Department, and Linda Garceau, dean of ETSU's College of Business and Technology, for their support of Ed's 2008–9 noninstructional leave, which gave us the time we needed to successfully complete this project.

Our sincere thanks also go to our graduate assistants—Ashley McMurray, Jason Kuan, and Phillip Carney—who put in many hours gathering and synthesizing information for this new edition of *Management for a Small Planet*. Also, our special thanks to both Ashley and Jason for taking their valuable time to read and comment on each chapter. Their efforts added significantly to the content of this book, and their comments added significantly to its quality.

There are also some very important family members who deserve our thanks—"the cousins," Hank, Donna, Blakley, and Wil Appleton, Janet and Ken Payton, and Stanley and Susie Appleton. Over the past few years while this book was being gestated, researched, and written these kinfolk have given us their unconditional love, support, encouragement, and companionship. They will always have our deepest gratitude. They have enriched us, they have broadened our perspectives, they have been our true friends, and they have been there whenever we have needed them (which has been often). We are truly blessed by their presence in our lives.

Finally, we want to thank our all-important Auburn support group: Gregg and Martha Shepherd and Mike and Linda Davis. They have turned what could have been the drudgery of many long, lonely workdays into fun and meaningful companionship. Happy hours at Mellow Mushroom, beers and oysters at Touchdowns, gumbo and grits at Christopher's, cooking out, watching ballgames, talking on the phone, and just spending time together have all made the last several months a blast. Thanks so much for your friendship. To you and to the cousins we say, War Eagle!

As we come to the beginning of this book, we want to make the point that the world is rapidly reaching a crossroads. Since we wrote the first edition of this book in 1992, the population of the planet has grown from 5.4 billion to 6.6 billion. That means humankind has essentially added the equivalent of another China or India to its ranks in 16 short years. Unfortunately, this has happened (and is continuing to happen) on a small planet that has finite resources, such as water, topsoil, energy, and species, and a finite potential for continued economic growth. Thus managers are now faced with the need to dedicate the considerable wealth, power, and influence of their organizations to the development and implementation of more sustainable ways of doing business. We hope that this new edition of *Management for a Small Planet* offers them viable ways to do this.

Peaceful solutions,
Jean and Ed Stead

Part I

Business Happens on a Small Planet

For most of the Industrial Revolution, business organizations have operated as if they didn't exist on planet Earth. The economic models that have driven the rise of the global economy over the past 350 years have historically been based on the assumption that humans can produce, deliver, consume, and throw away billions upon billions of products every day forever without stressing either the Earth or the people and other species that inhabit it. The primary purpose of Part I, which consists of the first four chapters, is to debunk this assumption and replace it with a more realistic, twenty-first century view of the relationships among business organizations, society, and the natural environment. In this new view, business organizations function in an economy that coevolves with the planet and its people.

1

— 1 —

Management Meets a Small Planet

It is important that readers understand from the beginning that we are not in any way trying to convince business managers that it is their altruistic responsibility to help "save the planet." Nothing could be further from the truth. After all, as James Lovelock (1979) clearly demonstrated in his "Gaia hypothesis," the Earth does not need saving. It can take very good care of itself. Recall that 65 million years ago, a giant comet or meteor collided with the planet somewhere off the coast of the Yucatan Peninsula. Fallout from the collision covered the Earth with a huge layer of ash, and it created a nuclear winter that eventually wiped out 70 percent of the planet's species including what remained of the dinosaurs (Anonymous 2002). However, despite the massive collision and resulting fallout the Earth was not destroyed and has since renewed itself many times over.

Thus, even if all of the combined powers of every corporation and every nation on the globe were focused on destroying the planet, the Earth would survive and continue to thrive. What would be lost with such mass destruction would be a human-friendly habitat—farmable land; abundant natural resources; supplies of fresh water; rich, life-sustaining oceans; protective, biodiverse forests and wetlands; and a favorable climate—that make the Earth such a nice home for humankind. There is little doubt that the Earth itself will remain and continue to carry numerous living species, probably including some humans, as it rotates on its axis once every 24 hours and around its energy-giving sun once every year. However, if humans continue to foul their own nest through incessant global production, delivery, and consumption of products and services then the water, trees, land, atmosphere, and oceans that make this planet such a nice place to live will shrink. Thus, we see no need to offer managers some overly sentimental formula for saving the planet. Rather, what we are offering managers is an approach to managing their organizations that will help them to make positive contributions to improving and preserving humankind's habitat and quality of life now and in the future.

The Earth Is a Small Planet

Lovelock (1979, 1988) has shown that the Earth humans know today is neither a product of geology nor biology alone. Rather, it is the result of coevolution in which "the evolution of the species and the evolution of their environment are tightly coupled together as a single and inseparable process" (Lovelock 1988, 12). Before the Industrial Revolution began around 1650, these coevolutionary processes had resulted in an ecological balance between plant life, animal life, and the planetary systems that support both. Up to that point global human population was small, and people employed their machines in very limited ways—using wheels for wagons and grain mills, for example. Most of the population was engaged in agriculture, and most people spent their time simply trying to survive. Life was very hard and tenuous, and population growth was slow.

Then came the Industrial Revolution with its powerful fossil-fuel energy sources, mass-production techniques, and modern transportation and communication systems. Over the past 350 years humankind moved away from older forms of society whose primary activities were hunting, raising livestock, planting, gathering, and milling to the modern industrial society of today. During that time, survival has become much easier and more secure for those who can afford it. Modern farming techniques have made it possible to raise sufficient amounts of food for humans to consume. High-speed communications and transportation have made it possible to speak and carry on face-to-face conversations with almost anyone in the world in a matter of seconds and to be on their doorsteps in a matter of hours. Modern medicine has transformed deadly illnesses of the past into minor irritations today. During this time the human species has survived and thrived on the planet, growing to 6.6 billion people in 2008.

However, the Earth isn't getting any larger. This beautiful blue-green marble is still only 25,000 miles in circumference, 75 percent water, and much of the rest uninhabitable mountain, desert, and frozen tundra.

The Earth's natural resources are being depleted, and wastes are being generated at rates unheard of in human history. Ecologically the climate is changing, tropical forests are being cleared to make way for economic progress, water tables are being drawn down to dangerous levels throughout the world, and soil erosion is exceeding soil replenishment rates. Like the lemmings of Arctic Norway, human breeding and consumption are outstripping existing resources.

All of this would be acceptable if it were not for the fact that the life-giving and life-supporting processes of the Earth are currently operating in a rather closed ecosystem. The more open a system is—that is, the more it can exchange energy, information, and wastes with its environment—the more renewing it can be. This is because an open system is able to import sufficient amounts of energy from its environment, and it can expel the waste products back into the environment. However, the more closed a system is, the less renewing it can be because it can neither import sufficient quantities of energy, nor can it develop sufficient capacity to dispose of its wastes. Open and closed are relative terms. As a system, the Earth has only one significant energy input from its environment—solar flow, the sun. Through photosynthesis, solar energy provides the Earth with the power to feed its species; it also provides the basic energy for water and wind cycles. The remainder of the planet's energy is tied directly to terrestrial resources such as oil, coal, wood, natural gas, and uranium. Further, the Earth must absorb the wastes generated when energy is converted into products and services consumed by human beings. These wastes are often buried in the ground, dumped in the water, or spewed into the air.

For all but the last 350 years of the 4.5 billion-year history of the Earth, these mechanisms provided a more than adequate amount of openness to meet the needs of life on the planet. It has only been during the Industrial Age that humankind has been using the Earth's resources and discharging wastes at rates faster than renewal can take place. This means that the balance the planet once enjoyed has in 350 years—a split second of eternity—essentially disappeared. As humans are now learning the hard way, this unprecedented short-term human experiment has the potential for disastrous social and ecological consequences for both present and future generations. Climate change, poverty, human health, food security, water security, gender equity, literacy, the digital divide, urbanization, suburbanization, political instability, and failing states are some of the consequences.

As these environmental and social issues make clear, the Earth is indeed a small planet, one that must support a rapidly growing number of human beings seeking the improved lifestyles promised by the Industrial Revolution. By 2050 this planet will have 9 billion people or so, and that puts humankind in somewhat of a mathematical bind. Like the lemmings, humans are doing everything possible to squeeze more and more from less and less. In the process, the Earth's natural resources are being consumed faster than they can be renewed, and social issues are growing in terms of both quantity and severity. Although it has been known for years that the results for the human species may be nothing short of disastrous if civilization fails to adjust its rates of economic activity to the evolutionary processes of nature, the experiment continues at full throttle. Many believe that humans can save themselves from these problems with new technologies; however, this promise remains unfulfilled. Real change will require new values and new ways of thinking.

Becoming Part of Something Larger

Developing these new values and new ways of thinking in business organizations begins with the understanding that making positive contributions to quality of life while earning a profit is a critical part of doing business on today's small planet Earth. In his keynote address at the 1992 Institute of Noetic Sciences convention, engineer, psychologist, author, and philanthropist Charles Garfield talked in depth about his career which has included being an engineer on the first moon landing project, a venture capitalist, and a clinical psychologist working with indigent terminal cancer patients. His clear and profound message that day was that his career had been so fulfilling because he'd had so many opportunities to contribute to something larger and more important than just himself by helping put a person on the moon, providing opportunities for budding entrepreneurs, and providing comfort to those who needed him the most. In fact, contributing to something larger and more important has long been recognized as a primary pathway to fulfilling the human spirit. That is, contributing to the greater good provides humans with a sense of joy, happiness, satisfaction, enlightenment, peacefulness, self-control, and/or creative expression.

In fact, what Garfield did for himself is something that numerous scholars have advocated for years that organizations can and should do for themselves: contribute to the greater good (Halal 1986; Handy 1989;

Maslow 1962; Schumacher 1973, 1977; Senge 1990; Senge et al. 2008). They have said that organizations should focus more clearly on their roles in contributing to the quality of life in the larger community and they should create structures, processes, and outputs designed to fulfill the social and ecological as well as the economic needs of the humans whose lives they touch (employees, customers, etc.). The principles, frameworks, and practices we present in this book, which we collectively refer to as "sustainable organizational management," open up many opportunities for organizations to achieve such a higher purpose by allowing them to put economic success, social responsibility, and ecological protection in their proper perspectives.

There is definitely a rise in consciousness happening regarding the health of the planet and the people who inhabit it. Hawken (2007, 12) says that environmental, social, and cultural forces are currently converging into a worldwide "movement [that] expresses the needs of the majority of people on Earth to sustain the environment, wage peace, democratize decision making and policy, rejuvenate public governance . . . and improve their lives . . ." In researching his book, Hawken (2007) began with the idea that there are at least 100,000 environmental and social justice organizations across the globe that are part of this movement, but he soon discovered that the number is closer to a million. He found these organizations to be quite diverse, focusing on a wide variety of global, regional, and local issues.

Edwards (2005) also contends that there is a movement happening. He says that we are now making a transition from the Industrial Revolution to what he calls the "sustainability revolution." He justifies his stance by pointing to the fact that the sustainability revolution is currently going through the three phases typical of all social revolutions: genesis, critical mass, and diffusion. He says that the revolution had its beginnings (its genesis) in the 1970s and 1980s, and that it is currently in the process of building the necessary critical mass and worldwide diffusion. Speth (2008) echoes both Hawken and Edwards in their assertions that there is a new consciousness arising based on concerns for the Earth and its people.

Although both Hawken (2007) and Edwards (2005) present optimistic pictures of the kinds of changes that are happening, both along with Speth (2008) agree that things have not changed yet. Hawken (2007) says that the movement is currently long on ideas but short on solutions because it lacks the financial support it needs to develop and implement the solutions. Edwards (2005) sees the sustainability revolution moving toward but not yet reaching the critical mass and diffusion levels it needs to be truly world-changing. Speth (2008) expresses some disappointment regarding the impacts that the environmental movement has had to this point, and he (along with numerous others) expresses some doubts about humankind having enough time to change before real disasters occur.

We believe that business organizations pursuing the principles and practices of sustainable organizational management are the keys to the success of this movement. Dunphy, Griffiths, and Benn (2007, 4) say, "Corporations have contributed to the problems . . . and they must therefore be part of the answer." If business organizations across the globe were to universally adopt sustainable organizational management, it would infuse a huge force for change into the sustainability revolution (Senge 2007). The one million social and environmental groups working hard to move the world toward sustainability would be joined in the movement by millions of business organizations seeking ways to make social and environmental responsibility a larger part of doing business. The addition of these organizations would create the critical mass of people and organizations across the planet necessary for changing to a sustainable world. Also, it would infuse into the movement the desperately needed financial resources so critical for turning the good ideas of creative people into actions that lead to real change. That is why we say that the time is now for business organizations to expand their responsibilities and strategies beyond the economic to the social and ecological dimensions. If the assessments of Edwards (2005), Hawken (2007), Speth (2008), and others are correct then this is the ideal time for organizations to contribute to a planet that is fiscally, socially, and ecologically welcoming for all human beings now and in the future.

A New Perspective for Managers

What managers do has remained constant since the field emerged in the late 1800s and early1900s with the works of Frederick Taylor, Henri Fayol, Max Weber, and numerous other pioneers. Managers are as responsible today as ever for establishing strategies, building organizational structures, directing and leading employees, and establishing control systems that will allow their organizations to function in effective and efficient ways. However, while their responsibilities have changed very little the environment in which managers do their jobs has changed drastically. Since the days of Taylor and his colleagues, the environment has become more turbulent, more unpredictable, and more complex with more critical factors for managers to consider when making their decisions regarding the strategies, structures, and processes of their organizations.

Among the most critical environmental factors visible on the radar screen of managers in recent years are the impacts their products and services are having on the global community and the natural environment. Classic business education has erroneously informed managers over the years that their decisions are made in a closed economic system which functions independently of both the social and natural environments. By assuming away both society and nature, managers have been taught (at least implicitly) that the organizational decisions they make are unaffected by the physical laws of the universe, the natural processes and cycles of nature, or the values and conditions of society.

Assuming away society and the environment has led managers to believe that the economy can grow forever without any serious social and ecological consequences as insatiable consumers seek to buy more and more stuff from further and further away to satisfy their never-ending list of economic desires. Unfortunately, the data say otherwise. For example in 2005 alone, 9.3 billion tons of oil (over 1.4 tons per capita worldwide) was used to power a global economy that spewed 7.6 billion tons of carbon (almost 1.2 tons per capita) into the atmosphere (Assadourian 2007a). Annual figures like these clearly show why all of the ecosystem services that support life on Earth—the atmosphere, geosphere, hydrosphere, and biosphere—are stressed due to humankind's insatiable economic appetite; yet, huge numbers of people continue to live in abject poverty without having their basic needs met. According to Assadourian (2007a, 9), "The economy, like a cancer, is consuming the very systems that we need to survive."

Data like these strongly suggest that today's managers require a different perspective on the role organizations play in society and the ecosystem. Thus, managers practicing sustainable organizational management recognize that both society and nature are critical factors in managerial decision making. They understand that there are natural limits to economic growth beyond which human quality of life on the Earth is threatened, and they recognize that the economy functions within and serves the needs of society.

Sustainability: Transcending the Manager's Divergent Dilemmas

Sustainable organizational management is designed to provide managers with ways to integrate "sustainability" into the decision-making processes at every level of their organizations. The classic definition of sustainability is "development that meets the needs of the present without compromising the ability of the future generations to meet their own needs" (World Commission on Environment and Development 1987, 8). Sustainability is generally considered to have three interdependent, coevolutionary dimensions: the economy, the society, and the natural environment. The interactions among these three dimensions are complex, and many of these interactions lie outside the realm of traditional business models. As such, integrating sustainability into organizational-management principles and practices will require that managers think differently—not just act differently—about the relationships among the economy, society, and the natural environment.

It is well established that humans' thoughts and actions are framed and guided by their values. Thus, managers wishing to adopt sustainable organizational management will likely need to examine their organizations' values. Values serve both as data filters, determining what information managers attend to and how they interpret it, and as decision shapers, providing the frameworks upon which final decisions are based (Schwenk 1988). Values are generally arranged in systems, which are complex networks of related values. At the center of these networks are "core values," values that define the essence of the value system. Core values are considered good in and of themselves, are typically few in number, are enduring, and are difficult to change. Core values provide the overarching ideals upon which organizational ethical systems and behaviors are based.

E.F. Schumacher (1977) believed that quantitative measures and linear logic are quite sufficient for the plethora of linear, "convergent" problems that humankind regularly faces. He uses the modes of transportation that have developed over the centuries as examples of the power of applying quantitative analysis and rational thought to convergent problems. However, he pointed out that value-based problems are not convergent in nature; rather, they are "divergent." Thus, unlike convergent problems, divergent problems defy solutions attained with rational linear logic. The more straight-line logic applied to such problems, the more diametrically opposed and outrageous the solutions tend to become. Finding a meaningful solution to a divergent problem means finding values that transcend the polar opposite dichotomies that characterize the problem. Schumacher used the slogan of the French Revolution, "liberty, equality, fraternity," to demonstrate this. The slogan represents two diametrically opposed forces—liberty and equality—that can only exist together under the transcendent value of fraternity. That is, only when a society's members value brotherly love and respect for one another can they be both free and equal; without fraternity, the freedom versus equality dichotomy will ultimately lead to the domination of the weak by the strong.

The divergent problems focused on most extensively in the writings of Schumacher (1973, 1977, 1979) are the seemingly dichotomous dilemmas posed by the relationships among the economy, society, and ecology. Growth versus no growth, wealth versus beauty, wealth versus poverty, jobs versus the environment, economic development versus local culture, people as means versus people as ends, and nature as means versus nature as ends are but a few of these dilemmas. Bipolar positions like these create the perception that there are inherent, unsolvable conflicts among economic success and social responsibility, economic success and ecological health, and social responsibility and ecological health. Schumacher said that operating within these dichotomies creates pathways to resource depletion, environmental degradation, worker alienation, and violence.

Schumacher (1973) coined the phrase "small is beautiful" to symbolize his belief that humankind's solutions to these problems lie in transcending these destructive dichotomies. He referred to the process of searching for values that can transcend such seemingly unsolvable divergent problems as seeking the "middle way." Sustainability—the belief in a high quality of life for posterity—provides the middle way for transcending the perceived economy-society-ecology dichotomies. Via sustainability the façade of these dichotomies can be penetrated and debunked, allowing society to seek sustainable economic development that provides citizens with good jobs while protecting and promoting the environment and culture. This is why we refer to sustainability as the transcendent core value that anchors sustainable organizational management.

Organizations Coevolving with Their Environments

Coevolution is a term that originated in the biological sciences. Ehrlich and Raven (1964) first used the term to describe their observations that different species of butterflies and plants evolve together. The research of Lovelock (1979, 1988), Margulis (Margulis and Hinkle 1991), and others extended the idea of coevolution beyond the symbiotic relationships among living organisms by showing that the Earth's life forms have coevolved not only with one another but also with the Earth's geosphere, atmosphere, and hydrosphere. For example, Lovelock (1988) demonstrated that animal size has coevolved with the oxygen content in the atmosphere over the eons of Earth's existence, eventually creating enough oxygen in the atmosphere to support the breathing needs of large mammals such as humans.

Coevolution is currently emerging as a major framework in the organizational sciences (Lewin, Long, and Carroll 1999; Lewin and Volberda 2003b; T. Porter 2006). In the late 1800s, Max Weber implied that organization-environment relationships are coevolutionary when he posited that bureaucracy emerged from social conditions created by the Industrial Revolution. A century later, both Senge (1990) and March (1991) demonstrated what is rapidly becoming a commonly held belief in the field of management: Organizations learn and change through coevolutionary relationships with their environments (Lewin, Long, and Carroll 1999). These organization-environment relationships are interdependent, mutually causal (circular), and iterative (Baum and Singh 1994). Terry Porter (2006, 5) and Lewin and Volberda (2003b) point out that the underlying principles and processes of coevolution are at the "conceptual nexus" of several well-established organizational science frameworks including systems theory, contingency theory, organizational ecology theories, institutional theory, complexity theory, and others.

Using literature from both the biological and organizational sciences, Terry Porter (2006) develops six criteria necessary for organization-environment relationships to be considered coevolutionary: The first three—specificity, reciprocity, and simultaneity—originate from the biological roots of coevolution. Taken together, these three criteria say that each entity in a coevolutionary relationship must affect the others in specific ways leading to simultaneous changes in and among all the entities in the relationship. Porter's next three criteria—which originate from the organizational sciences—say that coevolutionary relationships between organizations and their environments typically involve boundary-crossing interrelationships at multiple levels, are more adaptive and responsive than planned and deliberate, and generally lead to permanent change in all the entities involved.

At the heart of this book is the assumption that there are coevolutionary relationships between organizations, the people they employ and serve, the economy they participate in, the society they are a part of, and the planet they exist on. Figure 1.1 depicts these coevolutionary relationships. In this model, the Earth is a living system whose survival is dependent on achieving a sustainable balance within its various interdependent subsystems. At the center of the model are the planet's most dominant species, people. Because of their dominance, the decisions made by people are major forces influencing the ultimate state of the economy, society, and nature. Of course, humans make their decisions in a variety of contexts, including families, religious organizations, educational institutions, governmental agencies, and interest groups. In the economic realm, people make decisions as members of organizations that produce goods and services, and they make decisions as consumers who purchase and use those goods and services. Collectively the organizations that produce the goods and services and the consumers who purchase them make up the economy, the system that encompasses the global production-consumption cycles. The economy is embedded in the greater society it serves, and society, in turn, is embedded in the natural environment, the biophysical system to which all life on Earth is bound. The model also shows the flow of solar energy that provides fuel for the systems to operate, it depicts the terrestrial resources in nature that provide the materials and energy necessary for economic activity, and it shows that the wastes generated during economic activity are absorbed back into the natural environment.

A cursory examination of the model demonstrates that the relationships among its variables meet the criteria for coevolutionary relationships discussed above. For example, changes in population have specific, interdependent, reciprocal, circular, iterative, simultaneous impacts on the number of consumers, the number of organizations, the amount of economic activity, the size and complexity of society, the availability and cost of terrestrial resources, and the amount of wastes generated on the planet. These relationships cross all the model's boundaries, and they lead to permanent changes in all variables at all levels of the model.

Pursuing the Triple Bottom Line

As mentioned above, managing organizations in the open coevolutionary environment depicted in Figure 1.1 requires a very different mental framework from the one grounded in neoclassical economics that says

Figure 1.1   **The Coevolutionary Economy**

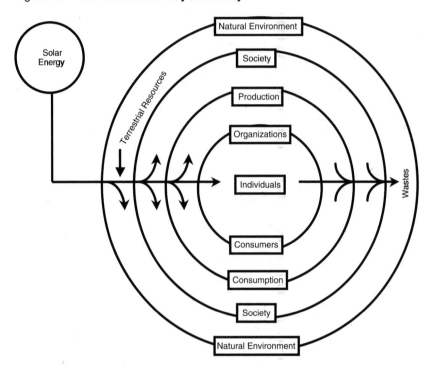

Source: W. Edward Stead and Jean Garner Stead. 1996. *Management for a Small Planet.* Thousand Oaks, CA: Sage Publications.

organizations function in a closed economic environment that is separate from the social and natural environments. This new mental framework is founded on the three dimensions of sustainability discussed above: the economy, society, and nature. Thus, whereas in the neoclassical framework managerial success is defined solely by managers' contributions to the financial profits of the firm, in sustainable organizational management managerial success is based on earning profits in ways that also contribute to the good of society and the natural environment.

A popular sustainable organizational management framework used by several organizations (such as Royal Dutch Shell, Ford, and KPMG) to capture their commitment to all three dimensions of sustainability is the "triple bottom line" (Elkington 1997; see Figure 1.2). Firms pursuing the triple bottom line are committed to economic success that both enhances and is enhanced by their concerns for the greater social and ecological

Figure 1.2   **The Triple Bottom Line**

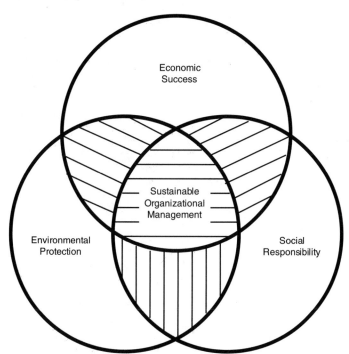

contexts in which they exist. Because organizations are generally familiar with the bottom-line concept, the triple-bottom-line image can be
more easily integrated into current organizational cultures. Further, the
framework allows managers to more clearly focus their organizational
initiatives at those points where economic success, social responsibility,
and/or ecological health intersect. Thus, using the triple bottom line as a
managerial framework allows organizations to map out a future that is
consistent with the three tenets of sustainability, and it allows organizations to more clearly define the roles and responsibilities of managers
in achieving that future.

Transforming to Sustainable Organizational Management

It is clear from the above discussion that successfully implementing
sustainable organizational management will require that organizations
learn to effectively manage the endless stream of mutually causal,

simultaneous changes they face in their coevolutionary relationships with their economic, social, and natural environments. Thus, managing organizational change effectively is a critical requirement for successful sustainable organizational management. There are three basic requirements for successful organizational change efforts. First, they require the active support and participation by managers at all organizational levels from the strategic level down to the operational level. Second, they require collaborative open dialogue and consensus-building processes that allow all relevant stakeholders (internal and external) to have a say about what issues exist, what changes are to be made, and how those changes are to be made. Third, they require that both the changes made in the organization and the processes used to make those changes are effectively integrated into the culture of the organization.

With regard to the third requirement, cultural integration, an organization's culture is composed of the artifacts (language, rituals, symbols, etc.), norms, values, beliefs, and assumptions shared by its members. These cultural elements exist in a hierarchy ranging from the more surface-level artifacts and norms to the deeper-level values, beliefs, and assumptions (Schein 1985). There are varying degrees of organizational change depending on the level of organizational culture targeted by the change effort (Bartunek and Moch 1987). Change efforts targeted at the shallower levels of the organization's culture involve more adaptive, incremental changes, focusing on changing surface-level artifacts and norms so that the organization can do what it currently does better than before.

However as change touches the deeper, value-based levels of culture, change efforts are required to be more transformational requiring organizations to employ dialogue processes that allow them to closely examine and change the underlying values, beliefs, and assumptions that define the essence of who they are and what they do. Transformational change is discontinuous, requiring that organizations achieve and perpetuate an entirely different qualitative state. Organizations attempting transformational change cannot expect to be successful by taking the slow, linear steps associated with incremental organizational-change efforts. Rather, transformational change requires fundamental efforts designed to completely shift the consciousness of the firm to a different level based on new values. This shift to a new consciousness can only be accomplished by changing the values that underlie the current organizational consciousness (Beckhard and Pritchard 1992; Senge 1990).

Scholars have long held that successfully implementing sustainable organizational management requires organizations to implement transformational-change processes that allow them to examine and redefine their core values, the nature of their work, and their relationships with their stakeholders at all levels—economic, social, and environmental (Dunphy, Griffiths, and Benn 2007; Freeman, Pierce, and Dodd 2000; Gladwin, Kennelly, and Krause 1995; Post and Altman 1992, 1994; Stead and Stead 1994). Post and Altman (1992, 13) said years ago, "Internal paradigm shifts and transformational change are necessary as companies attempt to adjust to the rapidly changing world of green politics and markets." More recently, Dunphy, Griffiths, and Benn (2007) pointed out that business organizations have been largely responsible for transforming the planet into the hyper-growth, environmentally and socially challenged planet we know today. Now it's time for these organizations to transform themselves in ways that will allow them to better contribute to planetary health, social responsibility, and human quality of life. Thus, as social and ecological concerns continue to move into the forefront of the issues facing humankind, organizations across the globe wishing to join the sustainability revolution will need to become adept at designing and implementing socially and ecologically responsible transformational change processes.

Plan of the Book

The book is divided into two parts. Part I, Business Happens on a Small Planet, is designed to provide an in-depth, sustainability-based picture of today's business environment. In addition to this chapter, Part I includes Chapters 2, 3, and 4. In this chapter, we have stated the purpose of the book, we have introduced the idea of sustainability—the central concept around which the book is built—and we have introduced some of the critical sustainable organizational management concepts that will be developed as we proceed. The next three chapters are dedicated to discussing the three dimensions of sustainability in some depth. In Chapter 2, we discuss the ecological dimension of sustainability. We examine some key biological and physical frameworks, and we discuss how the "human footprint" is exceeding the planet's "carrying capacity." In Chapter 3, we discuss the economic dimension of sustainability. We examine the inadequacy of neoclassical economic assumptions so prevalent in today's world to account for the social and ecological dimensions of the environment in which business organizations operate. We follow that with a discussion of some modern economic perspectives that are designed to remedy these inadequacies. In Chapter 4 we discuss the social dimension of sustainability including the distribution of wealth, food insecurity, gender inequity, educational inequity, environmental injustice, and numerous others, and we follow this with a discussion of ways that these social issues may be addressed.

In Part II of the book, Managing on a Small Planet, we explore the processes, values, structures, strategies, tools, and behavior patterns necessary for making the transformation to sustainable organizational management. The focus of this part of the book will be to identify and explain the transformational changes that organizations will need to make if they are to successfully transcend from mere economic institutions into sustainable corporations that earn their economic profits by contributing in lasting ways to a better society and a more pristine natural environment. In Chapters 5 and 6, we will explore established management theory as it applies to sustainable organizational management. We will expand the discussions of coevolution and transformational change introduced in this chapter, we will explore the structural requirements for successfully adopting sustainable organizational management, we will examine the role of stakeholders in the transformation process, we will explore the importance of attitudes and values when transforming to sustainable organizational management, and we will examine the roles and responsibilities of leaders in these transformational processes. In Chapters 7 and 8, we will focus our attention more directly on the strategic management dimensions of transforming business organizations into sustainable corporations. We will present the closed-loop value chain, we will discuss several functional-level sustainability strategies for achieving competitive advantages along the closed-loop value chain, and we will build a model of sustainable strategic management designed to make such sustainability strategies an institutional part of how the organization is managed. In Chapter 9, the book culminates with our summarization of what we believe are key capabilities necessary for effectively implementing sustainable organizational management in twenty-first century organizations.

— 2 —

Management Happens on Earth: The Biophysical Dimension of Sustainability

As seen in Chapter 1, this book is based on the core assumption that the universal adoption by business organizations of sustainable organizational management values, principles, processes, and practices will significantly contribute to humankind's pursuit of a human-friendly Earthly habitat for both current and future generations. Thus, it's important as we begin our discussion of sustainable organizational management to examine the concept of sustainability more closely. Recall from Chapter 1 that sustainability has three broad coevolutionary dimensions: the economy, society, and nature. In the next three chapters, we will discuss each of these dimensions in some depth. Please note that although each of the three chapters is designed to focus primarily on one of the three dimensions, the coevolutionary nature of these dimensions dictates that they often be discussed together. For example, population growth is a serious social problem with huge biophysical and economic implications, and climate change is directly related to economic activity and has potentially serious social consequences. Coevolutionary relationships such as these demonstrate that sustainability is by nature complex, trans-disciplinary, and multidimensional. As such, we hope to demonstrate to managers that achieving sustainable organizational management will require that they think differently as well as act differently regarding the relationships among the economic, social, and environmental dimensions of their decisions.

The Coevolving Earth

The Earth—humankind's home—is a living bio-socio-physical system subject to constant coevolutionary change processes as it renews, reproduces, and regenerates itself and its component subsystems. As an open system, the Earth has processes in place that help it maintain a dynamic balance among its component subsystems, each of which is also open and in search of balance among its own component subsystems. These component subsystems are typically nested within one another, and they are highly interdependent and cannot be treated as isolated entities. Thus, the Earth is an irreducible whole whose survival is threatened if any of its component subsystems break down. Figure 1.1 in Chapter 1 represents a nested hierarchy of component subsystems associated with economic activity on Earth. As such, all of these subsystems—individuals, organizations, the economy, society, and the ecosystem—are qualitatively different from those below and above it, and the demise of any of these subsystems would gravely threaten the survival of the others. Thus, achieving sustainability in any of these subsystems means achieving a sustainable balance among all of them.

Due to the Earth's biophysical nature and reliance on the energy from the sun for its survival, the coevolutionary interactions among its component subsystems are subject to the entropy law (the 2nd law of thermodynamics), which essentially says that it is physically impossible for energy and resources to have value forever. They will degrade and become useless over time. However, whereas the Earth and its component subsystems will eventually degrade as the sun cools and burns out, there is little certainty about the actual path or time this process will take. That will depend on how efficiently humankind uses its available energy and resources and how well it responds to the changes in its environment. The Earth and its component subsystems can survive and increase in orderliness while there is sufficient power from the sun as long as people respond correctly to signals from the environment. Climate change, smog, cancer rates, water shortages, genocide, and energy crises are just a few signals that indicate the need for changes in how humans interact with the planet. The more serious these problems get, the more difficult they will be to deal with. However, if people respond appropriately to these signals, the species can survive and develop for eons to come.

Gaia theory provides a strong scientific basis for understanding the coevolutionary nature of the Earth's component subsystems (Ehrlich 1991;

Lovelock 1979,1988; Margulis and Hinkle 1991). In Greek mythology Gaia was Mother Earth, the wife of Uranus (the universe) and birth mother of life on the planet. Gaia theory founder James Lovelock chose the label because it best represented his idea that the Earth is a living super organism. Gaia theorists point out that the living system Earth was actually born with the big bang of creation some 15 billion years ago, when the energy necessary for the formation of the universe was released. Some 4.5 billion years ago the Earth became a discernable hot, gaseous ball, and since then it has changed dramatically in terms of chemical content, geological activity, and the evolution of life. Research in Gaia theory has demonstrated that these three have not changed separately but rather have coevolved on the planet. For example, the oxygen content of the atmosphere has increased over the eons to 21 percent—enough to support large mammals such as humans—as a result of interactions among the Earth's living and nonliving components. In this and many other ways, the Earth's living organisms have continuously interacted with their natural environments to change and regulate chemical, atmospheric, and climatic processes in much the same way that a plant or animal self-regulates its internal state. These symbiotic, coevolutionary relationships generally involve a complex choreography of both cooperation and competition. Thus, Gaia theory has clearly established that the relationship between the Earth's biological and physical forces is one of mutual influence.

Gaia theory also points to the fact that humankind's environmental sensitivity need not be altruistic. Although environmental debates are often couched in terms of "saving the planet," research results from Gaia theorists make it clear that the planet can take care of itself. What is threatened via ecological, social, and economic degradation is not the planet but humankind and its way of life. Thus achieving sustainability will require balanced, complex interactions involving both cooperation and competition among all of the planet's component subsystems, or the human condition will suffer as a result. Environmental scientist Daniel Chiras (1991, Gallery 1) says Gaia "is an elegant metaphor that underscores a key principle of ecology: that all living things operate together." It is a metaphor that can help human beings better understand their place in the overall ecological scheme. It brings the phrase, "system of systems" (Boulding 1956, 202) to life. If people were to perceive the Earth as a living, breathing, coevolving being which exists through a beautiful and intricate dance of forests, rivers, oceans, atmosphere, microbes, plants, and animals, their perspectives of human activities would likely change. Lovelock (1988, 14) says, "In

Gaia we are just another species . . . Our future depends much more upon a right relationship with Gaia than with the never-ending drama of human interest." Tolle (2005, 21) agrees, saying that the only way to avoid the environmental crisis generated from humans' egoistic pursuit of material wealth is to "evolve or die" as a species.

Carrying Capacity Meets the Human Footprint

From a biophysical perspective, sustainability is defined by the planet's "carrying capacity," which is essentially the amount of production, consumption, resource depletion, and waste generation the planet can realistically absorb without threatening the coevolving atmospheric, geospheric, hydrospheric, and biospheric processes that support human life. The Earth's carrying capacity dictates the maximum size of the "human footprint"—the resources, energy, and wastes used and/or generated by humans in the conduct of their daily lives on the planet. When the size of the human footprint exceeds the planet's carrying capacity, the human-friendly balance of the Earth's biophysical systems is threatened. In this section, we will attempt to elucidate why and how the current human footprint is out of balance with the Earth's carrying capacity and thus puts significant stress on the planetary subsystems.

Population, Affluence, and Technological Efficiency Coevolve

The current human footprint (see Figure 2.1) results from the interactions among three highly interrelated, coevolving variables: population growth, human affluence (as measured by the growth in per capita Gross Domestic Product [GDP]), and the impact of technology on the natural environment (as measured by the materials, energy, and wastes generated to create each unit of GDP; Ehrlich and Ehrlich 1990). We will demonstrate in this chapter that today's rapidly growing global population and GDP are creating worldwide production and consumption levels that are depleting the planet's resources and fouling the human nest.

Population

Global population in 2008 reached over 6.6 billion. The population has tripled in the last 72 years, and there were 10 times as many people

Figure 2.1   **The Human Footprint**

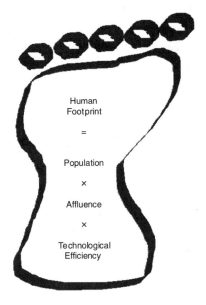

Human
Footprint

=

Population

×

Affluence

×

Technological
Efficiency

on the Earth in 2000 as there were in 1700. The world's population is forecasted to rise to 9.4 billion by 2050 with Asia accounting for 58.5 percent, Africa 20.2 percent, Latin America 8.6 percent, Europe 7.3 percent, North America 5.0 percent, and Oceania .5 percent. Population growth remains high in the Middle East, South Asia, Southeast Asia, Latin America, and especially sub-Saharan Africa. However, some countries and regions are experiencing net decreases in population, especially in Central and Eastern Europe (mainly due to low fertility rates) and Southern Africa (due to the high number of HIV-related deaths). Within the next decade, Japan and some countries in Western Europe are also expected to encounter negative population growth due to sub-replacement fertility rates. Even with these declines, worldwide population is still growing at an annual rate of 77 million (Brown 2008; Speth 2008; U.S. Census Bureau 2007).

Although overpopulation is primarily portrayed as a problem for developing markets, the human-footprint concept demonstrates that overpopulation is an issue in both the undeveloped, developing, and developed markets of the world. Overpopulation occurs when a region, nation, or community exceeds its human footprint and cannot sustain itself without rapidly depleting its resources, degrading its environment, and/or importing energy and resources from elsewhere. In the developing world the increasing size of the footprint is largely related to rapid population growth. However, in the developed world the increasing size of the footprint is largely due to the ecological excesses of affluence. For example, the most affluent 15 percent of the population creates almost half of the world's carbon dioxide emissions. Regardless of the source, today's 6.6 billion people are stomping all over the planet's carrying capacity. Given that by 2050 the planet will have 2.8 billion more humans "walking" on the planet, it seems crucial that humans quickly find ways to reduce the size of their collective footprint.

Affluence

In addition to exponential population growth, world GDP increased on average 46 percent per decade from 1980 to 2005 (Speth 2008). In 2007 global output rose by 5.2 percent to $53.64 trillion led by China (11.4 percent growth), India (8.5 percent growth), and Russia (7.4 percent growth). Between 2004 and 2030 world GDP is forecasted to increase by an average of 4.1 percent annually, primarily due to the projected increased consumption in China and India (U.S. Department of Energy 2007).

The fact is that such economic growth statistics are generally reported with glee because the global economy is currently functioning under the illusion that everyone on the planet can consume all they want forever. This has been a dominant assumption of economic theory since Adam Smith published *Wealth of Nations* in 1776. Of course, when Smith published his theories in the early days of the Industrial Revolution unlimited growth was a relatively harmless assumption. There were less than a billion people inhabiting the Earth, and very few nations were actually involved in significant economic activity. There was certainly plenty for everyone at that time. However, rapid population growth and the increased number of organizations and nations involved in economic activity since that time have changed the situation drastically. Today we live in a "full" planet. For example, China, the world's most populous nation, has the world's fastest-growing economy with an average annual economic growth rate of 6.5 percent forecasted between 2004 and 2030 (U.S. Department of Energy 2007). By 2015, 150 million cars are expected to clog the streets of China, 18 million more than were driven in the United States in 1999. If China's car ownership and oil consumption rates were equal to the U.S. rates, 80 million more barrels of oil a day above current production levels would be needed. These numbers are especially troubling because China's car population is expected to reach 1.1 billion by 2030 (Brown 2008).

Thus, if there are 9.4 billion people in 2050 living in growth-oriented economic systems, the human habitat will not be able to manage the stress without making significant changes in the way business is practiced. The Earth does not have the carrying capacity to absorb an exponential increase in its human footprint without suffering declines in the coevolving systems that support human life on the planet. Ironically, as Gaia theory has demonstrated, the Earth will survive these changes. It is humankind and its quality of life that will be threatened.

Technological Efficiency

One of the keys to stemming the size of the human footprint is to create production, transportation, and consumption technologies designed to have little or no impact on the Earth's biophysical systems as humans pursue perpetual economic growth. For many, improved technological efficiency provides the saving grace from planetary ecological catastrophe. They believe that the road to ecological salvation is paved with environmentally improved technologies that use less energy and resources and generate fewer wastes while churning out a never-ending stream of products and services. In fact, there have been and continue to be important advances in green technology. For example, enhanced energy efficiency from numerous sources ranging from improvements in lighting and air-conditioning technologies to improvements in automobile engine efficiency provides double dividends by lowering energy costs and carbon dioxide emissions. Research and development of alternative energy sources, such as solar collectors and hydrogen fuel cells, and improvements in current technologies, such as carbon capture and storage technologies (CSS) for coal-generated energy systems, hold serious promise for a more energy efficient future (United Nations Development Programme 2007).

However, as we will demonstrate in the next section, despite current improvements in energy efficient technology, there are still large global increases in carbon emissions. Further, statistics show that the Earth's temperature continues to rise, toxins and pollutants continue to plague the planet, species continue to disappear, and many critical natural resources such as clean air and water are declining. Thus, skepticism abounds with regard to the potential for technology alone to provide the way out of humankind's ecological ills.

Resulting Resource Depletion, Pollution, and Climate Change

In his classic article, Kenneth Boulding (1966) compared the Earth to a spaceship because it is a relatively closed system with little ability to import inputs or export outputs. As we noted in Figure 1.1 in Chapter 1, the Earth's only significant input is solar energy, and the Earth has no present way to dispose of wastes beyond its own boundaries. For billions of years, this limited openness was sufficient to support a robust biophysical balance. However, as discussed above, the increased production and consumption associated with a growing population in a growth-oriented global economy flies directly in the face of ecological balance. Thus, the planet's wild places are disappearing, its resources are being depleted at increasingly rapid rates, it is being degraded by an overflow of dangerous pollution and wastes, and its climate is changing at an alarming rate.

Depleting Resources

The 4.5 billion year coevolution of the Earth's biophysical systems has resulted in an abundance of natural resources such as fossil fuels, high-grade mineral ores, trees, rich agricultural soils, groundwater stored during the ice ages, and millions of species. Resources are critical to humankind's survival because, ultimately, these resources are the only capital humans have. They are the basic sources of material wealth, financial wealth, and psychological wealth.

The news on how well humans are protecting the planet's natural capital—its collection of life-supporting natural resources and processes—is not all that encouraging. There is the potential for severe water and cropland shortages in the coming years. Forests, wetlands, species, upper-atmospheric ozone, and fossil fuels are also disappearing at alarming rates. Speth (2008) reports data that show high global increases in consumption of numerous resources from 1980 to 2005. His data reveal a 41 percent increase in use of paper and paper products, a 41 percent increase in the fish harvest, a 37 percent increase in meat consumption, a

30 percent increase in the number of passenger cars, a 23 percent increase in fossil fuel use, and a 16 percent increase in water withdrawals.

Water security is a fundamental requirement for human survival and development. Today, around 1.4 billion people live in closed river basins where water use is greater than discharge levels, thus exceeding the area's carrying capacity for water and creating severe ecological damage. By 2025, 1.8 billion people could be living in countries and regions with absolute water scarcity, and two-thirds of the world population could be living under conditions of water stress (United Nations Environment Programme 2007). Groundwater levels are estimated to drop one to three meters in India and China, which possess the most irrigated lands in the world. Water withdrawals are expected to increase by 50 percent by 2025 in developing markets and 18 percent in developed markets. The Middle East and North Africa are considered the most water-stressed regions in the world. Together these regions have 6.3 percent of the world's population but only 1.4 percent of the world's renewable fresh water. Water stress is a serious human development problem with an alarming potential for geopolitical conflicts over access to water (Roudi-Fahimi, Creel, and De Souza 2002; United Nations Development Programme 2007).

Wetlands are also vital to the planet's ecological balance because they help to stem floods and erosion, replenish groundwater aquifers, and facilitate the settling or removal of inorganic matter and organic microbes. Further, wetlands are rich in biodiversity. Half of the world's coastal and inland wetlands have been lost over the past century, and 60 percent of the world's rivers have fallen victim to construction, channeling, draining and/or pollution. The devastation caused by Hurricane Katrina was significantly enhanced because the vast wetlands that once protected New Orleans and Baton Rouge from the brunt of tropical storms have largely disappeared due to stream channeling and development.

Species extinction rates today are estimated to be roughly 100 times higher than past ages based on analysis of fossil records. Estimates are that these extinction rates will increase to the order of 1,000 to 10,000 times over the coming decades (United Nations Environment Programme 2007). According to Brown (2008) we are experiencing the sixth great extinction in civilization, with the last one occurring 65 million years ago when an asteroid hit the planet. For the first time in history, a mass extinction is being caused by one of the planet's own species—human beings. The Millennium Ecosystem Assessment, a four-year study of the Earth's ecosystem services by 1,360 eminent scientists, found that 15 of the 24 primary ecosystem services were being degraded or pushed beyond their limits. For example, world fisheries have been depleted, with 75 percent of the world's fish stocks either fully or overexploited. This is of critical concern in terms of food security (discussed in Chapter 4) because fish are a major global source of human protein (Brown 2008).

In 2007, 20 percent of the world's mammals, 12.5 percent of all birds, 33 percent of all amphibians, and 70 percent of all assessed plants were considered at risk (Brown 2008). Plant and seed conservation has become a critical issue related to the ability of future generations to have both the biodiversity and the food supply they will need. That is why a vault was built under the Arctic ice in Norway to house millions of seeds that may otherwise become extinct or in short supply in the future (Mellgren 2008). Recent reports also indicate that one-third of the honeybee population in the United States has disappeared since 2006, leading to the potential for dire consequences in the stability of food crop yields. Research indicates that air pollution may be a factor in the loss, but in fact the reasons for the loss are still largely a mystery. There is also a major concern about the decline in genetic diversity in both plants and animals. For example, at least one breed of livestock has become extinct every month for the past seven years. The state of farm animal diversity is critical for the people in undeveloped and developing markets where farm animals are not only sources of food, but also are capital that can be sold in times of need (Nierenberg 2007).

Stratospheric (upper atmosphere) ozone depletion continues to occur everywhere except over the tropics. Huge holes in the planet's upper ozone layer, which shields the Earth's inhabitants from the debilitating effects of the sun's ultraviolet rays, have been discovered over the past several decades. Seasonal stratospheric ozone depletion is at its worst over the poles, especially the Antarctic, and the inhabited areas of Australia, New Zealand, Chile, and Argentina are the most affected by the resulting ultraviolet radiation. Though many are touting the recent decline in size of the ozone holes the total area actually varies from year to year, and it is not yet possible to say whether it has reached its peak. The largest holes occurred in 2000, 2003, and 2006. In September 2006, the hole extended over 29 million square kilometers (United Nations Environment Programme 2007).

About 4.2 percent of the world's natural forests—161 million hectares (398 million acres)—disappeared during the 1990s. Even more disturbing is that 152 million of these hectares were lost in the world's tropical rainforests, which were once referred to by Brazilian environmental martyr Chico Mendes as "the lungs of the planet" because they absorb so much carbon dioxide and produce so much oxygen. Between 1990 and 2005 the global forest areas shrunk at an annual rate of .2 percent with the greatest losses in Africa, Latin America, and the Caribbean (United Nations Environment Programme 2007). With these forests go the habitats of most of the Earth's species, the water and watersheds for billions of people, and an important line of defense against climate change. Tropical deforestation releases more than 1.5 billion metric tons of carbon into the atmosphere each year, which is 20 percent of greenhouse gases (Butler 2007).

This problem stems largely from the current nature of the interactions among the economic, social, and ecological systems. The forests are being harvested and shipped to developed markets where they are converted into paper and wood for furniture, homes, and so on. By 2030, China will have 1.46 billion people who will consume twice as much paper as is produced worldwide today (Brown 2008). Forest clearing is also occurring in order to convert the land for farming and raising livestock. Ironically the economic life span of a farm or ranch in a cleared tropical forest is only a few years because once the tree cover is lost the soil falls victim to the overwhelming tropical heat. Thus, farming and grazing activities can only be supported for a short time before the sun renders the land parched and useless.

Nonrenewable fossil fuels are also being exhausted at incredible rates, and this trend is predicted to continue. World energy consumption is projected to increase by 57 percent from 2004 to 2030, with energy demand increasing 95 percent in developing markets and 24 percent in developed markets. In terms of oil, the current consensus among oil-market experts is that the world will meet the 93 million barrel a day peak-extraction rate—the rate beyond which demand cannot be met—sometime around 2020 (U.S. Department of Energy 2007).

Coal is the most abundant fossil fuel. In 2004 coal accounted for 26 percent of energy consumption, and it is predicted to increase to 74 percent by 2030. Increased use of coal in developing markets will account for approximately 85 percent of the total growth in world coal consumption by 2030. Coal was the fuel that launched the Industrial Revolution, and it has continued to grow in use especially in developing markets. China, which already has many of the world's most polluted cities, was building about two coal-fired power plants every week in

2007 and these plants are not being built using new clean-coal technology discussed earlier.

Although natural gas is the fastest-growing energy source for electric power generation, the total amount of energy generated from natural gas will continue for the foreseeable future to be only about half of the total energy generated from coal. These trends indicate that there will continue to be a need for new sources of precious fossil fuels, and these sources will invariably be less accessible and more costly both economically and environmentally (for example, drilling for oil in the Alaskan National Wildlife Refuge). Further, largely because of the concentration of available supplies of these fossil fuels in a few of the world's nations, they are associated with myriad political, social, and environmental issues related to their control, pricing, and transportation (U.S. Department of Energy 2007).

Increasing Pollution

As mentioned above, the Earth has no significant potential for exporting its pollution and wastes beyond its atmospheric boundaries. In other words, humans are left to release their wastes into the air, water, and ground in the form of environmentally degrading pollution as a result of their consumption and production processes.

Access to clean air is a fundamental requirement for human life and human development. During the Industrial Age, there has been an unprecedented increase in the presence of potentially dangerous greenhouse gases in the atmosphere. In 2005 the global mean concentration of carbon dioxide in the atmosphere was around 379 parts per million, with other greenhouse gases adding about 75 parts per million to that total. Atmospheric concentrations of carbon dioxide are increasing by 1.9 parts per million annually. Over the past 10 years, the concentration of carbon dioxide has increased at a growth rate of 30 percent faster than it did in the previous 40 years. In fact, in the 8,000 years before the Industrial Revolution atmospheric carbon dioxide only increased a total of 20 parts per million (United Nations Development Programme 2007). Fossil-fuel burning, biomass burning (i.e., burning the rainforests to clear them for grazing land), agricultural activities, along with declining forest cover are infusing large quantities of toxins into the atmosphere every day. From 1980 to 2005, the planet was subjected to decade-average increases of nitrogen oxide of 18 percent, carbon dioxide of 16 percent, and sulfur dioxide of 9 percent (Speth 2008). More than 80 percent of China's cities have sulfur and nitrogen dioxide emissions above the World Health Organization's threshold. The World Bank projects that on average 1.8 million people will die prematurely from air pollution between 2001 and 2020 (Anonymous 2005b).

Humankind is being no kinder to its water than it is to its air. Besides using water at irreplaceable rates as mentioned above, toxic chemicals and other waste products have been poured into the Earth's waterways over the years as if they were humankind's personal dump. Human and animal wastes, agricultural wastes, and industrial wastes are too often dumped into the Earth's aboveground and underground waterways with little regard for those who are downstream. Many substances such as nitrates, pesticides, petrochemicals, arsenic, chlorinated solvents, radioactive wastes, and human wastes, find their way into rivers and waterways and eventually flow into the oceans. For example in Latin America and the Caribbean close to 80 percent of the wastewater discharged into the sea contains raw human sewage, and in large parts of Africa and Indonesia the proportion is as high as 90 percent. In the United States, more than 3.2 trillion liters of sewage gush into waterways each year. Not only are humans fouling their nests by dumping their human wastes into the water, they are also dumping solid wastes into the oceans at a rate that has increased threefold since the 1960s. There is an estimated 46,000 pieces of plastic litter floating on every square mile of the Earth's oceans. Conservation groups estimate more than a million seabirds and 100,000 mammals and sea turtles die globally each year by getting tangled in or ingesting plastics. There are more than 200 dead zones—areas so contaminated that they cannot support marine life—in our oceans, one-third more than there were two years ago. The most severe cases exceed 20,000 square kilometers (about the size of Maryland) and are located in such waters as the Gulf of Mexico, the Baltic Sea, the Arabian Sea, the Bay of Bengal, and the East China Sea (Halweil 2007b).

One of the most troubling water issues is the pollution of groundwater in agricultural regions due to the huge amounts of fertilizers, pesticides, and animal wastes that mix with rain and seep into the underground aquifers from which farmers and communities get their drinking water. Unfortunately, this problem shows no signs of abatement. For example, pesticide use has increased five times in Latin America since 1980 due to the increased demand for fresh produce all year in high-income countries. Americans pour approximately 2.2 billion pounds of pesticides on their farmlands each year, and fertilizer use is up 10 percent worldwide (Speth 2008). Contamination of groundwater is particularly troubling because once polluted it is expensive and sometimes impossible to clean.

Many of humankind's wastes are buried. The images of overflowing landfills and garbage barges looking for communities willing to take their trash are fresh in people's minds. In fact, the "throwaway society" we know today was deliberately conceived in the United States not long after World War II to generate more employment and economic growth by making disposable products. The rationale was that if more products are produced and thrown away, then more jobs will be created to replace them and more economic growth will result. Little did the decision makers over 50 years ago understand that the throwaway society would set the economy on a collision course with the planet's ecological limits. Most of the world's major cities have reached a crisis in waste disposal. For example, Toronto, Canada's last landfill closed in 2002, and it now ships 750,000 tons of garbage each year to Wayne County, Michigan (Brown 2008).

Not only are landfills overflowing, the economic and environmental costs of getting the garbage to the landfills is rapidly becoming prohibitive. The simple reality is that the world has run out of cheap oil to move things like garbage around from place to place. The city of New York, for example, is currently using 600 energy-intensive tractor-trailer rigs to move the 12,000 tons of garbage generated by its citizens daily (primarily to New Jersey). If these rigs were to be strung together each day, they would constitute a nine-mile long tractor-trailer truck convoy, contributing significantly to fuel consumption, air pollution, carbon emissions, and traffic congestion. In addition to oil, humankinds' current fascination with throwaway products will assure that future generations of humans suffer from shortages of numerous other natural resources discarded by their ancestors such as tin, lead, copper, iron ore, and bauxite. All of these minerals are being quickly depleted; the world has 17 years of remaining reserves for lead, 19 years for tin, 25 years for copper, 54 years for iron ore, and 68 years for bauxite (Brown 2008).

Although they don't come close to matching the amount of chemical and solid wastes generated, nuclear wastes represent a very serious hazardous waste-disposal problem. With the increasing price of oil, nuclear energy is seen by many (including some environmentalists) as a potentially cost-effective and safe alternative to fossil fuels. Developing markets are expected to see a robust expansion of nuclear power generation between 2004 and 2030, with China's annual growth rate forecasted to be 7.7 percent and India's 9.1 percent (U.S. Department of Energy 2007). Yet, many of the wastes and byproducts from nuclear-processing facilities, power plants, and so on are dangerously toxic and will be so for hundreds of thousands of years. Further, none of the countries that produce nuclear wastes have come up with an acceptable solution for their disposal. For example, in the United States a battle over the appropriateness of burying nuclear wastes under Yucca Mountain, Nevada, has raged for decades, and there really doesn't seem to be an end in sight. In the meantime, millions of containers of nuclear wastes are stored on the grounds of U.S. nuclear power plants and processing facilities waiting final disposal.

Changing Climate

Of the many insidious environmental issues contributing to the oversized human footprint of today, climate change is clearly the most notorious and immediate. Climate change is occurring because of the increases in greenhouse gases in the atmosphere discussed above—especially carbon dioxide. These gases trap solar heat in the Earth's atmosphere just as the transparent roof on a greenhouse traps solar heat (hence the term, "greenhouse effect"). Essentially, climate change is occurring because of changes in the "planetary carbon cycle"—the cycle by which carbon molecules are created and exchanged among the Earth's biophysical systems. The carbon cycle remains in balance so long as the amount of carbon in the cycle does not exceed the carbon budget, which is the amount of carbon that can be naturally absorbed by the cycle's carbon sinks (the atmosphere, waterways, plants, and soil). Because of the huge rise in carbon emissions from the burning of fossil fuels during the Industrial Revolution (discussed previously), more carbon is being trapped in the atmosphere. This creates an abundance of carbon dioxide that remains in the atmosphere, keeping more of the Earth's heat from escaping and resulting in rising temperatures now and into the future. Further, such excesses of carbon in the cycle have the potential to weaken the natural carbon sinks, reducing the carbon budget and stimulating even more rapid changes in climate.

When the current excessive greenhouse gas emissions of the developed world markets are combined with the emissions from the accelerating economic engines of China and India and other developing markets, aggregate carbon emissions are predicted to continue to increase world-wide during the twenty-first century. Predictions indicate a potential stabilization point for atmospheric carbon dioxide in excess of 750 parts per million, with possible resulting temperature increases in excess of five degrees centigrade. Such rates would exhaust the entire twenty-first century carbon budget by 2032. Beyond a warming threshold of two degrees centigrade above the pre-Industrial Revolution era, there could be a large-scale reversal in human development resulting in irreversible declines in social and human capital. According to the United Nations Human Development Report (United Nations Development Programme 2007), if the two-degree centigrade threshold is crossed, poverty, mal-nutrition, and serious health consequences will be encountered. The report identifies five specific risks for human development from climate change: increased oceanic temperatures leading to more climate-related disasters, reduced agricultural productivity, increased water insecurity, the reduction in ecosystems and biodiversity, and increased adverse human health consequences.

Several of these consequences are already being felt. The oceans have warmed significantly over the past 40 years, and much of that warming has taken place in the deepest regions. According to scientists, deep-water warming is a clear sign of impending temperature increases. Further, as the ocean waters warm, there is an increased likelihood in both the quantity and intensity of tropical storms because there is more warm water over which they can form and increase in intensity. Studies have found that hurricane winds have increased about 50 percent in the past 50 years. The increased tropical storm activity could have devastating consequences for many countries, including Pacific and Caribbean island states that could literally disappear because of the storms and the rising sea levels. Scientists believe that up to 330 million people could be displaced by storms and rising tides resulting from temperature increases in this century.

Warming seas have also already affected ice-based ecologies. Arctic ice has been melting at a rate of nine percent per decade, meaning that Arctic summers may be ice-free by 2050, threatening numerous species including the polar bear (Briggs 2003). Glacier loss is also an issue in several nations and regions. The Himalayan glaciers are retreating at an annual rate of 10 to 15 percent affecting water resources in Central Asia, Northern China, and the northern region of South Asia, and the glaciers in Greenland and Antarctica are melting at a must faster rate than originally forecasted (United Nations Development Programme 2007).

The risks from climatic disasters exist worldwide, but as with so many issues their impact will be felt predominantly in the lives of the poor. Ninety-eight percent of those affected by natural disasters from 2000 to 2004 lived in the undeveloped and developing markets of the world. Whereas developed markets have public health systems in place to deal with climatic shocks, undeveloped and developing markets have very limited public health systems with which to respond to such disasters. There are currently one billion people living in urban slums on fragile hillsides or riverbanks in undeveloped and developing markets, making them very vulnerable to the dire consequences associated with increasing storms and sea levels. Cropland loss from climate change—such as the potential 60 to 90 million hectare loss in sub-Saharan Africa that could impact the lives of 75 to 250 million people—also has potentially serious outcomes for the poor. Such cropland loss could raise the number of malnourished humans worldwide to 600 million. Further, global warming could expand the reach of major diseases affecting the developing world; millions of additional people could be exposed to diseases such as malaria, which already kills a million people annually (United Nations Development Programme 2007).

In short, climate change transforms ecosystems and reduces biodiversity. Although some species will be able to adapt to the warmer temperatures, a three-degree centigrade increase in warming could put 20 to 30 percent of land species at risk of extinction (United Nations Development Programme 2007). Ironically, one of Lovelock's (1979, 1988) most significant findings in his research on Gaia theory was that biodiversity is an important ingredient in climate regulation. So as species extinction rates increase due to climate change, the resulting loss in biodiversity may be reflected in more climatic disasters and rising temperatures. It's a coevolving, vicious reinforcing cycle that could easily spiral out of control if it hasn't already. If humankind doesn't find some way to effectively deal with climate change now, then future generations will suffer greatly from our lack of action. Clearly, this is a problem that humankind has already willed to its children.

Conclusions

The coevolving issues and patterns discussed in this chapter are but a few that indicate that current human activity is biophysically unsustainable. Clearly, the current and potential future human footprint is much larger than the planet's carrying capacity. In business terms, humans are violating a basic financial principle: They are living off capital rather than income; living off capital depletes the potential for future income generation, and ultimately is a sure route to poverty. Today humans are living off their natural capital, and the results are predictable—a coevolving downward spiral of the quality of the biophysical systems that support human life as we know it. Rising temperatures lead to heat waves, more destructive storms, more droughts, more forest fires, more ice melting, more refugees, and more food insecurity. According to Lester Brown (2008, 5) and numerous others, the time for reversing these trends is running out. Civilization is reaching the tipping points in both the world's ecological systems and political systems. Brown asks, "Which will tip first?"

— 3 —

Economics as if the Planet Mattered: The Economic Dimension of Sustainability

The discussion in Chapter 2 clearly supports our basic point that the Earth's biophysical systems are approaching their tipping points with regard to their ability to support the human species. At issue is humankind's perception that the planet's carrying capacity is sufficient to absorb the effects of an oversized human footprint forever. This perception emanates from the underlying assumptions of economic theory. Noted scholars have warned for decades that there are major discrepancies among the assumptions of economic theory, the preservation of the ecosystem, the happiness of the planet's human inhabitants, the dynamics of the global marketplace, and the preservation of civilization. E.F. Schumacher (1973, 1979) said that assuming unlimited economic growth is possible in a finite world is a dangerous illusion. Management pioneer Peter Drucker (1980, 160) agreed, saying, "Reality and the available economic theories have been moving further and further apart." Economist Herman Daly (1977, 89), a founder of ecological economics, said that applying the assumptions of modern economics is like "seeking the optimal arrangement of deck chairs on the Titanic," and Gus Speth (2008) said that the environmental crises of today can only be solved if current capitalism can be fundamentally transformed.

Inadequate Economic Assumptions

These scholars have had recent company in their criticisms of economic theory. In the spring of 2000, economics students at the Collège de Sorbonne, the elite academic institution in Paris, France, demanded reform within the economics profession. They called current economic theory "autistic," consisting of mathematical models operating under conditions that don't exist. They called for a "post-autistic economics." Students at Cambridge, Oxford, and Harvard universities joined their protest; students at Harvard even handed out alternative economics literature during the introductory economics courses on campus (McKibben 2007). The criticisms of these scholars and students range from the role of the individual and the firm to the true nature of international trade to the relationship between the economy, society, and the ecosystem. At the heart of their criticisms is that the basic assumptions underlying much of economic theory have outlived their validity in the world of business and beyond. In short, the realities of the global marketplace have outgrown the assumptions of neoclassical economic theory. Below we examine four key economic assumptions that are in need of change.

Unlimited Economic Growth Is the Goal

We chronicled in Chapter 2 the environmental costs of the unlimited growth assumption including the rapid depletion of nonrenewable energy, the depletion of natural resources, the pollution of the natural environment, and changes in the Earth's climate. A logical conclusion here is that the global economy has an optimal size beyond which the negative biophysical consequences of growth begin to outweigh the positive consequences.

Unfortunately the concept of optimal size is not a part of macroeconomic theory. Whereas microeconomic theory teaches that organizations should strive to maintain an optimal size beyond which their marginal costs will be greater than their marginal revenues, the idea of optimal size is somehow lost in the shift to macroeconomic theories of the total economy, where it is assumed that the benefits of growth will outweigh the costs of growth regardless of how big the economy gets. The concepts of optimal scale and diminishing marginal utility are virtually ignored. This growth mentality is reflected in politics across the globe, where economic growth is regularly seen as the answer to humanity's ills. Yet, as we will demonstrate in our discussions throughout this book, the data show that humankind's fixation on growth has produced more inequity than prosperity, more insecurity than security, and has pushed our natural systems supporting human life to their tipping points. In other words, we are now experiencing "uneconomic growth" (Daly and Farley 2004).

The pursuit of economic growth was formalized in 1929 when a statistical standard called the Gross National Product (GNP)—now generally referred to as the Gross Domestic Product (GDP)—emerged as an official measure of economic growth (Boulding 1970). GDP is in fact an undifferentiated measure of economic growth. That is, it is designed to account for all money spent in an economy whether it's spent on a new product to make someone happy, on salaries for employees, on a waste-disposal facility for what humans throw away, or on a chemotherapy drug to treat someone for cancer. Despite its undifferentiated nature, GDP has become the primary indicator by which societies measure human welfare. Efforts to show significant increases in the GDP drive virtually every monetary and fiscal action taken by the global political and economic machinery. Prevailing economic thought says that increasing GDP is the primary mechanism necessary for achieving prosperity and happiness for all the world's people. Yet increasing GDP and improving human welfare do not necessarily go hand-in-hand. In the United Kingdom, for example, per capita GDP grew 66 percent between 1973 and 2001, yet people's satisfaction with their lives did not change. The proportion of Americans who say they are happy has steadily decreased since its peak in the 1950s. Even though the United States trails only Luxembourg in per capita GDP, it comes in thirteenth in total quality of life (McKibben 2007). E.F. Schumacher (1979, 125) was quite graphic in his criticisms of society's fixation with GDP: "How can anybody assert that growth is [always] a good thing? If my children grow, this is a very good thing; if I should suddenly start growing, it would be a disaster. . . . Therefore, the qualitative discrimination is the main thing; it's far more important than some mysterious adding-up of everything."

Economists often use the technological efficiency arm of the human footprint to try and circumvent the argument that the economy can't grow forever. They argue that new technologies will continually appear to counteract the ecological problems. For example, they may assume that less intrusive oil-drilling methods can be developed that will allow oil exploration in wilderness areas with less environmental impact, or they may assume that the cleaner ways to mine and burn coal can allow its continued use as a primary energy source, or they may assume that as prices rise for the commodity someone will invent a substitute for the scarce resource. Sachs (2008) argues that if the world would adopt more sustainable technologies such as sustainable farming, improved seed varieties, and new forms of renewable energy the planet could sustain rising incomes and avoid environmental catastrophe.

Daly (1977), however, believes that changes must go beyond technological innovation. He said (1977, 105), "Technology is the rock upon which the growth men built their church." Technological innovations certainly need to be pursued because of their potential for improved energy and material use. However, humankind cannot expect sufficient technological advances to neutralize all of the negative impacts of increasing economic output for the growing number of people on the planet. Indeed, technology can often cause as many problems as it alleviates. For example, nuclear energy may be one answer to reducing greenhouse gases, but the technology to safely dispose of nuclear wastes is far from perfected. A massive steel container (taller than the Empire State building and as wide as the arch over St. Louis) has been built around the failed Chernobyl nuclear reactor to protect people from its radioactive fallout for generations to come.

Given the seriousness of our current environmental problems, it seems time for the field of economics to embrace proven concepts like coevolution, systems theory, and thermodynamics—all of which clearly point to the fact that unlimited growth on a finite space is destructive and ultimately impossible. Incorporating these concepts into economic theory means discarding the unlimited growth assumption in favor of a more realistic macroeconomic model that recognizes that the economy has limits defined by the ecosystem. Again quoting Peter Drucker (1989, 133): "Concern for the ecology, the endangered habitat of the human race, will increasingly have to be built into economic policy. . . . We still talk of 'environmental protection' as if it were protection of something that is outside of, and separate from, man. But what is endangered are the survival needs of the human race."

Natural Capital Can Be Ignored

Natural capital consists of the goods and services provided by nature, the sustaining system. Specifically, the goods (abiotic resources) from the ecosystem include fossil fuels, minerals, water, land, and solar energy; while the services (biotic resources) include renewable resources, ecosystem services to maintain human survival, and waste-absorption services. As Daly and Farley (2004, 77) say, "[B]iotic resources . . . are self-renewing, but human activities can affect their capacity to renew. Abiotic resources are either nonrenewable (fossil fuels) or virtually indestructible (everything else)."

The assumption of unlimited growth can exist only if the limits of the Earth's natural capital are ignored. Unfortunately, because energy provided by biotic resources provides the power for economic activity, the economic subsystem is governed by the entropy law, which imposes absolute biophysical scarcity on economic activity. Despite this biophysical reality, the mechanical economic models of the past century assume away the ecological contexts in which economic activity occurs, leading to a social science that is unable to deal with the dynamics of the natural environment. Thus, natural capital in current economic theory is assumed to be virtually unlimited. As such, natural capital is considered to be a near-perfect substitute for human-produced capital. Without natural or human-produced capital limits, there are no limits to growth (Boulding 1966; Capra 1982; Georgescu-Roegen 1971).

The market is relied upon to reflect the full cost of products and services. If the market gives society poor information by not recognizing the value of natural capital, then poor decisions are made in the allocation of these scarce resources. A key issue in including the value of natural capital in the cost of products and services is the common practice of discounting the value of assets and liabilities in the future. When managers make investment decisions, they weigh future benefits and costs as less valuable than present ones. Although this is sound for short-term financial decisions, when applied to natural capital, discounting distorts the ecological costs and benefits of decisions. Further, the choice of the discount rate can determine the quality of life for future generations. For example, using the discount rate of six percent, one study recommended that we not spend $300 million today to prevent $30 trillion of ecological damage from climate change in 200 years (the world's GDP is around $30 trillion today). However, using the discount rate of two percent, another study indicated that we should make substantial investments now to reduce the impacts of global warming (Daly and Farley 2004).

As Daly and Farley (2004, 183) say, "The public good problem appears beyond the scope of market allocation." Nicholas Stern (2006), the former chief economist at the World Bank, agreed. He said that the gap between the climate change costs and the market prices for fossil fuels is huge. For example, he said that including the costs of climate change in the market price of gasoline would add approximately $12 per gallon to the price at the pump. In other words, the market is grossly undervaluing the price of gas by failing to fully account for the environmental costs of burning fossil fuels (Brown 2008). Such examples demonstrate the fallacies of relying solely on Adam Smith's "invisible hand" for market allocation. Commenting on this, Ray Anderson, founder and chairman of Atlanta-based Interface, an industry leader in the production of industrial carpet, asks, "Can we really trust a blind invisible hand to allocate resources rationally?" (as quoted in Brown 2008, 8).

Selfishness Is the Road to Fairness

One of the most often criticized economic assumptions is that self-interest is the "invisible hand" that efficiently guides the market system toward a fair allocation of resources. In current economic theory, self-interest is interpreted as the selfish pursuit of individual goals. This assumption of selfish individualism is supported because, in theory, maximizing individual wealth is the most direct route to maximizing the welfare of society. Thus, in simple terms the assumption says that selfish individualism will lead to the common good. Individuals are depicted in economic theory as self-contained entities that have no need to consider anything beyond themselves when they make their choices. Further, it is assumed that individuals are essentially value neutral; they are perceived to have no values except those that can be expressed monetarily. Thus, in economic models human beings are only satisfied when they are consuming goods and services.

In his classes at Louisiana State University, Herman Daly used to say that selfish individualism is the "invisible foot that kicks the heck out of the common good" because morality, quality time, meaningful relationships with others, and spiritual fulfillment play no part in human satisfaction in the model. As Daly and Cobb (1989, 86) say, the radical individualism of current economic theory "excludes concerns for other people's satisfaction and sufferings that do not express themselves as one's market activity . . . [It] knows neither benevolence nor malevolence, only indifference." Etzioni (1988, 13) agrees, saying, "There is more to life than a quest to maximize one's own satisfaction." He says that morality, which evolves from the greater community, is as important as individual pleasure in guiding human behavior.

McKibben (2007) goes even further, saying that there has been a transition from individualism to hyper-individualism that isolates people even more from community. According to McKibben, plenty of data back this up. Americans are spending less time with friends and family. Younger adults today (20 to 30 year olds) are half as likely to join a group of some kind as their grandparents. This isolating individualism can be attributed to the pursuit of two-career households and the spread of suburbanization as well as increased time spent on television and the Internet. Consider just one of these trends: the impact of suburbanization in America. At the heart of suburbanization is the idea of providing more space for each individual. Whereas in 1920 the average density of U.S. cities was about 10 persons per acre, by 1990 it had dropped to four persons per acre even as the U.S. population doubled. Americans multiplied by eight times the amount of land they occupied during that period. Americans are now more isolated from one another than ever before.

Etzioni (1988) points out that exchanges seldom occur among equals; usually one party has a power advantage over the other. This means that powerful individuals and firms can often dominate the free market. If this domination is not tempered with the imperative to do no harm to others, then powerful executives and organizations can easily conclude that their primary purpose is to serve their own personal interests, implementing what Freeman and Gilbert (1988) call "managerial prerogative strategies." The commitment to hyper-individualism has allowed us to tolerate and even celebrate such strategies and the often gross-income inequities they produce (McKibben 2007). The results of this distorted neoclassical economic view of self-interest has had predictably dire consequences.

Examples abound of negative outcomes related to this hyper-individualism in today's business organizations. Corporations have "for the good of the company" left closed plants, unemployed workers, devastated communities, and environmental disasters in their wakes. Wall Street's greed during the sub-prime mortgage crisis of 2008, which caused a meltdown in the financial markets and required worldwide governmental intervention, reflects the investment community's obsession with hyper-individualism and high pay. Executives took imprudent risks in hopes of making big profits. Of course, who can forget the Enron debacle where the greedy hyper-individualism of CEO Ken Lay along with his COO, Jeffery Skilling, and CFO Andy Fastow, brought this blue-chip energy company, which reported earnings of $50.1 billion in July of 2001, into bankruptcy by December 2001. The deregulation of the sale of electricity and natural gas in the United States during the 1990s provided the perfect climate for these managers to pursue their hyper-individualism and greed through irregular, fraudulent accounting procedures in conjunction with their auditors from Arthur Andersen. Thousands of investors and employees lost all their savings, pensions, and children's college funds. Arthur Andersen was convicted of obstruction of justice, and 16 Enron managers and five others (including four employees of Merrill Lynch) pleaded guilty at trial. As a direct response to the Enron collapse, the U.S. Congress created the Sarbanes-Oxley Act in 2002, which is considered one of the most significant changes in federal securities laws since the 1930s. In an analogy, Lester Brown (2008, 8) equates Enron to the planet's ecological collapse, saying, "Enron was bankrupt. The collapse was complete. It no longer exists."

One of the most interesting aspects of the neoclassical economic assumption that social welfare will improve if human beings will behave as selfish profit maximizers is that it is a fundamental misinterpretation of what Adam Smith meant when he described the invisible hand in both *Wealth of Nations* and *Theory of Moral Sentiments*. Adam Smith indeed warned us from the beginning to do no harm in our business dealings. He made it clear in his writings that self-interest did not mean selfishness. According to Smith, self-interest is the rational pursuit of human desires constrained by considerations of justice, morality, and the impact of one's actions on others. By contrast, Smith defined selfishness as the immoral pursuit of one's goals without regard for the interests of others (Collins and Barkdull 1995).

Globalization and International Trade Are Synonymous

Michael Porter (1990) says that the economic theories of comparative advantage that guided free trade for decades do not even address the right questions, much less provide the right answers. These theories focus on understanding why some nations are more competitive than others, but Porter points out that nations do not compete. Instead, industries and industry segments are the competitors in the global market. The role of the nation is to serve as a supportive "home base" for the competitors. Thus, the proper question is, why do particular nations provide favorable conditions (a good home base) for the emergence of globally competitive firms and industries?

In answering this question, Porter (1990) dispels many fallacies related to the theories of free trade. For example, he points out that many nations are quite well off despite high trade deficits or high exchange rates for their currencies. He also shows that an abundance of cheap labor or natural resources is usually a poor mechanism for achieving advantages in the global marketplace. For example, since 2000 approximately ten thousand jobs in the maquiladoras along the Mexican border have been shifted to China due to the lower wage rates (Mitchell 2006). The advantages once provided by low wages and cheap natural resources are being replaced by the ability to adopt new technologies that bypass or reduce dependence on these factors. Porter (1998) points out that the competitive advantages in the global economy now come more from local clusters such as relationships, knowledge, and motivation that competitors are unable to match.

Other economic assumptions of international trade have been criticized as well. Michael Porter (1990) points out that the current theory of comparative economic advantage among nations assumes that capital and labor cannot cross international boundaries, technologies everywhere are identical, products are undifferentiated, no economies of scale exist, and the pool of factors of production in a nation is fixed. The absurdity of these assumptions renders the theory of comparative advantage virtually useless as a tool for understanding international trade. Porter says (1990, 13), "It is not surprising that most managers exposed to the theory find that it assumes away what they find to be most important and provides little guidance for appropriate company strategy."

Daly and Farley (2004) agree with Porter that the current mobility of financial capital renders the theory of comparative advantage useless. They point out that transportation costs in the theory are implicitly assumed to be zero even though transportation is energy intensive. Thus, the full costs of energy are not accounted for in the theory. Further, they criticize the theory for assuming that the costs of nations choosing to specialize in the production of particular products and services at the exclusion of others are negligible. In fact, countries that specialize in nonessential commodities (i.e., toys) are often left to trade for essential commodities (i.e., food and energy) making them dependent on people from different cultures with different values, interests, and political agendas for the products and services they need for survival. Therefore, the original guarantee of mutual benefits of trade on which the theory of comparative advantage is grounded no longer holds true.

Daly and Farley (2004) explain that the key issue with the theory of comparative advantage is that it doesn't recognize the difference between internationalization and globalization. They point out that internationalization involves the nation state as the basic economic unit, whereas in globalization, all national economies are integrated into one global economy. The theory of comparative advantage is based on the concept of internationalization and has been fallaciously applied to the global, integrated economy. Daly and Farley (2004) argue that the global economy is based on absolute advantage rather than comparative advantage, which provides both winner and loser nations. In fact empirical evidence indicates that an important unintended consequence of globalization is the increased concentration of wealth within and between countries (which will be discussed further in Chapter 4; Daly and Farley 2004).

Global free trade is seen by most economists as the best way to allocate worldwide resources and increase global economic growth. Thus, the concept of globalizing free trade clearly reflects the dominance of the assumption that unlimited economic growth can take place on a finite sphere. Yet, as noted above, many countries are not free to trade because they lack essential commodities and are therefore forced to trade even when trade is not favorable. Evidence suggests that globalization, by creating fewer and bigger firms and by limiting a nation's ability to regulate negative external costs, may be undermining competitive conditions for efficient market allocation, which contradicts the basic assumption that globalization leads to the most efficient allocation of resources (Daly and Farley 2004).

A New Economics for a Coevolving World

Thus, current economic theory is having a destructive impact on the natural environment; it favors egoism over the moral standards of the greater community, has led to abuses of power, has led to greater inequity and insecurity, and provides an inaccurate picture of global trade. Drucker (1989, 157) was very pessimistic about the role that economic theory would play in the future. He said, "To give us a functioning economic theory, we need a new synthesis. . . . And if no such synthesis emerges, we may be at the end of economic theory."

Numerous economists and non-economists alike have labored diligently over the last several years to find this new synthesis, seeking to foster new economic theories based on more realistic assumptions about the greater environment and social system in which the economy is embedded. Daly and Farley (2004) call the new economics coevolutionary because the economy is embedded within the culture (see Figure 1.1 in Chapter 1), and the ability to adapt to the environment through cultural evolution is a distinguishing characteristic of the human species. Below we present a brief summary of some of the key ideas in the new coevolutionary economics, organizing our discussion around the four issues of current economics identified in the first part of the chapter: pursuing unlimited growth, ignoring natural capital, being hyper-individualistic, and misunderstanding the dynamics of trade and globalization.

Replacing Unlimited Growth with Sustainability

E.F. Schumacher (1973) was one of the earliest economists to bring the world's attention to the problems of unlimited economic growth. He said that the first assumption of economics should be that there is such a thing as enough. Once such an assumption is in place, then economists and other scientists can go about the business of defining what enough is. Herman Daly (1977) proposes that "enoughness" needs to be a primary value upon which economic theory is based if humankind is to achieve a sustainable balance between the economic system and the ecosystem. Enoughness is based on sufficiency, implying that there is a sufficient level of economic consumption beyond which human welfare and ecological balance are significantly eroded. Defining sufficiency is no easy task. However, the results of ignoring sufficiency are a great deal more ominous than assuming that it exists, albeit imprecisely. Daly (1986, 43) says, "Perhaps the only thing more difficult than defining sufficiency is our present attempt to get along without the concept by pretending that there is no limit to either the possibility or desirability of growth."

Daly (1977, 1993) asserts that it's important to differentiate between physical, quantitative growth and nonphysical, qualitative development. He says (Daly 1977, 243), "Limits to growth do not mean limits to development." Making such a distinction allows for an economy that develops but does not grow, just as the planet develops but does not grow. Whereas a development-based economy requires stabilizing the growth of both the population and the quantity of goods produced, it does not require stabilizing such things as culture, knowledge, genetic inheritance, and technology. These can develop and change. Further, both the mix of products in the economy and the distribution of capital can be adjusted to accommodate a development-based economy.

Daly (1977) believes that if the scarcity and aesthetic value of resources and the relationship between economic satisfaction and human fulfillment can be added into the economic formula, then the concept of sufficiency would take on real meaning. Enoughness will be definable when economic models include the following assumptions: (1) Human beings want happiness, fulfillment, enlightenment, and a sense of purpose—not just more things; and (2) the Earth is a finite sphere with a limited amount of resources and a limited waste-processing capacity (Daly 1977). Thus, optimal scale replaces unlimited economic growth as a goal, followed by fair distribution (Daly and Farley 2004).

Though the ideas of Daly, Schumacher, and others were ignored for decades, there is now a loud call to design a new economy that operates within its ecological limits. Lester Brown (2008, 22) says, "The challenge is to build a new economy and to do it in wartime speed before we miss so many of nature's deadlines that the economic system begins to unravel." So how does humankind design an economy where global population is stabilized, forests are increasing, and carbon emissions are falling? Brown (2008), Daly and Farley (2004), and Speth (2008) offer policy solutions that can take humans in that direction if they have the will to change.

Brown's (2008) vision of the new economy in his "Plan B 3.0" includes macro policies and micro-market mechanisms designed to stabilize population and eradicate poverty, to restore the Earth, to increase energy efficiency, to increase the use of renewable resources, to redesign cities for people, and to feed a population of 8 billion. Brown provides convincing data that civilization is at a crisis point, and unless humanity mobilizes, the tipping point will be close. He sets forth specific ecological and social goals that need to be achieved and action plans to achieve them.

Daly and Farley (2004) provide a framework for a steady state economy (described below). They point out that there are three goals of such an economy—sustainable scale, efficient allocation, and fair distribution—and they suggest that each of these goals requires specific economic policies. These policies should provide macro control with the maximum of micro freedom and variability, and they should err on the side of conservation when dealing with impacts on the natural environment (following the precautionary principle of ethics). Such policy development requires that those involved engage in continuous learning and be willing to question fundamental assumptions and beliefs about the kind of world that exists and the kind of world that can be created for future generations.

Accounting for Nature

In 1977, Daly proposed a model called a "steady state economy" (SSE). Like traditional economic models, a SSE is based on the physical stock of capital (comprised of both people and products), but unlike traditional economics it also accounts for the flow of matter and energy through the economy. By adding this throughput into the formula, a SSE is able to operate on the assumption that the entropy law imposes absolute limits on the capacity of the economy. Daly (1977, 199) says, "To deny the relevance of the entropy law to economics is to deny the relevance of the difference between a lump of coal and a pile of ashes."

As we discussed previously, there has been a massive market failure when valuing the worth of natural capital. Daly and Farley (2004, 122) say, "[E]conomic activities increasingly take place in a full world and the whole system is governed more by thermodynamics and photosynthesis than by prices and GNP." In this regard, Daly (1977, 1986) takes issue with the neoclassical assumption that reproducible capital is a near-perfect substitute for land and other low-entropy resources. He notes that capital requires natural resources (matter and energy) for its production; that is, it requires throughput. Since current macroeconomic theory ignores the role of throughput, human-produced capital and low-entropy resources are seen as almost perfect substitutes. In reality, however, the entropy law places limits on factor substitution. For example, the evaluation of land based solely on monetary terms improperly equates human capital (people) and natural capital (land) with the nonliving assets of the firm, such as buildings and equipment. This exposes land, which embodies life, to the potential for undue exploitation, and it makes people potentially vulnerable to corporate actions taken purely for financial gain.

A number of environmental scientists and economists have suggested that land could be more easily accounted for in living-systems terms if energy rather than money was used to express its value. H.T. Odum (1983) said that using energy to determine land value allows humankind to account for land in terms of its potential to provide energy on a sustainable basis. This encourages economic decisions that are compatible with the Earth's long-term survival. Daly and Cobb (1989) agree and suggest that by replacing the term "land" with "nature" in economic theory, the differences between reproducible economic capital and non-reproducible natural capital can be taken into account more easily. After all, whereas land is something humans can buy, sell, and live on they can never own nature; they must live with her.

Given the importance of these non-market goods and services in human survival, achieving sustainability will require the development of meaningful economic models and tools for including the value of nature. One approach, commonly referred to as "environmental economics," tries to internalize the environmental costs of doing business, which in the past have been considered external to the economic system. Environmental economics proposes that regulations, taxes, and market incentives can be used as mechanisms for assigning value to resources, pollution, and wastes. Once this occurs, the natural environment is brought into the closed, circular-flow model allowing for the application of neoclassical economic theory in determining the optimum levels of resource depletion, pollution, and waste generation that the planet can bear (Costanza 1989).

One example of an environmental economics approach is the use of market incentives to control environmental problems. Such approaches as cap and trade are designed to reward firms for controlling wastes and pollution before they occur. One approach is to issue pollution credits that allow a firm to emit a certain amount of pollutants into the environment. These credits are tradable assets; that is, companies whose emissions are below that allowed by their credits can sell the excess credits to other firms. For example, the 1990 Clean Air Act provides for tradable sulfur dioxide credits and carbon emission trading is one of the ways countries can meet their obligations under the Kyoto Protocol (the international agreement on greenhouse-gas emissions). The metric tons of carbon emissions traded increased 240 percent between 2004 and 2005, and the carbon-emissions market was valued at $60 billion by 2007. The London financial market is now the center of carbon trading, and by 2007 over 150 global businesses had signed the G8 Climate Change Roundtable's statement calling for governments to establish clear price signals through a policy framework (Capoor and Ambrosi 2006).

Another approach that has had more success than the cap and trade systems is the European ecological tax reform that taxes the "bads, not the goods." Rather than taxing what we want more of—value added by labor and capital—we tax what we want less of—throughput and its associated depletion and pollution (Daly and Farley 2004). Although this system has been relatively successful, European governments are concerned that internalizing these external costs will raise resource prices and thus reduce their competitive advantages in the global economy.

Depletion quotas are another mechanism that can used to internalize environmental costs (Daly1977). Depletion quotas impose limits on the absolute amount of resources that can be extracted in a given period of time. Such quotas recognize the value of resources in their natural state. Like pollution credits, depletion quotas would be tradable on the open market providing positive incentives for organizations to save resources. Thus, these depletion quotas would provide a macro control over scarce resources such as the world's fisheries, while maintaining a free-market system to allocate them.

As discussed earlier in the chapter, the common financial practice of discounting the value of assets in the future creates serious issues when accounting for natural capital. Recall that such discounting implicitly assumes that future generations have no rights to resources, energy, clean air, clean water, and abundant land; therefore, the present generation has no obligation to preserve them. To remedy this issue, ecological economists suggest that a social discount rate lower than the individual discount rate be created that allows for the preservation of natural capital, thus protecting the rights of future generations who will need them to survive (Daly and Farley 2004).

Costanza (1989), Daly (1977, 1991), and Daly and Farley (2004) believe that these micro-market mechanisms are good ideas, but they don't think they go far enough in internalizing environmental costs into the economic system. They say that environmental economics alone cannot be counted on to solve all of our ecological ills because it doesn't directly address the issue of absolute scarcity of resources. Speth (2008) agrees saying this kind of sustainability is "weak sustainability." Market mechanisms, however, can be used to allocate the relative scarcity of energy and other natural resources. In this regard, evidence indicates that micro-market mechanisms that allocate energy and natural resources within smaller local and regional markets provide lower costs to society than regulations aimed at large national/global macro-markets. These micro-market mechanisms, however, must be subject to macro controls based on the planet's carrying capacity (Daly and Farley 2004).

Daly, Speth, and others are now calling for an evolution from environmental economics to "ecological economics," which suggests adding the basic principles of ecology to the tenets of economics so that natural capital is not only sustained but also renewed. Speth (2008) calls this "strong sustainability." Whereas environmental economics is based on relative scarcity, ecological economics is based on the fact that the entropy law imposes absolute scarcity on the economy. Essentially, ecological economics is based on: (1) a dynamic, holistic coevolutionary view of the world; (2) multi-scale time frames that recognize both the short-term dimensions of day-to-day economic decisions and the long-term coevolutionary dimensions of nature's processes; (3) the recognition that humans are a part of nature; (4) a macroeconomic goal of sustainability (sustainable scale) and appropriate microeconomic goals to support this; (5) a belief that technology is important but not a panacea for achieving sustainability; and (6) a belief that solutions to ecological problems must transcend traditional disciplinary boundaries (Costanza, Daly, and Bartholomew 1991).

One of the most enlightening frameworks for understanding the impacts of a high-entropy economy is "industrial metabolism" (Ayres 1989, 1994). Just as living organisms have metabolic processes for transforming the energy they import from their environment into life-maintaining processes, economies can also be viewed as metabolic because they extract large quantities of energy-rich matter from the environment and transform it into products for consumption.

Whereas the metabolic processes necessary to maintain life in the ecosystem are balanced and self-sustaining, metabolism in the economic system is grossly out of balance with its environment. Resources that literally take eons to renew (such as oil) are being used at nonrenewable rates because only a small percentage of the resources used in economic activity remains in the system for any length of time (basically as durable goods). Most materials are used to produce food, fuel, and throwaway products that pass through the economic system from extraction to production to consumption to waste very rapidly. These wastes are often toxic and harmful to the natural environment. The damage is done not within the economic system per se, but in the atmosphere, land, water, and gene pool that have no current economic value.

Entropy occurs at all points in the metabolic process including extraction, production, and consumption. However, most of the loss comes at the point of consumption. Most foods, fuels, paper, lubricants, solvents, fertilizers, pesticides, cosmetics, pharmaceuticals, and toxic heavy metals are discarded as wastes after a single use as are thousands of other products. Many of these are very difficult and expensive to recycle, so not only do people use too many of them, but they are also not likely to use them again.

The basic message from the industrial-metabolism framework is that the metabolic processes in the economy need to achieve the same type of balance that is possible in the ecosystem when it is absent of economic activity. Just as the ecosystem can sustain itself indefinitely by importing sunlight and using it to power a system that operates almost totally by recycling materials, economic systems also need to incorporate sustainable energy-transformation processes. Achieving this balance will require processes such as recycling, remanufacturing, and reconditioning. Achieving this balance will also require creating a sustainable worldwide energy system. Contrary to popular belief, the Earth has an abundance of energy. The issue with energy is not the quantity of the energy but its sources and generation processes. Humankind's current dependence on fossil fuels and nuclear fission is not sustainable because of the environmentally degrading nature of these energy sources. Developing a sustainable energy system will require developing a worldwide mix of energy sources and technologies that are more renewable, less dissipative, and more ecologically sensitive than the current fossil-fuel and nuclear-based systems. The transition to such a system will be neither easy nor cheap. However, as investments in these technologies continue to grow and prices continue to rise for fossil fuels, these energy sources will become more economically competitive.

Achieving a worldwide sustainable balance in industrial metabolism will require that the global economy transcend through three progressively difficult stages of industrial evolution (Richards, Allenby, and Frosch 1994). The first stage of this evolutionary process is the type I industrial ecosystem, which is the classical industrial model. In this stage the global production and distribution systems operate on straight linear processes in which virgin raw materials and energy are converted into goods and services. The byproducts of this process are heat and material wastes that either dissipate or must be disposed of in the natural environment. The second stage of evolution is to a type II industrial ecosystem, which involves some recycling of materials and energy in production processes but still requires some linear transformation of virgin inputs and energy into products and wastes which must be absorbed by nature. The third stage of evolution is to a type III industrial ecosystem in which the only inputs are renewable energy and renewable resources, and operations are totally closed-looped with virtually total materials reuse and recycling. Type III industrial ecosystems export only heat and biodegradable wastes into the external environment. They mimic mature natural ecosystems that are generally quite stable, operating on minimal amounts of entropy.

Today, industrial systems seem to be in transition from type I to type II systems. We believe that sustainable organizational management can provide pathways to type III systems.

Replacing Hyper-individualism with Living in Community

Amitai Etzioni (1988) proposes that the assumption of hyper-individualism in current economics should be replaced with what he refers to as the "I/We paradigm." This paradigm recognizes that human beings make rational economic choices designed to satisfy their individual needs and desires, but it also recognizes that individual economic satisfaction can only occur within the moral dimensions of a meaningful community structure. The I/We paradigm makes three assumptions that foster a more realistic perspective of human beings. First, it assumes that people have many needs and wants. In addition to economic desires that can be measured in monetary terms, people also hold values that are unrelated to the economic system. Second, the paradigm assumes that people typically make their choices primarily on the basis of value judgments and emotions and only secondarily through empirical logic. Third, it assumes that people exist as parts of communities that impose moral standards of conduct, and that individual relationships are largely molded by the community in which they take place. Thus, human beings are perceived in the I/We paradigm to be multi-directed, emotional, value-laden, and guided by the moral limits of the community.

Daly and Cobb's (1989) "person-in-community paradigm" is similar to the I/We paradigm. They point out that people are both consumers and workers in an economic community where relationships with one another are important. Further, the economic community is a smaller part of larger social, political, and ecological communities, and thus it should reflect the moral priorities of these larger communities. The foundation unit of the economic system within this paradigm is the self-sufficient community rather than the selfish individual.

Daly and Cobb (1989) have two recommendations that address the problems associated with extreme egoism. First, they suggest governmental policies be designed to prevent consolidation of economic power into the hands of a few individuals and organizations. For example, tax and ownership laws should be structured to encourage spin-offs and discourage mergers. Second, they propose that income tax laws be modified so that income differentials are less extreme. They clearly state that income differentials are important free-market incentives that should not be abandoned; however, extreme income differentials ignore the important interdependencies among the members of the community.

One feature of the person-in-community paradigm that is of particular interest to business managers concerns labor-management relations. Daly and Cobb (1989) say that management and labor constitute a single community of mutual interests. They advocate small, employee-owned organizations that are energy efficient and provide real opportunities for personal employee satisfaction with the work. Such organizations tend to do less environmental damage, foster the group over the individual, and help to restore thought, skill, and initiative to the workplace.

Building Local Economies in a Global World

There is a growing movement across the globe to build economies around small, locally owned organizations like Daly and Cobb (1989) describe. Research indicates that locally based, independent organizations contribute not only more to the social and natural capital of the community than do big-box retailers; they also contribute more to the local economy (Mitchell 2006). According to Mitchell (2006, xii), "[M]ega-retailers impose a variety of hidden costs on society and contribute far less to our economic wellbeing than they take away." She equates the mega-retailers to the European colonial system designed to extract the community's wealth and resources, leaving it less self-reliant and viable. Of course mega-retailers and the global marketplace are not going away, so communities today are attempting to "go local" (Shuman 1998) in the midst of a thriving global market.

"Glocalization" is a term popularized by Thomas Friedman (1999, 2004) to recognize the need for local communities to maintain strong local cultural and economic identity as the global economy grows. Thus, glocalization is the recognition that the integrated global economy is here to stay, and in order to be competitive, communities must keep their local economies strong by building them around local enterprises. Michael Porter (1998, 77) says, "Paradoxically, the competitive advantages in a global economy lie increasingly in local things—knowledge, relationships, and motivation that distant rivals cannot match."

Over 20 years ago, bioregionalism emerged as a way to place the economic development of land into a living systems perspective. Bioregionalists advocated dividing the land into natural regions based on native vegetation, geology, watersheds, and distinctive life forms. Along with the region's natural capital, the social capital of the region would be sustained as well recognizing the importance of local traditions, educational systems, workforce skills, healthcare systems, civic organizations, and interest groups. These bioregions would develop their economic systems around their regional resources and would be responsible for processing their own wastes in ways most suited to the unique characteristics of that region. This self-reliance would encourage regions to promote economic systems geared toward long-term sustainability (Sale 1985).

The idyllic vision of bioregionalism has taken practical root in the going-local movement. Community action groups of every political, religious, and economic ilk are attempting to block firms that are perceived to be threats to their community's sustainability. In fact since 2000, around 200 big-box development projects have been stopped because ordinary citizens mobilized, even though the myth exists that these corporations are unstoppable (Mitchell 2006). For example, in the central Appalachian Mountain region in the United States there is a coalition of community groups from five states called the Central Appalachian Network with a goal of promoting sustainability in the region. Members of this network have lobbied against Wal-Mart locating in a Virginia town, kept a nuclear processing plant from being located in the mountains of Northeast Tennessee, and currently provide a co-op for distribution of organic food grown by local farmers.

Michael Shuman (2006) argues that there is an "epoch struggle" going on between two opposing views of capitalism. One view is that "there is no alternative" (TINA) to globalization in the free-market economy. Thus, conventional economic developers only have one alternative: "[G]et Toyota to locate in your backyard and export your goods as far and as widely as possible" (Shuman 2006, 8). This economic development philosophy is based on the mainstream economic belief that regional development and growth depend on a strong export base; the rationale goes that recruiting large manufacturers brings in new capital flows into the state so citizens can buy imported goods from other regions and countries. In keeping with this belief, most communities in the United States offer businesses incentives or subsidies to come or to stay. For example, Wal-Mart, one of the world's wealthiest companies, received more than $1 billion from state and local governments within the last ten years to locate distribution centers in various communities (Shuman 2006).

The other view is what Shuman (2006) calls the "Small-Mart Revolution," which is much more than just fighting chain stores; it is about supporting quality local businesses in all sectors of the economy. The focus of economic development is on local ownership and import substitution. Import substitution means that if it is economically feasible for a community to produce a good or service, then it should be produced locally. Thus, the focus is to build entrepreneurial capability within the community and to only rely on the global economic system for goods and services that cannot be produced locally; therefore, building communities from the inside out—from the local to the global. So in Michael Porter's (1990) terms, it is necessary for communities and nations to build a strong "home base" in order to have a competitive advantage in the global economy. Using this economic development policy will not only strengthen the community, it will (among numerous other environmental benefits) reduce the carbon emissions from transporting goods from place to place. Currently, even products such as organic foods that are thought to be ecologically sensitive are packaged in plastic containers and transported a thousand miles or more before they are ever consumed (McKibben 2007).

Paul Hawken (2007) says that there is currently a "blessed unrest" among the citizens of the world, a bottom-up revolution that recognizes the absolute scarcity of both our natural and social capital. There has been an explosion of activities that supports local entrepreneurial activity. The cities of Austin, TX, Raleigh, NC, and Bellingham, WA, for example, have all embraced the concept of strengthening and rebuilding their local independent businesses through specific policy measures. Slogans such as "Break the chain habit" and "Shop locally owned" are visible across the globe as community is being recognized not only as a cultural value but also as an economic value (Mitchell 2006). However, there is an important point for communities to remember as they go about the task of building healthy local economies. People have migrated to the large global chains at the expense of local businesses because they provide a wider variety of quality goods at lower prices. Further, many are good employers and good corporate citizens that contribute to local wellbeing in numerous ways. Local entrepreneurial efforts must be able to do the same things, or they will likely fail.

Conclusions

We would like to conclude with a story. A cruise ship sank in a storm several years ago, and one of its rafts was left adrift with three people aboard—a physicist, an engineer, and an economist. The raft was stocked with a survival kit that included canned goods, but the can opener was missing from the kit. The physicist said that this presented a very perplexing problem because they had no way to separate the strong metal molecules of the cans in order to get to the food inside. The engineer agreed, lamenting that there were no sharp instruments on board which they could use to open the cans. The economist, however, dismissed the pessimistic realities of his fellow passengers, saying, "All we have to do is assume that the cans are already open. Then we can eat to our hearts' content."

The fallacious assumptions that frame a great deal of our current economic thought make it extremely difficult to apply traditional economic models with any degree of success. In this chapter, it has been documented that new economic models are springing forth from both inside and outside the discipline of economics. Because managers in business organizations make the vast majority of the decisions within the global economic system, they are the ones most in need of new models. Concerns for the Earth and future generations are now being expressed passionately to business organizations by a plethora of stakeholders. Managers are left with no choice but to apply new models, values, and methods to deal effectively with these concerns. The survival of their firms and their species depends on it.

— 4 —

Searching for Equity:
The Social Dimension
of Sustainability

Socially, achieving sustainability will require effectively dealing with a plethora of social issues facing communities and nations worldwide. Included among these issues are population growth, the economic gulf among developed, undeveloped, and developing markets, human rights, human health, gender equity, education, food security, urbanization, and community viability. As discussed at length in Chapter 3, unlimited economic growth is a cornerstone assumption of conventional economics. From a social perspective, the logic of this assumption goes something like this: If the economic pie gets bigger, then more people can get wealthier until eventually everyone has enough therefore solving the issue of distributive equity both within and between nations. Thus, conventional economics teaches that the fair distribution of wealth will happen when the whole world gets aboard the economic-growth train.

However, ecological economics provides a very different view of this issue. In addition to addressing the appropriate scale of the economy and the efficient allocation of natural resources, ecological economics directly addresses the distribution of wealth within and between countries because inequitable wealth distribution results in so many social (and environmental) injustices. As Daly and Farley (2004, 267) explain, the distribution of wealth and income is "a fundamental dimension of justice in society." Distributive inequity and injustice are primary contributors to overpopulation. Increases in income eventually lead to decreases in both mortality rates and fertility rates. In today's world, many regions have increased incomes enough to reduce mortality, but they have not yet increased incomes enough to reduce fertility. Thus, a situation develops "where rapid population growth begets poverty and poverty begets rapid population growth. In this situation countries eventually tip one way or the other. They either break out of the cycle or they break down" (Brown 2008, 5). For example, in Sudan women have five children each on average, and the population of 39 million is growing by 2,400 per day. "Under this pressure, Sudan—like scores of other countries—is breaking down" (Brown 2008, 124). In fact, a billion people live in countries where the population will double by 2050 (Brown 2008).

Rapid population growth like this means that approximately 85 percent of the world's population will live in developing markets by 2025 (Schmidt 1999). The average age of the population in these markets is very young, so the working-age population will grow rapidly. Ironically, markets facing rapid population growth provide business organizations with opportunities for new labor and consumers not available to them in the slow-growth developed markets of the world with their aging populations. Unfortunately, these new sources of labor and consumers come with myriad social issues exacerbated by their rapid population growth such as poverty, discrimination, violence against women, infant mortality, inadequate access to reproductive healthcare, and urbanization. Further, as these issues worsen, they coevolve with natural resource issues such as water and cropland scarcity, deforestation, and species diversity. These coevolving issues make improving the quality of life of citizens in markets experiencing rapid population growth a tough uphill battle. Thus, in order for organizations to take advantage of these new, emerging consumer and labor markets, they will have to add healthcare, education, water scarcity, social equity, and so on to their management agendas in the twenty-first century.

The Injustice of Distributive Inequity

Wealth is defined as the total value of the assets held by an entity—such as a person, household, organization, or nation—at a given point in time. The wealth created from global economic activity has come at high human and environmental costs that are borne disproportionately by the poor and marginalized people of the world. According to Brown (2008, 107), "The social and economic gap between the world's richest one billion people and its poorest billion people has no historic precedent. Not only is this gap wide, it is widening." It is the poor that bear the majority of the costs of global economic growth through the contamination of ecosystems, child labor, disease, and loss of natural capital that support their livelihood.

Daly and Farley (2004, 262) say that wealth is a "historical result of whose ancestors got there first, of marriage, of inheritance, plus individual ability and effort and just plain luck." They don't take issue with these per se, but they strongly believe that without also accounting for the huge distributive inequities of wealth that exist in the world today, achieving sustainability will be impossible. Unfortunately, even though environmental and social justice have been endorsed over the past 60 years by numerous international conventions, including the United Nations, millions of people are still denied these rights daily. Life expectancy is now declining in many parts of the poverty-stricken world indicating that even the most basic human right, that of survival, is threatened in places. For example, the 40-year life expectancy of people living in Botswana and Swaziland is only half the 80 years that those living in Sweden and Japan are expected to live (Brown 2008). Further, there is a swelling flow of impoverished environmental refugees fleeing their homes because of land degradation, water scarcity, and climatic disasters. Some societies are so stressed over basic resources and their inability to meet the basic needs of their people that their political systems are failing. Brown (2008) believes that these are the early signs of decline in our civilization.

Economic Injustice

As previously mentioned, the gap between the rich and the poor is widening in this full world. Research shows that the richest 25 percent of the world's population receives 75 percent of the world's income even when adjusted for purchasing power (Milanovic 2002). In fact, the gap between the rich and the poor citizens of the world has been identified as the "twin peaks" (Quah 1997), reflecting the fact that the world is socially divided into polar opposites. One pole consists of the world's poorest citizens. Approximately 2.4 billion people have a mean income of less than $1,000 a year, and 4.6 billion make less than $1,500 annually (Hart 2005; Sánchez, Ricart, and Rodríguez 2005). These people live in the poorest regions and countries especially in India, sub-Saharan Africa, Indonesia, and rural China. Poor nations and regions comprise

42 percent of the world's population, yet they receive only 9 percent of the world's income. At the other pole are the 500 million people whose income exceeds $11,500 annually. They account for only 13 percent of the world's population, yet they earn 45 percent of the world's income. This pole includes markets in such countries as France, the United States, Japan, Germany, and the United Kingdom.

Further, even though the citizens of these affluent countries earn 45 percent of the global income, they have their own internal distributive inequity issues. For example, in the United States the income gap is widening. Data indicate that the top one percent of American wage earners is currently capturing more of the real national income gain than are the lower 50 percent (McKibben 2007). More and more average Americans are struggling to get by while the rich are getting richer. The working poor, primarily dual-income families that still cannot make ends meet, are being "nickeled and dimed to death" while trying to provide food for their families as global food prices continue to rise.

Given their clear coevolutionary relationship, it is no surprise that statistics on the distribution of wealth (defined above) mirror those for income distribution. Wealth is an important measure of economic wellbeing for several reasons: It provides the citizens who hold it with a cushion against adverse events such as illness and unemployment; it provides them with capital for entrepreneurial efforts and other investments; and it increases the income they have available for food, shelter, and other needs and wants. There is a very high disparity of wealth among the citizens of the world, even though there have been rising incomes in the developing markets of the world such as in urban China. In fact, global wealth is more concentrated than income both within and between countries, with the lowest level of wealth in the poorer countries that lack any sort of social safety nets. Not surprisingly, 90 percent of the world's wealth is concentrated in North America, Europe, and the rich Asian Pacific countries. India and China, if current growth continues, will move up in the global distribution of wealth, while Africa, Latin America, and the poor parts of the Asian Pacific region will continue in poverty. "Thus wealth may continue to be lowest in areas where it is needed the most" (Davies et al. 2008, xii).

Food Insecurity

The stresses on the ecosystem are having a serious effect on global food security. Brown (2008) notes that food insecurity is a tipping point that has brought many civilizations down over the ages. He explains that several converging trends are impacting farmers' abilities to meet the world demand for food. Falling water tables, loss of cropland to non-farm uses, and extreme climatic events such as droughts, heat waves, fires, and floods have resulted in world grain production that has fallen short of consumption for the last eight years. World grain stocks are at their lowest level in 34 years (Brown 2008).

Declining grain stocks combined with increasing demand for grain has led to the highest grain prices ever. Wheat prices nearly tripled between late 2005 and 2007, which is just one of the reasons why grain import costs for undeveloped and developing regions were five percent higher in 2006. Further, the United States is now taking close to one-third of its grain harvests out of food production and using it for the production of fuel-grade ethanol, putting that much more pressure on grain prices. Rising prices like these will force many undeveloped and developing markets to cut back on food imports, placing them under a greater risk for political, social, and/or economic failure due to food insecurity (Halweil 2007a).

Cropland is decreasing because farming has become so efficient. Since 1945, primarily because of improved efficiency, an American farm has been lost about every half hour on average (McKibben 2007). There are so few U.S. farmers that since 1980 the Census Bureau hasn't even listed farming as an occupation. Further, as farms have declined so have the rural farming communities that supported them. Today, due to the intense consolidation and specialization of the industry, sociologists have designated many areas in rural America "food deserts" because the population is totally dependent on convenience stores without access to fresh produce (McKibben 2007). Consider the irony of midwesterners going to local food banks for cornflakes to feed their children, all the while surrounded by fields of corn grown to feed livestock for meat consumption. The results for rural communities in undeveloped and developing markets in other countries could be even more devastating than in the United States as farming communities decline and the rural poor migrate to urban slums.

There are three major problems associated with growing crops on a centralized industrial scale that add to the world's food insecurity: There are limited water resources, the entire system is fossil-fuel based, and there are increased risks of spoilage and disease. Regarding the first, water scarcity, we discussed in Chapter 2 that the depletion of aquifers is happening at frightening speeds across the globe, and 70 percent of the water used by humanity goes for crop irrigation. Regarding the second, agriculture has become totally fossil-fuel dependent at every stage of the production and delivery chain. McKibben (2007, 63) says, "Our food arrives at the table marinated in oil—crude oil. Cheap and abundant fossil fuel has shaped the farming system we've come to think of as normal." The processing, packaging, and distribution of food around the world uses four times as much energy as farming itself. Food travels an average of 1,500 miles from the farm to the table. The grapes from Chile in the supermarkets on the east coast of the United States have traveled almost 5,000 miles, mostly by air, before they are consumed. Airfreight not only contributes from 10 to 30 times more carbon per mile than trucking, it also increases the price of food, putting even more pressure on global food security (Anonymous 2008c). Regarding spoilage and disease—the third issue—the recent cases of E. coli and salmonella bacteria in fruits, vegetables, and meats sold in the United States demonstrates that the centralized food system provides inherent risks of disease. The consolidation of the poultry industry, for example, is the underlying culprit for the spread of Avian flu, and more than half the poultry sold in Britain is contaminated with salmonella because of the industrialized process of stacking the bird cages on top of one another, thus forcing the birds to consume the wastes from the cages above (McKibben 2007).

The United Nations reports that close to one billion people, mostly in poorer nations, get fewer calories than they need for proper nutrition, while approximately 1.6 billion, mostly in wealthier nations, get more calories than they need. Humans, on average, obtain about 48 percent of their calories from three grains—wheat, corn, and rice. In the United States, the average grain consumption per person is 800 kilograms; most of this grain is actually consumed by livestock that is in turn consumed by people. On the other hand, in India each person consumes only 200 kilograms of grain, but most of that is consumed directly with little available for feeding livestock (Brown 2008).

Statistics like these make it clear that there is s strong coevolutionary relationship between wealth and food security. As Lester Brown (2008, 107) says, "Hunger is the most visible face of poverty," and the faces that it can be seen on the most are those of children. There are six million Ethiopian children under the age of five that are at risk from malnutrition, and some 120,000 only have a month to live (Dinnick 2008). There is also a strong coevolutionary relationship between the natural environment and food security. For example, the severity of the Ethiopian situation was exacerbated in 2008 when rains that allow Ethiopian farmers to plant a second crop did not come. Also, desertification is spreading in Ethiopia providing little hope that the land can sustain the expanding population.

Zakaria (2008, 3) says, "The 50 countries where the Earth's poorest people live are basket cases that need urgent attention." This raises an important question: Should the rest of the world try to save them from sinking by foreign aid or should the world engage in what Garrett Hardin (1974) calls "lifeboat ethics," where each of the more affluent nations, like lifeboats with limited capacities, must decide whether or not to pull these 50 struggling nations to safety? Hardin argues that the carrying capacity of the lifeboats is just like the carrying capacity of the Earth, and if all 50 of these countries swimming in the water are allowed in, it will overload the lifeboats resulting in complete justice coupled with complete catastrophe. According to Hardin (1974), the harsh ethics of the lifeboat become harsher when considering the reproductive differences between countries along with the land's carrying capacity to feed expanding populations. Most of these 50 countries also have failing social and political systems. How should the world respond? These are difficult ethical questions that must be asked by a global community moving toward a sustainable world. Politically, global poverty and income inequity exacerbate tensions between the rich and the poor leading to increased geopolitical conflicts and stresses that create a politically unstable world.

Health, Gender, and Educational Inequity

The gap between the rich and poor of the world is also reflected in disease patterns. The poorest billion suffer the most from infectious diseases such as malaria, dysentery, tuberculosis, respiratory infections, and HIV/AIDS. Infant mortality in the 50 poorest countries is 85 per 1,000 newborns, while in affluent countries it averages eight per 1,000 (Brown 2008). The HIV/AIDS epidemic has taken its toll on the poor who lack basic healthcare, especially the children. For example, in 2006 there were 39.5 million people infected with the HIV virus, and 25 million of them lived in sub-Saharan Africa. Of those, only one million were being treated with antiretroviral drugs (Brown 2008). The virus impacts all facets of these peoples' lives. Families break down when an adult becomes infected, and currently more than 20 percent of adults are infected in the region.

And the most heartbreaking impact may be the orphans created by the epidemic. It is predicted that there will be 18 million AIDS orphans by 2010 in sub-Saharan Africa. As Brown (2008, 111) says, "There is no precedent for the number of street children in Africa." Another serious impact of the HIV/AIDS epidemic in sub–Saharan Africa is that it is breaking down the ability of many of the region's communities to resist famine, so the spread of the virus and the spread of hunger are caught in a deadly reinforcing downward spiral.

In 2006, more women were affected with HIV than ever before in every region of the world (Jordan 2007). In the regions where women do not have a position of power in making decisions about sexual relations, the infection rates are rampant. This gender inequity is a widespread global problem because in many cultures women are seen as inferior persons whose primary purpose is to serve as vessels for male sexual pleasure and childbearing. Women brave enough to acquire birth control pills in developing regions often have to hide them from their husbands or lovers for fear that they will be accused of interfering with the men's right to control their fertility. In many parts of the world, women have no choice but to continue to have unprotected sex (Jordan 2007). Undervaluing, abusing, and otherwise discriminating against women is also a worldwide problem. One of the most egregious outcomes of gender inequity is violence against women whether it is verbal, physical, sexual, or economic. In many parts of the world, women are seen as mere property with no rights. Levels of income, education, legal rights, and political involvement are lower for women than men throughout the world.

Another rich–poor nation gap exists in literacy rates. Whereas the wealthy regions of the world can boast that almost all of their adult citizens are literate, the illiteracy rates in many undeveloped and developing regions are alarmingly high. Two-thirds of the 785 million illiterate adults are concentrated in the three regions of the world—south and west Asia, sub-Saharan Africa, and the Arab states—where one-third of men and one half of women are illiterate (Central Intelligence Agency 2008). Access to the Internet is a tool with the potential to diffuse education into the farthest corners of the globe. Whereas nearly 70 percent of the population in North America has access to the Internet, only 3.6 percent has access in Africa. This digital divide will likely continue until some of the underlying social, political, and economic issues are addressed in poor countries (Guillén and Suárez 2005). The irony revealed in statistics like these is that those who could benefit the most from Internet access—the poor with little or no access to schools, libraries, and the like—are the ones with the least Internet access.

It's also important to note that literacy rates within the wealthiest nations often vary significantly with levels of income, thus creating undeveloped markets within their borders. For example, functional illiteracy is a serious problem in the southern Appalachian Mountains of the United States, one of the nation's most poverty-prone regions. Adult functional illiteracy rates of 30 to 50 percent are not uncommon in rural areas of this region (Stead, Stead, and Shemwell 2003). Research indicates that poverty level is clearly related to literacy rates. For example, research on entering kindergarten students revealed that the average math and reading scores for African-American children, 36 percent of whom live in poverty, and Hispanic children, 29 percent of whom live in poverty, was 20 percent lower than the scores for white children, 11 percent of whom live in poverty. The researchers note, "By age four the average child in a professional family hears 35 million more words than a child in a poor family" (Winerip 2007). Thus, by the time children from lower income families turn five years old, they are already so far behind in school that they stay behind through high school, reinforcing the cycle of poverty and illiteracy within one of the wealthiest countries in the world.

Globalization, Capitalism, and the World's Undeveloped and Developing Markets

As discussed in Chapter 1, the global corporation today has the ability to influence the world on a scale never seen before. With globalization have come the rise of the giant corporation and the consolidation of global industries. In 2007 there were 63,000 multinational corporations employing about 90 million people, generating a quarter of the world's GDP and generating half of the greenhouse gases responsible for global warming. ExxonMobil, for example, is larger than the economies of 180 nations (Speth 2008).

The trend toward global industry consolidation continues as multinational corporations attempt to reduce costs via economies of scale. Industries such as energy, transportation, financials, automobiles, information technology, agriculture, and many others have seen major consolidation. Agribusiness, for example, has seen consolidation along every aspect of the food chain, from input providers to food processors to retailers. This trend is squeezing small farmers at every stage, from the availability and cost of seeds and fertilizers to the low prices paid for the food by the huge retail food chains. Three firms—Bayer, Syngenta, and BASF—control half the agrichemical industry, and 88 percent of the genetically modified seeds are controlled by Monsanto. Many undeveloped and developing markets are having a difficult time obtaining the improved seed varieties and breeding technology from multinational corporations, which now have the intellectual property rights to genetic resources once considered a global commons. At the retail end, global supply chains give large supercenters like Wal-Mart the power to squeeze producers for lower prices. This squeeze on both the input and output ends has resulted in a decline in farmers' income to some of the lowest levels in decades (Starmer and Anderson 2007). The rise of the global corporation in contemporary capitalism has resulted in the consolidation of economic and political power in the hands of the corporation, often at the expense of nations and communities. This consolidated corporate power is generally accountable to relatively few people.

Globalization, capitalism, and global corporations are all tightly linked and inherently grounded on the unlimited economic growth assumption and the ideology of free trade. Between 2000 and 2007 the world economy grew at its fastest pace in almost four decades, and global income per person rose by 3.2 percent—the fastest rate in history (Zakaria 2008). Globalization and contemporary capitalism are fueled by hyper growth, searching for new markets, cheap labor sources, and access to new resources. Such an economic system favors deregulation so corporate activity can expand as quickly as possible. This growth mentality is reflected in the behavior of corporate managers with their obsession on quarterly profits and the share price of stock. If the corporation doesn't experience growth in new markets and expanding profitability, it is penalized by the market with the CEO and Board of Directors held accountable by shareholders. Extreme pressures to cut costs and expand profits often deter organizations from accounting for the full environmental and social costs of their products or services. To do so may lead to higher prices, making the organizations uncompetitive in the global marketplace. According to Speth (2008, 116), even though challenging the unlimited economic growth assumption is like challenging capitalism itself, "The planet cannot sustain capitalism as we know it." Besides the carrying capacity issues already discussed at length, capitalism is also currently facing threats from global terrorism, geopolitical conflicts, global environmental change, and a social backlash against globalization itself (Hart 2005).

Urbanization

A large proportion of the economic activity becomes centered in urban areas due to the lack of infrastructure in rural areas (M. Porter 1998). According to the United Nations, by 2009 more of the world's population will live in cities than in rural areas. Although urbanization is slowing in the already urbanized nations of North America, Europe, and Latin America, 88 percent of the world's population growth between 2000 and 2030 will be in the cities in undeveloped and developing markets. Further, in Latin America where the highest level of social and income inequity in the world exists, megacities such as Mexico City and Buenos Aires have stable populations, but their slums are growing rapidly as the poor crowd into the cities (Lee with Mastny 2007). For the urban poor, the stress of living in overcrowded slums is incredible. Ecopsychologists argue that the lack of contact with nature in urban slums leads to a measurable decline in human wellbeing. Such declines have the potential to threaten political and social stability, tipping societies into chaos (Delgado 2007).

Africa and Asia will experience a doubling of their urban populations by 2030. Africa, which has only 38 percent urban population, has seen rapid growth in its urban areas due to rural poverty, wars, and population growth. People are migrating into the cities looking for ways to meet their basic needs, but these urban areas lack infrastructure and public health facilities for the increasing number of poor. The result is expanding urban slums where disease, hunger, violence, and a high risk for environmental disasters like flooding are prevalent. In Asia, the most populous region of the world, 40 percent of the population is urban. The regions in Pacific Asia, from Japan to Southeast Asia, have undergone an economic transformation in the past decades, experiencing rapid urbanization. Interior Asia, southern Asia, and western China have seen the rapid increase in their urban populations as well. Unfortunately, both poverty and pollution are becoming more critical with the urban growth in these regions; currently, 16 of the 20 most polluted cities in the world are in China (Lee with Mastny 2007).

In fact, there are approximately one billion people living in urban slums worldwide, areas where people live without their basic necessities—sanitation, shelter, clean water, or sufficient living space. More than 200 cities in undeveloped and developing markets have grown beyond one million inhabitants stressing the local, political, economic, and social infrastructures (Lee with Mastny 2007). Economically, an informal economy composed primarily of semi-legal or illegal ventures thrives in most urban slums as the basic means of economic survival for the poor. Informal employment accounts for one-half to three-quarters of the non-agricultural employment in poorer countries, with the greatest growth in sub-Saharan Africa, Asia, and Latin America. In some countries, informal employment accounts for more than one-half of the total GDP (Delgado 2007).

Other issues related to urbanization include indirect costs such as unsafe working conditions in factories and the use of child labor (children between five and 11). The International Labor Organization estimates that 1.2 million children are sold into labor each year with transactions totaling around $10 billion. One-sixth of these are African children from families who earn less than one dollar a day (Chafe 2007a). Also, urbanization is directly related to increased traffic congestion that is a major culprit in increasing air pollution, rising fossil-fuel costs, and increasing pressures on personal time (Lee with Mastny 2007).

Environmental Injustice

When members of poor communities and regions suffer disproportionate risks from environmental threats, there is environmental injustice. Much of the hazardous wastes generated in the more affluent countries is shipped and disposed of in the poorer countries of the world. For example, there has been a rapid increase in the consumption of electronic equipment, resulting in a three to five percent increase in electronic wastes (e-wastes) over the past decade. Of the 20 to 50 million tons of e-wastes generated, more than 90 percent end up in Bangladesh, India, and China, despite the Basel Convention of 1989 that was designed to stop the shipment of hazardous substances across international borders (United Nations Environment Programme 2007).

Environmental injustice is tightly linked to economic and social injustice. Natural disasters and environmental degradation affect the poor to a much greater extent than they do the rich. For example, the flow of environmental refugees in poorer nations is rising due to falling water tables and expanding deserts, and this rise is creating stress on both the social and political systems in cities. Whereas three million people were displaced during the U.S. dust bowl of the 1930s, the expanding desert in China is creating a dust bowl that could displace tens of millions of people. Maybe even more serious is that the majority of the three billion people who will be added to the planet by 2050 will be born in water scarce countries. Millions of villagers in Mexico, western China, and numerous countries in the Middle East and northern Africa may become refugees of "hydrological poverty" (Brown 2008, 123).

The changing climate and resulting increase in weather-related disasters such as floods, wildfires, heat waves, droughts, tornados, cyclones, hurricanes, and winter storms, will be a major source of environmental refugees in the future. Weather-related natural disasters were responsible for almost $220 billion in losses in 2005, and in 2006 5.4 million people worldwide were made homeless as a result of weather-related disasters. Floods affected 87 countries that year, and Africa experienced the worst flooding during monsoon season ever recorded. The potential number of refugees from rising seas and storms related to climate change could eventually reach the hundreds of millions, disproportionately affecting the poor and disadvantaged (Brown 2008). Most vulnerable may be people who live in the crowded slums of the planet's many densely populated coastal cities. Twenty-one of the world's coastal cities are expected to reach the eight million mark by 2015. Besides their initial disastrous effects, climate-related natural disasters leave myriad serious social issues in their aftermath including loss of jobs, separation of families, destruction of schools, hospitals, and places of worship, domestic violence, disease, sexual harassment in refugee camps, child labor, and trafficking of children (Chafe 2007b). If temperatures continue to rise as expected, then these problems are bound to worsen.

The wealthy industrial regions seldom have all the natural resources they need to fuel their economic machines. Japan, for example, has almost no resources of its own, and the European Community is not much better off. Also China, the world's fastest growing economy, lacks many of the resources necessary to fuel its economic growth engine. A large amount of these resources are imported from developing regions that often have an abundance of natural capital but few financial resources.

Under the current economic system, the rational thing is for the cash-rich industrial regions to purchase their natural resources from the cash-poor developing regions. However, this solution is flawed for two reasons. First, the resources being traded by these developing regions, for the most part, are natural capital that are limited and being depleted at unsustainable rates. As discussed earlier, under the current economic assumptions these natural resources have no value unless they are sold, so developing regions unwittingly transfer huge amounts of their nonrenewable resources to industrialized markets in return for financial capital. Of course, these undeveloped and developing regions can only collect cash so long as the resources last and remain affordable. Once they are gone their income source is gone, and the land is usually left scarred and devastated. This is precisely what is happening to rainforests all over the world; they are being cut for short-run financial gain only to be lost forever.

Second, the cash paid to undeveloped and developing regions for these resources seldom contributes much to the social welfare of the citizens. The resources are normally owned by a few landowners who may become wealthy themselves, but who often invest little of their money back into the economy. The jobs that result from trading nonrenewable resources for cash are typically low paying, and the returns on their investment are normally below average (M. Porter 1990; 1998). New firms in these resource-rich developing countries are normally tied to the excavation of the resources, and human rights violations are frequent as corporations seek ways to lower labor costs for their operations. Thus, those regions willing to trade their natural capital for financial capital will often deplete both their natural and social capital as they struggle to participate in the global economy.

Shifting Geopolitical Power, Conflicts, and Failing Political Systems

The expanding global economy has resulted in a diffusion of political power within the world. Zakaria (2008) contends that the great transformational growth in economic and political power in countries such as China, India, and Brazil signals that the political and economic power long held by the developed nations of the world, particularly the United States, is now shifting to emerging markets. Consider the fact that by 2040 the emerging-market countries of China, India, Brazil, Russia, and Mexico will generate more economic output than the historically dominant G-7 countries of the United States, the United Kingdom, Italy, France, Germany, Japan, and Canada. Currently, emerging-market countries own 75 percent of the world's foreign exchange reserves; China alone holds $1.5 trillion in its accounts (Zakaria 2008). Zakaria calls this future the post-American world where rising powers reject being integrated into the global system the "western way" and are instead choosing to enter on their own terms, thereby reshaping the system itself.

Jeffrey Sachs (2008) says that the real paradox of rising globalization is that the global economy is integrated while global society is politically divided. Sachs believes this provides the greatest threat to the survival of civilization because it makes it virtually impossible to get the global political cooperation necessary for dealing with the issues created by the rapid growth of the global economy. Sachs (2008) says that we are now crowded into an interconnected society of global trade, migration, geopolitical conflicts, pandemics, and global terrorism.

Global warfare has declined dramatically over the last two decades, decreasing over 60 percent since the mid 1980s. Although the public perception is that war is on the rise, the reality is that there is a broad trend away from wars among major countries (Zakaria 2008). Although the number of high-intensity conflicts has declined over the years, medium-intensity (sporadic rather than continuous violence) and low-intensity conflicts (nonviolent) have risen steeply. Sudan's Darfur region, the Republic of the Congo, and Iraq all rank among the deadliest of conflict zones (Renner 2007). Many of these conflicts are associated with scarce resources. The U.S. involvement in Iraq began when the Iraqis seized the Kuwaiti oil fields in the early 1990s. The allocation of scarce water among countries sharing the same water source, such as the Nile River, has led to conflicts among Egypt, Sudan, and Ethiopia, whose populations are experiencing exponential growth.

In Sudan, for example, declining rainfall and overgrazing have destroyed most of the grasslands. Sudan's population has increased more than four times, from 9 million in 1950 to 39 million in 2007, with a forecasted population of 73 million by 2050. Along with this increasing population is a six-fold growth in cattle production and an eight-fold growth in sheep and goat production. The grasslands have not been able to sustain this increase in livestock grazing. This type of shrinkage of cropland leads to tensions within communities as subsistence societies attempt to live off smaller parcels of land. In the Darfur region, the issue of food insecurity combined with the political conflict between Muslim groups—camel farmers and subsistence farmers—has led to a wholesale slaughter of black Sudanese in an effort to drive them off the land. This conflict so far has killed 200,000, and another 250,000 have died due to hunger and disease in the refugee camps in Chad (Brown 2008).

Research indicates the state failure rate is increasing. "Failing states are now an integral part of the international political landscape" (Brown 2008, 123). States fail when governments can no longer provide for the basic needs and security (education, healthcare, food, and so forth) for their people. Revenues cannot be generated to finance government, so the society becomes fragmented and disrupts into civil war. When this happens, groups such as the warlords in Afghanistan, the tribal chiefs in Somalia, and the street gangs in Haiti are often left to rule the failing state. Currently the CIA estimates that more than 20 states are failing, and the British government classifies 46 states as fragile. It is not surprising that 17 out of the top 20 failing states are experiencing rapid population growth, and that in 14 of them 40 percent or more of their populations are under the age of 15.

There is a tight coevolutionary link among insurgency movements, unemployment, environmental degradation, and failing states. The top three failing states are Sudan, Iraq, and Somalia; however, state failure is not always confined to national boundaries. For example, the genocide in Rwanda spilled into the Republic of the Congo drawing several other countries into the conflict. The war eventually claimed the lives of 3.9 million people. Of course, at some point, political instability such as this has the potential to spread and to disrupt the global economy (Brown 2008).

Distributive Equity: Searching for Economic, Social, and Environmental Justice

As we hope the above discussion has made clear, distributive equity—the fair distribution of resources and wealth—is a very contentious issue with numerous interdependent political, social, ecological, and ethical dimensions. If people are poor and are not having their basic needs met, they will have little concern for sustainability and the interests of future generations. In order to survive, the excessively poor are forced to overgraze grasslands, clear forests for fuel, and tolerate excessive pollution, which impacts both the local and global environment. On the other hand, people who are excessively rich over consume finite resources, jeopardizing future generations' abilities to meet their basic needs. Caring about sustainability means caring that future generations do not live in poverty, yet it is very difficult to ask people to care about the wellbeing of future generations when so many of the present generation's basic needs are not being met. Further, as previously discussed, the planet cannot sustain unlimited growth on a finite sphere. Given that the pie must stop growing, humankind is ethically obliged to address the numerous complex issues related to distributive equity (Daly and Farley 2004).

Stabilizing Population and Alleviating Poverty

As previously discussed, poverty and population growth are coevolutionary forces. Thus, slowing population growth will help alleviate poverty and alleviating poverty will help to slow population growth. Given the number of nations whose survival is threatened, population stabilization and poverty eradication have become national security issues across the globe.

At the beginning of the twenty-first century, the United Nations set a goal of decreasing by half the number of people living in poverty by 2015. Due to the vast economic improvements in the planet's two most populous countries, China and India, the world is on track to meet this ambitious goal. India is attacking poverty by making investments in infrastructure in villages that target the poorest of the poor. Many believe that if the rest of the international community would follow India's lead of targeting the poorest of the poor, hundreds of millions more could be lifted out of poverty. Unfortunately, even though China and India are both having some success in reversing their poverty trends, sub-Saharan Africa is slipping deeper into poverty. Also, as a group the failing states discussed above have extreme poverty rates that generally exceed 50 percent, and these rates continue to worsen (Brown 2008).

Education is one of the great economic equalizers. Formal education is one of the most effective ways to free oneself from a life of poverty. Unfortunately, there are currently 72 million children worldwide getting no formal education. Universal education is a key to eradicating poverty by narrowing the gap between the rich and the poor. The World Bank has taken the lead in resolving this issue with its Education for All Plan, which gives financial support to those countries that submit well-designed plans for achieving universal primary education of their populous. The goal of the World Bank plan is for all children in poor countries to get a primary school education by 2015, thus helping them to break out of the cycle of poverty (Brown 2008).

Historically, one of the major issues related to achieving universal education has been gender inequity. In short, women generally receive less education than men and in some cases are banned from formal education altogether. However, gender equity in primary education has improved. Of the 181 countries reporting educational data in 2004, two-thirds had achieved gender equity in primary education. And it seems that these investments in female education are having an impact on poverty reduction. It's been shown that children with an educated mother are twice as likely to be in school as children whose mother has no education. Also, improved female education rates have been related to such positive social outcomes as higher crop yields, increases in per capita income, lower HIV rates, lower infant mortality rates, and lower fertility rates (Herro 2007).

Regarding fertility rates, stabilizing global population will require achieving a replacement fertility rate of 1.6 children per couple. Achieving this will require widespread open access to family planning services. Governments supporting family planning can have a major impact on slowing population growth and eradicating poverty. Iran, for example, passed a national family planning law in 1993 and has cut its population growth rate by half between 1987 and 1994. This was accomplished through establishing 15,000 family planning clinics in rural areas, increasing the literacy of women from 25 percent in 1970 to over 70 percent in 2000, using broadcasting to increase awareness in rural areas, and involving religious leaders in the crusade for smaller families (Brown 2008).

Achieving Food Security

As previously discussed, the centralized global food system currently in place is leading the world into greater food insecurity because it aggravates water scarcity, it is fossil-fuel intense, and it contributes to the spread of bacteria and disease. That is why there is a "going local" movement afoot in agriculture designed to move away from a consolidated global food system toward a food system in which most of the food sold in local markets is grown, raised, and processed locally. For example, in 1978 China dismantled its collective farms and replaced them with family farms with long-term leases. This shift from centralized control to more local control has been very effective in increasing land productivity (grain harvests doubled in eight years after the policy was instituted) and reducing water usage. In another example Mexican farmers have organized local water associations, and these are helping to manage 80 percent of Mexico's irrigation systems more efficiently (Brown 2008; McKibben 2007). In July 2008 Wal-Mart, the U.S.'s largest grocery chain, announced its intention to move toward local sources for its produce and meats.

Other strategies to address food insecurity include rethinking how to make the land more productive for growing food crops, increasing water efficiency, producing protein more efficiently, and eating lower on the food chain (Brown 2008). Increased land productivity could result from breeding crops that are more drought and cold resistant or from increasing the amount of land used to produce more than one crop per growing season. Water efficiency can be improved significantly by adopting more efficient irrigation systems. Moving from flood and sprinkler irrigation systems to drip irrigation can greatly reduce water use and raise crop yields. According to Brown (2008, 181), "These simple systems can pay for themselves in one year."

Producing protein more efficiently is an important strategy for addressing food insecurity. Currently 37 percent of the world's grain supply is being used to produce animal protein from beef, pork, poultry, and fish. From 1950 to 2005 the world's meat consumption per capita doubled. Since beef and pork are the least efficient means of producing protein from grains, eating protein from fish and poultry that uses grain more efficiently can raise the productivity of both land and water. In fact, worldwide aquaculture has a great potential for producing efficient animal protein. China, for example, generates approximately two-thirds of the global fish-farm output from its fish poly-culture that mimics natural aquatic ecosystems. As Brown (2008, 187) says, "The world desperately needs new protein production techniques such as these. Meat consumption is growing twice as fast as population, egg consumption is growing nearly three times as fast and growth in demand for fish—both from the oceans and fish farms—is also outpacing that of population."

Eating lower on the food chain will also contribute to global food security as well as help curb global climate change. Whereas the animal protein based, high-food-chain American diet can only feed 2.5 billion people, the plant-based diet of India can feed 10 billion people. Not only that, "[A] plant-based diet requires roughly one-fourth as much energy as a diet rich in red meat. Shifting from a diet rich in red meat to a plant-based diet cuts greenhouse emissions as much as switching from a Suburban SUV to a Prius" (Brown 2008, 189).

Shifting Taxes and Subsidies

Critical as it is for sustainability, distributive justice is a contentious issue in free-market economies where the dream is to create wealth by working hard and being ingenious. It is a well-established ethical principle that distribution according to effort and ability is both just and necessary to provide the human motivation that drives the economic system. However, nature, society, the workforce, and government services also contribute to economic success and should be valued fairly as well. Thus, the market must get the prices right in terms of both the value of ecosystem services and social capital. If the distribution of income becomes more equitable additional benefits may accrue to society such as lower crime rates, economic stability, better healthcare, and more viable communities in general. Economists suggest that distribution policies should address income and wealth as well as market and non-market goods. Some of their policy proposals to address distributive equity include caps on income and wealth, a progressive consumption taxation policy, a progressive income taxation policy, a minimum income requirement, and increased inheritance taxes (Daly and Farley 2004).

In addition to developing more equitable government wealth and income distribution policies, there is also a need to put an end to government subsidies that support the destruction of the natural environment. Research indicates that the world's taxpayers provide approximately $700 billion annually in subsidies to environmentally destructive industries such as unsustaintable forestry and mining. These subsidies reduce firms' financial risks and increase their financial rewards, thus providing them with incentives to continue their environmentally destructive activities. In the United States alone, federal subsidies of $74 billion went to fossil-fuel based energy development in 2006. Thus, humankind is currently spending billions of tax dollars annually to subsidize the destruction of its own habitat (Brown 2008; Daly and Farley 2004; Speth 2008).

Creating Sustainable Communities

As discussed in Chapter 3, globalization and free trade pose an ominous threat to communities when they become too reliant on global corporations with their mobile capital for their economic base. Shuman (1998) points out that because global corporations today are so large and free to search the world for lower priced resources and cheaper labor, they are more likely than ever to close operations and move to areas where labor and materials are less expensive to acquire. Shuman identifies four ways that this threatens the stability and survival of communities: First it causes a decline in the quantity and quality of jobs; second, it poses huge costs on all levels of government; third, it contributes to the gradual decline of local culture; and fourth, it undermines the capacity of communities to plan for the future.

Shuman (1998) believes "going local" is the best strategy for communities to buck these trends and remain viable. By finding ways to create and maintain locally owned businesses that use local resources, employ local workers at decent wages, and serve the needs of local consumers, communities can protect their cultures and natural environments while keeping more of their money at home. In addition to being more economically, socially, and environmentally viable for the community, research indicates that entrepreneurs from locally owned organizations contribute more to the community in both time and resources than do global corporations because the community is their home, providing them with much more meaning than just cheap labor and resources. Further, as mentioned earlier, the resulting social ties and interactions from living in a close community contribute much more to individual wellbeing and life expectancy.

Part of strengthening local communities is reducing their carbon footprint and better preserving their natural capital, while stimulating the economic viability of the community. Sustainable communities, often called "eco-villages" or "smart-growth communities," have become more popular avenues to build economically viable communities that are environmentally sound and socially responsible. Sustainable communities may be found in rural, urban, and suburban areas in both wealthy and poor nations. The ideal is a community where human activities are integrated in the natural environment in ways that mimic nature and support human development for the present and the future. The vision is for the community to move to a type III industrial ecosystem (discussed in Chapter 3) where closed-loop, interconnected networks of firms and community organizations operate on renewable energy, export only absorbable heat and byproducts that can be used as inputs in other processes, engage in total materials recycling, and create zero non-biodegradable wastes.

Currently there are around 400 or so eco-villages around the world, and the movement is becoming increasingly popular. In the Findhorn eco-village located near Findhorn, Scotland, a study revealed that the village's ecological footprint was only 60 percent of the average footprint in the United Kingdom; and in another eco-village, Sieben Linden, Germany, carbon emissions were found to be only 28 percent of the German average. Many communities in the United States have adopted the concept of sustainable communities, such as those in the Puget Sound and the San Francisco Bay Area (Assadourian 2007b).

Building Cities as if People Mattered

As discussed above, the majority of the additional three billion people that will be added to the planet by 2050 will live in urban slums. Many of these slums will be squatter settlements because the poor often have no other options but to reside on vacant land wherever they can find it. Although many political leaders just hope they will go away, issues related to the growing number of urban poor—such as social unrest, rising resentment, and increased violence—will rapidly expand in the next decades. Rather than sticking their heads in the sand, nations are going to have to develop effective strategies to address the problems of the urban poor. For example, they need to provide better services in the rural areas in hopes of reducing migration to the cities, they need to upgrade the sanitation and drinking water in the urban slums to limit disease as much as possible, and they need to find ways to integrate the urban poor into the life of the community (Brown 2008).

In addition to solving issues related to the urban poor, cities across the globe also must work to solve problems of traffic congestion. If not, both human health and economic productivity will be seriously jeopardized in many cities. In Atlanta, Georgia, for example, 95 percent of the city's workers commute to work by automobile (Brown 2008). There are signs of change, however. The number of passengers on public transit has increased recently in the United States. The older European cities, with narrower streets and older infrastructures than most U.S. cities like Atlanta, have far less traffic congestion due to the use of alternative modes of transportation. In Amsterdam, for example, only 40 percent of workers commute by car while 35 percent walk or bike and 25 percent use public transit (Brown 2008).

Another indication of change is that a group of eminent Chinese scientists questioned the government's policy of building an automobile-based transport system. "They noted a simple fact: China does not have enough land to accommodate the automobile and to feed its people" (Brown 2008, 210). This fact is true for India and many other developing economies as well, and it is encouraging that at least the Chinese government allowed the questioning of their transportation policies. The big challenge is to reverse the trend in the developing economies to emulate the automobile-based transportation system in the United States.

Transforming Capitalism and the Global Corporation

Many believe that contemporary capitalism must be transformed in order to move toward more economic, social, and environmental justice within the world. This means that the global corporation, the driver of capitalism, must be transformed because it is the most dominant institutional and environmental force on the planet today. According to Speth (2008), the limited-liability, publicly traded corporation will have to be dramatically changed by this generation, just as previous generations set out to limit monarchy. He says that more voluntary initiatives on the part of corporations as well as more command-and-control regulations promoting corporate accountability are necessary to achieve this change. Ultimately, according to Speth (2008), the corporation must be transformed into a sustainable enterprise based on the philosophy of the triple bottom line.

Laszlo (2008) believes that capitalism is already being profoundly changed by a growing number of global industry leaders who are adopting sustainability as the core value for their organizations. He found that firms such as Wal-Mart, DuPont, GE, and Unilever are "doing well by doing good." By finding business opportunities that address social and environmental issues, these firms are demonstrating the coevolutionary nature of the triple bottom line. Global corporations such as these have the resources, market reach, responsiveness, and power to be major agents of change, providing "timely solutions that will allow [them] to regain [their] place as an agent of world benefit" (Laszlo 2008, 75).

Thus, it is again important to emphasize that global corporations are the primary entities that will determine which way civilization tips. If enough corporate leaders can transform their corporations quickly enough, then there is a good chance that they can tip the world toward sustainability. But will enough corporations participate so that this transformation can become a reality? Both Laszlo (2008) and Hart (2005) think they will. Both optimistically predict that corporations across the globe will continue to move toward new sustainable products and technologies that can increase profitability, reduce poverty, and protect the natural environment.

Conclusions

In this chapter we have examined the social dimension of sustainability, focusing on several critical coevolutionary social issues that face the small planet Earth. We have examined the economic, social, and environmental injustices that exist in today's world, especially those related to population growth, food security, income and wealth inequity, educational inequity, gender inequity, urbanization, and the problems of failing communities and nations. We followed our examination of these issues with a discussion of some ways that they may be addressed and, hopefully, alleviated. We discussed some ideas for stabilizing population, dealing with poverty, establishing global food security, creating income, gender, and educational equity, building healthy communities and nations, and transforming corporations into global change agents.

This is the last chapter of Part I. At this point, the reader should be rather familiar with the concept of sustainability, from the social dimension discussed here to the ecological and economic dimensions addressed in Chapters 2 and 3. As we come to the end of this part, we want to re-emphasize its most important message. Business organizations are the most critical of all change agents in today's society. The only way that the world can achieve the Bruntland Commission's beautiful vision of humankind meeting its own needs now and for posterity (World Commission on Environment and Development 1987) is for global corporations to join in and lead the parade. That is going to require that corporations make fundamental transformations to a business model based on triple-bottom-line thought and action.

Part II

Managing on a Small Planet

We discussed in Chapter 1 how business organizations, the people they employ, the customers they serve, the economy they participate in, the society they are a part of, and the planet they exist on are all coevolving together in a mutually causal process that has and will continue to permanently change each of the elements over time. In Chapters 2 through 4, we discussed how this perpetual coevolutionary dance has resulted in an ever-growing human footprint produced by a geometrically expanding population seeking insatiable economic gratification, and we discussed how this growing human footprint is threatening the economic, social, and natural systems that encompass humankind's home.

In the second part of the book, we turn our attention directly to the field of management—specifically to the theories, processes, and practices of sustainable organizational management. It is our goal to build a strong theoretical and practical base for managers interested in managing in triple-bottom-line ways thereby adding their considerable knowledge, resources, creativity, and wealth to the task of sustaining and improving the human habitat for both the present and future generations.

— 5 —

Coevolution and Sustainable Organizational Management

The field of management emerged during the second half of the nineteenth century as the machines of mass production captured the minds and hearts of the industrialized world. As true of all disciplines that emerged during that time, management's beginnings were heavily rooted in the mechanistic worldview pioneered by the father of modern physics and mathematics, Sir Isaac Newton. Just as Newton visualized the universe as working like a clock driven by unbending physical laws, organizations of the late nineteenth and most of the twentieth centuries were seen as manufacturing firms with long, impersonal assembly lines with workers performing narrow, mindless tasks under the direction of managers who relied on formal authority, precise procedures, financial incentives, and unyielding rules to control workers' behavior.

Adam Smith shaped the economic thought from which these mechanistic organizational structures appeared. He espoused the concept of division of labor based on the mechanistic view that a person's behavior can be broken down into small, standardized parts. Modern management emerged when Max Weber's bureaucracy and Frederick Taylor's scientific management provided the organizational structure and job-engineering techniques necessary to make division of labor an operational concept that could be meaningfully applied in large-scale manufacturing organizations. Other management scholars and practitioners such as Henri Fayol, Frank Gilbreth, Lillian Gilbreth, and Henry Gantt followed closely on the heels of Taylor and Weber. They added their own frameworks, processes, and techniques to the growing body of management literature supporting the idea that organizations require authority-driven mechanistic structures.

Explanations of human behavior that emerged in the early and mid-twentieth century were also highly mechanistic, including those espoused by Ivan Pavlov, John B. Watson, Edwin Thorndike, and B.F. Skinner. Taken together, these theories espoused that human behavior and learning are entirely shaped by the influence of external stimuli and consequences. Such theories leave little room for the influence of values, culture, and human thought processes in explaining human behavior, even though these are the very characteristics that separate humans from other species.

However, there was a dramatic paradigm shift in science in the twentieth century. The clockwork universe of Newton was replaced by the theories of quantum physics and relativity. These theories led scientists to understand that the universe is not simply a deterministic machine made up of individual parts. Rather it is a holistic system of interconnected, coevolutionary processes that have manifested into the universe as we know it today. These theories have also shown that reality is not an absolute; rather it is relative, depending on the always limited and imperfect perspectives of an observer.

Some different perspectives on business organizations and the people they employ and serve have accompanied this new scientific paradigm. Today's organizations are no longer seen as rule-driven machines with automaton-like labor being financially rewarded for performing minute monotonous tasks exactly as instructed. Rather, they are understood to be dynamic, interconnected networks of internal and external stakeholders (managers, employees, suppliers, customers, shareholders, and others) that both influence and are influenced by each other and their external environments. They are culture-based systems made up of creative, value-driven humans seeking economic, social, and spiritual fulfillment by contributing from their heads, hands, and hearts to organizational goal accomplishment. These people's behavior is based on perceptions resulting from a complex array of cognitive processes that, along with environmental stimuli and consequences, help explain how and why they behave as they do both in and out of organizations.

Noted management historian Daniel Wren (1994) points out that whereas the field of management is a mere century and a half old, the practice of management goes back to the beginning of humankind. Human survival throughout history has depended on people being able to effectively deal with the environmental threats and opportunities they face in ways that help them meet their physical, social, and economic needs. In their efforts to meet these needs, humans have historically developed organizations, whether they be hunting parties in 10,000 BCE or multinational corporations in the twenty-first century CE. The success of these organizations has forever depended on their ability to efficiently and effectively allocate their scarce resources so that they can accomplish their objectives, and doing this has naturally led to the rise and development of the practice of management. Thus, from time immemorial humans have managed each other and their resources in ways that allowed their organizations to effectively and efficiently accomplish their goals in order to meet the needs of their stakeholders in hostile yet opportunity filled environments.

Interestingly, the explanation Wren (1994) presents of the rise of management clearly demonstrates that management as practiced today is the result of age-old, coevolutionary processes. The relationships and interactions among the variables Wren identifies as being key to the rise of management—environmental opportunities and threats, human needs, organizations, and management processes—clearly meet the criteria for coevolution outlined by Terry Porter (2006) discussed in Chapter 1. Each of the variables both influences and is influenced by changes in the others. These influences are specific, mutually causal, simultaneous, multilevel, adaptive processes that have led to permanent changes in all the variables over the ages of human existence. Thus, management as we know it today is, in fact, the result of ancient coevolutionary processes that were literally set in motion at the dawning of human civilization.

Coevolution: Meta-Theory for Sustainable Organizational Management

Recall from Chapter 1 that coevolution is a biologically rooted theory demonstrating that interdependent entities evolve and change in concert with one another over time. Since its inception, coevolutionary theory has crossed its biological boundaries into other academic domains, including the field of management in general and sustainable organizational management in particular (Flier, Van Den Bosch, and Volberda 2003; Lampel and Shamsie 2003; A. Lewin, Long, and Carroll 1999; A. Lewin and Volberda 2003a; A. Lewin and Volberda 2003b; T. Porter 2006; Volberda and A. Lewin 2003). Management scholars refer to coevolution as a meta-theory, an overarching theoretical umbrella that encompasses numerous, often contradictory, established management frameworks and theories (Lewin and Volberda 2003b; T. Porter 2006). As we proceed with this chapter, we want to examine this meta-theory in some depth, especially as it relates to the ascent of sustainable organizational management.

Transcending the Adaptation Versus Selection Dichotomy

A review of contemporary management theories leads to an interesting realization that, despite their sound intuitive logic and solid research support, they provide very different explanations of why some organizations survive and others do not. Some of the theories advocate that environmental selection is the primary determinant of firm survival. These theories support the idea that environmental forces such as resource scarcity, institutional and competitive dynamics, and rates and predictability of change in the environment determine which firms survive and which firms do not. They imply that intentional managerial decisions and actions designed to adapt to these changing environmental forces are relatively insignificant factors in long-term organizational survival (A. Lewin and Volberda 2003b; Volberda and A. Lewin 2003).

However, other contemporary management theories advocate that organizational adaptation is the primary determinant of firm survival. According to these theories, organizations are able to adapt to their environments and survive by choosing and implementing effective competitive strategies, by creating learning loops that allow them to discover new and innovative approaches to the issues they face, and by having effective structural and change-management systems in place that allow them to continuously renew themselves. These theories imply that firms can develop the adaptive capabilities to survive in most any type of environment (A. Lewin and Volberda 2003b; Volberda and A. Lewin 2003).

Ironically, whereas both the selection explanations and the adaptation explanations of organizational survival are logical and supported by quality research, they are divergent in nature. Pfeffer (1993) referred to this divergence in the management literature as a "weed patch" of contradictory theoretical frameworks. The logical conclusion of the selection argument is that organizations are essentially victims of their environments with little or no control over their survival regardless of their management efforts. On the other end of the spectrum, the logical conclusion of the adaptation argument is that organizations that do a good job of strategizing, innovating, changing, and renew-ing themselves can survive regardless of what kinds of ripples and shockwaves shake up the environment. As with all divergent problems, these explanations totally contradict one another at their extremes. Recognizing this dialectical conundrum, management scholars have sought an overarching meta-framework capable of encompassing both environmental selection and firm-adaptation explanations of firm survival. The framework that emerged from this search is coevolution (Flier, Van Den Bosch, and Volberda 2003; A. Lewin and Volberda 2003b; Volberda and A. Lewin 2003). According to Flier, Van Den Bosch, and Volberda (2003, 2164) "Coevolutionary theory argues that the concurrent operating of adaptation and selection explains processes of [organizational] change and renewal."

According to this coevolutionary perspective, the relationship between selection and adaptation is circular. Changing environmental dynamics creates the need for new organizational forms with new capabilities. If successful, these new capabilities become a part of the environment, which in turn changes the environmental dynamics, which in turn starts the process anew. Organizations whose new forms give them the capabili-ties they need to adapt to the changing environmental dynamics remain viable and are selected by the environment to survive, while organiza-tions that do not change forms because of inertia or that change to forms with inadequate capabilities fail and are selected out of the environment (Flier, Van Den Bosch, and Volberda 2003).

Thus, firm survival cannot really be fully explained from either an adaptation perspective or a selection perspective. Explaining it fully requires accounting for the coevolutionary interrelationships between the two. Occasionally firms may do everything managerially correct but have the market collapse under them (e.g., the collapse of the real estate market), bringing them down and selecting them out despite su-perior adaptation capabilities, and occasionally some windfall market will blow in (e.g., the market for motor scooters when the price of gas spiked), giving even very poorly managed firms a chance to be selected by the environment to survive. However, these are extreme examples. For the most part, good management makes a difference when it comes to firm survival. Organizations that can create flexible, self-renewing organizational forms that allow them to continuously modify, update, and change their capabilities to meet the demands of a changing envi-ronment are much more likely to successfully adapt and remain viable competitors in their environments than are organizations that give in to structural inertia, failing to adapt, and eventually disappearing from the environmental landscape (Volberda and A. Lewin 2003).

As we have demonstrated throughout the book, the sustainability movement with its worldwide cries for economic equity, fair trade, social justice, clean water, clean air, greenhouse gas reduction, safe food supplies, safe consumer products, living oceans, species protection, and local economic development has become a major environmental force influencing the survival of business organizations both in the short term and the long term. The coevolutionary relationships between environmental selection and organizational adaptation provide a framework that can inform managers concerning their decisions to institute sustainable organizational management systems in their organizations. The framework highlights the point that organizations that develop self-renewing sustainable organizational management structures and processes will have the capabilities to survive in the new sustainability-infused business environment. On the other hand organizations that do not develop these critical capabilities, giving in to the inertia of doing things as they have always done them without regard for the environmental and social impacts of their actions, will eventually disappear.

Management Theories Under the Coevolutionary Umbrella

Thus as a meta-management theory, coevolution has the potential to bring numerous management theories expressing seemingly conflicting explanations of the relationships between organizations and their environments under one conceptual umbrella (A. Lewin and Volberda 2003b; T. Porter 2006). Eight management theories that fit under the coevolutionary umbrella are population-ecology theory, the contingency theory of structure, strategic choice theory, resource-based theory, institutional theory, organizational change theory, organizational learning theory, and stakeholder theory. Below we discuss these theories and demonstrate their relationships to the understanding and practice of sustainable organizational management.

Population-Ecology Theory

Population-ecology theory probably best epitomizes the selection side of the coevolutionary organization-environment relationship (Flier,

Van Den Bosch, and Volberda 2003; A. Lewin and Volberda 2003b; McKinley and Mone 2003; Volberda and A. Lewin, 2003). In this theory, the external environment of organizations, specifically the resource scarcity and competitive dynamics of that environment, determine the capabilities that firms need in order to survive. The environment retains those firms that successfully develop these capabilities, and it selects out the firms that do not. Ironically, according to population-ecology theory, the firms retained by the environment are likely to eventually become victims of their own success because they entrench the capabilities that have made them successful in the past into their cultural and operational cores, creating inertia and the inability to adapt to future environmental changes that are beyond their current capabilities. Thus, according to the theory, the door is always open for new firms with the capabilities necessary for the new environmental dynamics. Unfortunately, the theory predicts that most of the new firms that succeed will also eventually fall into the inertia trap and disappear from the competitive landscape. Thus, in a nutshell, population-ecology theory predicts that the business environment will always be characterized by firm turnover tied directly to changes in environmental dynamics—the more rapid the change rate the more rapidly firms will turnover (Hannan and Freeman 1977, 1984).

From a sustainable organizational management perspective, population-ecology theory predicts that as the competitive business environment evolves to encompass the need for effective social and ecological as well as economic performance, managers will be faced with the need to develop triple-bottom-line capabilities that allow their organizations to survive. Further, those firms that successfully adopt these capabilities will also have to develop organizational-renewal structures and processes that allow them to keep these capabilities sharp if they are to avoid the inertia trap that comes from success with their initial adaptations. Thus, population- ecology theory suggests that, as the sustainability revolution takes hold, there will be significant turnover in the population of firms operating in the economy with the new firms entering the environment being more sustainability savvy than the firms that are disappearing from it.

Contingency Theories of Structure

Taken together, the classical contingency theories of structure essentially say that the organizations most likely to survive and thrive are those whose structure is appropriate for the dynamics of the environment in which the organization operates. According to these theories, hierarchical, authority-driven, rule-driven, rigid, mechanistic structures and production processes are best for firm survival in stable, predictable environments; whereas knowledge-based, idea-driven, value-driven, flexible, organic structures and production processes are best for survival in turbulent, unpredictable environments (Burns and Stalker 1961; Emery and Trist 1965, 1973; Lawrence and Lorsch 1967; Woodward 1965). These theories fall primarily on the selection side of the coevolution process because environmental dynamics are the primary determinants of how organizations should be structured in order to survive (A. Lewin and Volberda 2003b).

More recent contingency theories of structure, referred to by McKinley and Mone (2003) as neo-contingency theories, demonstrate more adaptive relationships between organizational structures and the environmental contingencies they are affected by and/or have an effect on (Donaldson 1995, 2003; Drazin and Van de Ven 1985). According to these theories, organizations engage in a continuous process of structuring and restructuring in order to adapt to changes in relevant contingencies such as organizational size, manufacturing technology, or the state of their environment. When these structural adaptations result in a fit between organizations and the contingencies they are responding to, the organizations will be operating at optimum efficiency, thus creating slack resources for further capability development such as the development of new products and services that give them competitive market advantages. These new capabilities eventually find their way into the industry environment, thus changing the competitive dynamics of that environment, and at that point the cycle starts anew. Thus, neo-contingency theories of structure demonstrate circular, mutually dependent coevolutionary relationships between organizational structure and the environment.

Throughout the book we have made it clear that the rapid, pervasive rise of a sustainability consciousness has added and is continuing to add significant turbulence to an already hyper-changing business environment. As we discussed in Chapter 1, successfully responding to these changes will require that organizations adopt change-oriented organizational structures and processes that allow them to continuously adapt to the paradigm-level environmental shifts resulting from the sustainability revolution (Dunphy, Griffiths, and Benn 2007; Post and Altman 1992, 1994; Stead and Stead 1994; Winn and Angell 2000). In accordance with the tenets of neo-contingency theory, organizations whose structural adaptations provide them with new capabilities that fit these sustainability-based environmental shifts will survive and thrive. These new adaptive organizational capabilities will, in turn, create further sustainability-based shifts in the environment beginning the circular process again. Clearly implied here is that the organizations that become victims of structural inertia and try to live off of past successes in the sustainability arena, as well as organizations whose adaptation efforts fail to find a structural fit compatible with the new sustainability-based environmental challenges, will be selected out by the environment and disappear in the future.

Strategic Choice Theory

Just as population-ecology theory best epitomizes the selection side of organization-environment coevolutionary processes, strategic choice theory best epitomizes the adaptation side of the equation. According to Lewin and Volberda (2003b, 575), "the strategic choice perspective assumes that organizations have the discretion and the strategic capacity to select, enact, and shape their environments." Child (1972) first proposed the idea of strategic choice. He said that strategic managers in organizations have the power and responsibility to choose the environments in which their firms compete, the strategies their firms pursue in order to capitalize on the opportunities in the chosen environment, the performance criteria their firms use to define their success in implementing those strategies, and the appropriate structures for achieving these performance criteria.

Miles and Snow (1978) explained that there are a wide variety of ways to prosper in a particular environment, and it is the job of strategic managers to make the choices that will successfully align their firms' strategies, structures, and processes in ways that will take advantage of those ways to prosper. In doing so, strategic decision makers follow what Miles and Snow call an "adaptive cycle." They explain that firms are faced with continuous cycles of critical decisions related to what market domains to select (entrepreneurial problems), how products and services should be produced and delivered (engineering problems), and how the organization should be structured to best accomplish all of this (administrative problems). By continuously cycling through these questions, firms eventually fall into one of four strategic patterns: defenders, in which firms choose narrow, stable environmental niches that they can defend via efficiency and reliability; prospectors, in which firms choose broader, more dynamic environmental niches that allow them to compete via innovation and market leadership; analyzers, in which firms exploit established stable, reliable market niches like defenders but also seek new market opportunities when they arise like prospectors; and reactors, in which firms follow no apparent strategic type choosing to simply react to environmental changes as they occur. Managers in reactor firms are more like firefighters than strategic thinkers and actors, always reacting to the latest crisis. Miles and Snow point out that the strategic choices that managers make during these adaptive cycles are the primary determinants of how well their organizations are able to align their strategies, structures, and processes with their chosen environmental domains and, thus, survive.

Michael Porter (1985) pointed out that regardless of the specific type of strategy chosen by a firm, its success in helping the firm to adapt to its environment depends on its ability to provide the firm with one of two types of competitive advantages: those based on lower product/service creation, manufacturing, and/or distribution costs; and those based on product/service differentiation in the marketplace. Thus, firms attempt to develop core capabilities that align their chosen functional-level strategies (marketing, finance, operations, etc.) with their pursuit of sustained cost and/or differentiation competitive advantages.

Strategic choice theory has major implications for sustainable organizational management. Recall that we discussed in Chapter 1 how important it is to humankind's quest for sustainability that business organizations contribute their considerable knowledge, talent, people, and wealth to the pursuit of social and environmental responsibility. If, as strategic choice theory claims, strategic managers—managers at the upper echelons of organizations, such as chief executive officers (CEOs)—have the power to "select, enact, and shape their environments" (A. Lewin and Volberda 2003b, 575), then they clearly have the power to shape their organizations into forces for change to a more sustainable world. After all, strategic managers are the ones who make the final decisions regarding how organizations adapt to their external environments. Collectively then, strategic managers in global corporations have the power to make social and environmental responsibility a part of doing business, and if they do so they have a chance to leave a legacy of economic, social, and environmental justice and wellbeing for generations to come. Because of the key role played by strategic managers in humankind's pursuit of sustainability, we have dedicated Chapters 7 and 8 to exploring the strategic dimensions of sustainable organizational management in more depth.

Institutional Theory

Institutional theory essentially says that the number and types of strategic choices that managers actually have are limited by the boundaries, expectations, norms, rules, and beliefs that are institutionalized in the environment in which they are embedded, which Scott (1991) calls their "organizational fields." According to the theory, organizational adaptation is a process of conforming to the ever-evolving institutional demands placed upon them by their organizational fields. This conforming process naturally leads to homogeneity among organizations. Thus, institutional theory explains why organizations in particular markets and industries tend to be so similar, and it predicts that firms that are able to rapidly mimic emerging new market capabilities will be the most likely to survive. On the darker side, institutional theory also predicts that the similarities among firms eventually lead organizations to resist change, develop organizational inertia, and inevitably be selected out of the environment as the capability demands of their organizational fields change around them (Hoffman 1999; A. Lewin and Volberda 2003b; Volberda and A. Lewin 2003).

Hoffman (1999) points out that organizational fields are not monolithic, unchanging entities that reign over organizations until they give in to sameness, inertia, and eventually death. Rather they are dynamic, multifaceted, changing environments that form and re-form around shifting technologies, markets, or issues. In this view, "organizational fields and institutions coevolve" (Hoffman 1999, 351). To demonstrate this, Hoffman develops a model of how the organizational field and the institutional context of firms in the chemical industry coevolved around the issue of environmentalism between 1962 and 1993. He shows how as the organizational field surrounding the industry demanded more environmental responsibility, the organizations in the industry embedded environmentalism more deeply into their cultures which in turn led to further embeddedness of environmentalism in the organizational field and so on. Bansal and Roth (2000) support the conclusions of Hoffman, finding in their research that the more salient and deeply embedded environmentalism is in an organizational field the more legitimate environmental responsibility becomes for firms in that field.

Resource-Based Theory

Resource-based theory asserts that firm survival is a function of heterogeneity rather than homogeneity (A. Lewin and Volberda 2003b). At the heart of the theory is the idea that firms can best create sustained (long-term) competitive advantages by building their organizational capabilities on resources that are scarce, difficult to duplicate, and have no direct substitutes (Barney 1991, 1995). Hart (1995) provides an overall view of the theory, demonstrating that by converting rare, difficult to copy, non-substitutable resources into unique internal procurement, design, production, distribution, and service capabilities, firms can develop both cost and differentiation competitive advantages that can be sustained over a long period of time. Thus, resource-based theory explains some of the coevolutionary processes involved in the continuous cycles of emergence, maturity, and decline of competitive capabilities in the environment.

Hart (1995, 1997) contends that resource-based theory needs to focus more directly on natural resources as a source of sustained competitive advantage. He says that if firms will develop the capabilities to prevent pollution and wastes at their source, to produce and deliver ecologically sensitive products and services, and to penetrate developing markets in socially responsible ways, they will be rewarded with sustained competitive advantages. Russo and Fout's (1997) findings support Hart's contentions. They found that organizations that develop natural resource-based capabilities can improve both their performance and profitability. Further, Richard (2000) found that racial, cultural, and social diversity in organizations can be valuable social resources that add to firms' long-term competitive advantages.

Organizational Change Theory

Organizational change theory is actually comprised of a wide array of behavioral science frameworks and techniques related to managing planned organizational change efforts (Weick and Quinn 1999). Recall we discussed in Chapter 1 that successful planned organizational change efforts require active involvement by managers at all levels, open organizational dialogue and consensus-building processes, and effective integration of the changes into the culture of the organization. We also discussed that the nature of the planned change effort is determined by the depth of cultural integration required; surface-level changes focus on integration at the shallower artifact and norm levels of culture, while transformational-level changes require integration at the deeper values and beliefs levels of culture.

Organizational change theory has its roots in the works of Kurt Lewin

(1946, 1947). Lewin identified three stages of change: unfreezing, changing, and refreezing. Unfreezing is the diagnostic stage of change where the existence of issues is recognized and the need for change is accepted. Data regarding the nature of the issues facing the organization are gathered, analyzed, and fed back to the relevant organizational members in this stage, and psychological contracting regarding the use of the data and the roles of the organizational members also takes place in this stage. In the changing stage, changes designed to allow the organization to successfully adapt to the issues identified in the unfreezing stage are planned and implemented by the organization, and feedback loops are established to measure the effectiveness of the changes so that adjustments can be made if necessary. In the refreezing stage, the newly implemented changes are stabilized and institutionalized in the routines, processes, and structures of the organization. Organizational change processes themselves are also stabilized and institutionalized in the organization in this third stage so that it is capable of continuous renewal and change in the future. Weick and Quinn (1999) found that these stages vary slightly depending on whether the change is based on a specific event or is continuous in nature. They said that whereas event-based changes follow Lewin's three stages pretty closely, continuous-change processes tend to be more organizational rebalancing processes with less discrete stages than found for event-based changes.

Kurt Lewin (1947) focused much of his attention on the role of group dynamics in change. He explained that the forces (or dynamics) at work within a group are the primary determinants of the outcomes achieved by that group. Group dynamics characterized by effective self-disclosure and feedback, open dialogue, risk taking, active listening, and consensus-building will lead to group success; whereas group dynamics characterized by closed-mindedness, defensiveness, playing it safe, power plays, and bickering will stop a group in its tracks. Lewin demonstrated in his research that groups with positive dynamics in place are a powerful means of social change. He developed "action research" (K. Lewin 1946), a still popular process in which groups of people work together through continuous cycles of unfreezing, changing, and refreezing in order to develop effective ways to deal with the issues they face. Due largely to Lewin's work, group processes such as focus groups and team-building are at the heart of organizational-change efforts to this day. According to Senge (1990), effective group dynamics are more critical than ever in organizational change. He says that team-learning processes in which organizational teams engage in dialogue designed to uncover, question, and change underlying organizational values and beliefs are the primary organizational mechanisms for successful transformational change in today's turbulent global business environment.

Effective organizational change processes such as those described above will be critical for firms wishing to successfully adapt to the rapidly evolving, sustainability-based business environment (Waddell 2007). As discussed in Chapter 1, organizational renewal efforts will need to focus on reaching the deepest levels of organizational culture where sustainability can be integrated into the core values and beliefs of the organization. Further, managers will need to establish action-research cycles in their organizations that are calibrated to recognize, analyze, and act on data related to performance in and among all three dimensions of sustainability. To do all of this, managers will need to establish effective group processes capable of focusing on, questioning, and if necessary changing their organizations' underlying value and belief systems (Senge 1990, 2007; Waddell 2007).

Organizational Learning Theory

Effective organizational learning processes are crucial for organizational adaptation because they make it possible for organizations to continuously learn (and unlearn) the knowledge, innovations, processes, skills, values, and norms they need (or no longer need) to efficiently and effectively manage the myriad coevolutionary organization–environment relationships critical to their long-term survival (A. Lewin and Volberda 2003b; Senge 1990). Learning, as discussed earlier, was once considered a simple process of shaping human behavior through the manipulation of external stimuli and consequences. Today learning is recognized as a complex, cognitive process whereby a person perceives environmental data through the five senses; searches a complex web of mental models composed of data, norms, values, beliefs, memory, knowledge, opinions, attitudes, and cultural mores in order to give meaning to the perceptions; and then bases his/her actions on these interpretations.

Organizational learning theorists say that organizations learn in essentially the same way as individuals. Cyert and March (1963) introduced the organizational-learning construct by observing how organizations adapt to changes in their environments through cognitive-learning processes such as problematic search (A. Lewin and Volberda

2003b). Learning theorists describe organizational-learning processes as either single-loop learning or double-loop learning (Argyris and Schön 1978; Senge 1990). Single-loop learning is essentially a process by which organizations search their environments for relevant data, interpret these data by filtering them through familiar, well-established organizational mental models, and then take actions to adapt to their environment based on these interpretations. This single-loop learning process is generally effective when firms make familiar or routine adaptations. However single-loop learning leaves little room for questioning the efficacy and accuracy of the familiar mental models, so when thinking in new and different ways is called for in organizational adaptation, double-loop learning becomes necessary. In double-loop learning, familiar mental models are examined and, if necessary, changed before they are applied to the new, novel environmental data. Conducting such an examination of currently held organizational mental models requires a deep examination of the underlying values and beliefs upon which these mental models are based. Given today's turbulent, unpredictable environment, organizations are being faced more and more with the need to replace their familiar mental models with new and different ways of thinking, making double-loop learning a critical coevolutionary skill.

According to Senge (1990), systems thinking—thinking in long-term, circular, holistic ways—is critical for effective organizational learning. Systems thinking rests on the notion that in the long term, relationships tend to be circular and mutually causal as opposed to linear and unidirectional. As discussed previously, long-term mutual causality is a central characteristic of all coevolutionary relationships, whether these relationships are between honeybees and the plants they pollinate or global corporations and the customers they serve. Thus, systems thinking means looking for circular patterns of dynamic interrelationships rather than linear patterns of discrete cause and effect.

These circular dynamics are sometimes reinforcing and sometimes balancing. Reinforcing dynamics begin as small changes that amplify over time, potentially spiraling out of control if not checked. These cycles can be either vicious reinforcing loops, in which things go from bad to worse over time, or they can be virtuous reinforcing loops, in which things go from good to better over time. Balancing dynamics are those processes that act to maintain stability and status quo in systems. A balancing process generally includes some goal, target, or natural limit that holds the system in check. Although they are simple enough to understand, both reinforcing and balancing processes are often implicit, subtle, and very hard to detect. Yet they are ever present in the dynamics of these organizational coevolutionary relationships.

Effective organizational learning is obviously directly related to successful strategic choice processes, and thus to successful adaptation processes. Organizational-learning processes are in fact the mechanisms organizations use to identify, gather, interpret, and act upon accurate, relevant internal and external data thus helping managers to make strategic choices that better fit the environmental dynamics they face (A. Levin and Volberda 2003b; Volberda and A. Lewin 2003). Specifically, single-loop learning processes give organizations the potential to develop effective, efficient routines for dealing with familiar environmental vacillations, and double-loop learning processes give organizations the potential to be innovative and do things differently (think out of the box). Both are significantly enhanced by effective systems-thinking processes that give organizations the ability to better perceive the underlying and often hidden circular dynamics that characterize the long-term interrelationships between organizations and their environments.

It is now generally recognized that novel, unexpected, nonlinear change is a primary characteristic of today's global business environment, and as we have already demonstrated in much depth, the changing social and environmental demands related to the sustainability revolution are major contributors to that turbulence and change. It will be necessary for managers following the practices and principles of sustainable organizational management to establish single- and double-loop learning processes that allow them to accurately interpret the social and ecological environmental dynamics affecting them (Senge, 2007; Waddell 2007). This will require them to develop systems-thinking processes in their organizations capable of perceiving the complex long-term, nonlinear relationships that exist within the data.

Stakeholder Theory

Stakeholder theory provides another explanation of how effective strategic-level organizational managers can help organizations successfully adapt to their environments. Freeman (1984, 46) defines stakeholders as "Persons or groups that can affect or are affected by the achievement of the organization's objectives." He points out that stakeholders include customers, shareholders, employees, regulators, suppliers, competitors, activist and advocacy groups, and so on, all whom have an interest in the practices of the corporation. Stakeholder theory basically says that successful firm adaptation is a function of serving the varied, often conflicting needs of these multiple stakeholders.

Stakeholder theorists advocate that in addition to economic interests, strategic managers should give weight to the ethical, social, political, and ecological interests of organizational stakeholders when making their decisions (Ansoff 1979; Carroll 1995; Clarkson 1995; Donaldson and Preston 1995; Freeman 1984; Freeman and Gilbert 1988; Hart and Sharma 2004; Hosmer 1994; Jones 1995; Starik 1995). Stakeholder theory is structured so that managers can discover the ethical core that underlies their strategic decision-making processes—known as their "enterprise strategy"—by assessing the interactions among the key values, key stakeholders, and key societal issues of their organizations (Freeman 1984; Freeman and Gilbert 1988; Stead and Stead 2000). Strategic managers following the tenets of stakeholder theory will include in their assessments who is affected, how they are affected, what rights they have, and so on.

Thus, stakeholder theory ethically encourages managers to broaden their strategic processes to include societal and ecological concerns. Doing so requires that the Earth and its people be given stakeholder status. Recognizing the significance of the Earth and the broader society as stakeholders is critical in integrating sustainability into the ethical core of organizations, allowing managers to recognize that the long-term survival of business and the long-term survival of the human species and its quality of life are intricately interconnected coevolutionary processes. After all, the Earth includes and supports all of humankind within its sphere; it is the geographical location of all business activity; it is the source of the resources and energy necessary to make the economic engine purr; it is the sink into which the wastes of economic activity are poured; and it is humankind's home (Gladwin, Kennelly, and Krause 1995; Post 1991; Shrivastava 1995; Starik 1995). From this perspective, the Earth and its people are the ultimate stakeholders of business organizations.

Of course the planet and its six billion plus inhabitants cannot all be active stakeholders, sitting on boards of directors, or attending shareholder meetings of the world's global corporations. Many exist on the fringe of the economy and have little traditional stakeholder power

(Hart and Sharma 2004). However, the Earth and its inhabitants have a growing cadre of friends in the world's communities, boardrooms, executive suites, retail stores, financial markets, courtrooms, media, halls of government, and factory floors that are representing the interests of society and the natural environment. These include environmentally and socially conscious consumers, investors, employees, legislators, regulators, litigators, interest groups, lenders, insurers, and industry standards setters, among others (Edwards 2005; Hawken 2007; Starik 1995). The worldwide growth in the influence of these sustainability-conscious stakeholders will ensure that they will be increasingly significant players in the coevolution to sustainable organizational management in the global economy.

Many of the socially and environmentally motivated stakeholders such as the poor, physically weak, isolated, and many animals remain on the periphery of traditional corporate stakeholder power circles despite their pervasiveness in both numbers and interests represented. Finding productive ways of communicating with them is no easy task. Hart and Sharma (2004) and Gregory (2000) encourage the development of value-based, open-dialogue processes that allow the voices of these hard to identify and reach stakeholders to be heard and accounted for in managerial decisions. Hart and Sharma (2004) believe that if such processes are put into place, these "fringe" stakeholders provide real sources of imaginative new capabilities for corporations doing business in a sustainable world.

Coevolution, Organizational Renewal, and the Rise of New Organizational Forms

In sum, coevolutionary theory explains that organization-environment coevolution is a continuous, circular selection-adaptation process. Through this process, coevolutionary theory overarches and synthesizes numerous seemingly contradictory contemporary management theories related to organizational selection and adaptation. One of the most prominent conclusions of scholars in the organizational sciences is that, over time, the coevolutionary selection-adaptation cycles that occur and reoccur in organization-environment relationships result in the rise of new, more self-renewing organizational forms. These new organizational forms arise from new entrepreneurial activities and new creatively destructive technologies that change the fundamental capabilities necessary for survival in the environment (Flier, Van Den Bosch, and Volberda 2003; Hart and Milstein 1999; Lampel and Shamsie 2003; A. Lewin and Volberda 1999, 2003a, 2003b; T. Porter 2006; Rodrigues and Child 2003; Schumpeter 1950; Volberda and A. Lewin 2003). According to Lampel and Shamsie (2003, 2189), "Coevolutionary research on strategic adaptation and change has focused on the emergence of new organizational forms. Technological innovation, global interdependence, and new managerial mindsets are combining to create organizations that are more efficient, more flexible, and quicker to adapt to change."

Lewin and Volberda (2003b) point out, as mentioned in Chapter 1, that Weber provided a coevolutionary explanation of the rise of the bureaucratic organizational form as large-scale industrialization replaced small-scale cottage industry as the foundation of the economy. Although by today's organizational standards bureaucracy is a stable, change-resistant structural form, from the late 1800s until the early 1970s the bureaucratic form provided an efficient, orderly, authority-based system that was capable of dealing with the stable environmental dynamics that existed during the rise of large industrial organizations. Lewin and Volberda (2003b) tell a similar story of the rise of the M-form (multidivisional form) of organization introduced by Chandler (1962). According to Chandler, the M-form coevolved with changes in the transportation and communication industries, "which enabled business enterprises to manage across time and space and to diversify their business interests" (A. Lewin and Volberda 2003b, 579).

In their research on the coevolutionary capabilities of self-renewing organizational forms, Volberda and Lewin (2003, 2125) conclude that too often "prescriptions for speeding change, counteracting resistance to change, installing heroic leaders, empowering bottom up processes, creating boundary-less structures, [and so forth] . . . focus on a single variable, process or strategy," which more often than not creates partial one-time solutions that are not easy to duplicate. Their review of the effectiveness of various self-renewing mechanisms and processes led them to three principles for organizational self-renewal designed to help organizations to synchronize their internal self-renewal efforts to the pace and type of selection-adaptation coevolution going on in the environment.

The first of the three principles is "the principle of managing internal rates of change" (Volberda and A. Lewin 2003, 2126), which says that internal organizational change-management structures and routines that track and act on changes in environmental capabilities should function at rates of change equal to or greater than the rates of change in the external environment. The second principle is "the principle of optimizing self-organization" (Volberda and A. Lewin 2003, 2126), which says that managers should eschew the use of bureaucratic outcome-control mechanisms in favor of self-organizing principles that stress self-responsibility and self-control and push decision making down to the lowest level possible in the organization. In these self-organizing systems, "managers function as stewards of the evolutionary process and focus their managerial role on devising and articulating critical values and on establishing boundary conditions that enable and guide decision making at lower levels of the organization."

The third principle of organizational self-renewal is "the principle of synchronizing concurrent exploration and exploitation" (Volberda and A. Lewin 2003, 2127), which means that managers should seek to balance their organizations' efforts to enhance their current competitive capabilities via product and process improvements (exploitation) with their efforts to find new ideas and innovations that will improve their competitiveness in the future (exploration). Overemphasis on exploitation creates the potential for the "competence trap" in which organizations fall behind the coevolutionary pace of their competitors' innovations. Overemphasis on exploration creates the potential for the "renewal trap" in which organizations expend energy and resources on the future, but in doing so lose their current identity in the market. Interestingly, exploitation is essentially a single-loop learning process whereby organizations learn how to improve their current products and processes, and exploration is essentially a double-loop learning process whereby organizations seek innovation and change. Thus, implied in this principle is that finding a balance between single- and double-loop learning is a key to effective organizational self-renewal.

It has long been recognized that interactions between business and the social and natural environment are significant features of environmental turbulence, and thus they are significant drivers for self-renewing organizational forms (Emery and Trist 1973; Schumacher 1973, 1979). The adaptation of organizational forms to meet the changing social and ecological demands placed on organizations was probably first considered by E.F. Schumacher (1973), who in his book, *Small Is Beautiful: Economics as if People Mattered,* developed his "theory of large-scale organizations," which focuses on creating self-renewing structures that are explicitly designed for sustainable organizational management. We will discuss this theory in more depth in the next chapter.

Conclusions

Coevolutionary management theory makes it clear that organizations can either adapt to their environments by actively creating and maintaining new organizational capabilities that encourage and support continuous cycles of organizational change and renewal, or they can sit passively by and allow organizational inertia to promulgate a culture of resistance to change and organizational sameness. Coevolutionary management theory also makes it clear that those organizations that allow themselves to be consumed by inertia are the ones most likely to disappear from the competitive landscape. Organizational survival is never assured, but its chances are much improved for organizations that create management processes and structures that encourage long-term strategic thinking, learning, change, and renewal.

We have made the case throughout the book that the interactions among the economic, social, and ecological dimensions of the global environment are currently threatening the quality of life for many people today and for generations to come. As we pointed out in Chapter 1, there is now a global movement of people and organizations afoot that is working to change this. These people and organizations are working for a sustainable world—a world with global economic, social, environmental, and intergenerational justice. As with any movement, this one started out small, but it is now a worldwide movement that is snowballing in terms of its numbers of people, its represented issues, and its represented groups (Edwards 2005; Hawken 2007; Senge et al. 2008). This movement and the concerns it brings with it are now primary drivers in the changing competitive landscape of business organizations. Issues such as climate change, energy efficiency, fair treatment of people, limits to growth, preservation of natural beauty, support for local products and services, and community philanthropy are already large landmarks on the competitive landscape of today's corporations, and the reinforcing dynamics among these various landmarks means that they only promise to get bigger and more significant in the future.

If coevolutionary theory is accurate then organizations that change their strategies, structures, and processes in order to integrate the pursuit of sustainable organizational management into their cultures and capabilities will be better prepared to adapt to the rapidly evolving sustainability issues now crowding the competitive business landscape. Unfortunately, this will not be true for organizations that do not develop such capabilities, opting instead to continue doing business as usual. Thus, as the sustainability movement continues to snowball, more and more organizations that are capable of renewing themselves in sustainable ways will survive (will be retained in the environment) while more and more business-as-usual organizations will likely disappear (will be selected out of the environment).

— 6 —

Leading the Way to Sustainable Organizational Management

We established in Chapter 5 that surviving in the complex, coevolution-ary adaptation-selection dynamics of the twenty-first century business environment requires that managers effectively and efficiently maneuver their organizations through continuous cycles of transformational change. These cycles involve discovering, designing, refining, and redesigning myriad sustainable organizational management capabilities in order to meet the increasingly demanding sustainability-oriented environmental capabilities emerging today. As we progress with our discussion of sustainable organizational management, it is critical to understand that ultimately it is the responsibility of the people that make up organiza-tions to develop, use, and continuously change their organizations' sustainability-based capabilities. After all, the common denominator for all organizations is people. Organizational structures are dynamic networks of people, organizational change requires that people change their behaviors, new technologies and processes are developed and implemented by people, and strategic choices are made by people. In short, successful organizational adaptation is ultimately a function of human behavior.

Human behavior, whether it be individual or organizational, results from a process in which humans sense signals from their environments, interpret these signals through complex cognitive webs of knowledge, values, beliefs, memories, norms, and attitudes, and behave in ways that are consistent with these interpretations. Clearly, the relationships among the variables in this process—environmental awareness, cognitive interpretation, and human behavior—are specific, reciprocal, and lead to permanent changes in each over time. In other words, these variables coevolve.

There is a rich body of research that supports the important role of human behavior processes in the effective implementation of sustainable organizational management. Sharma (2000) demonstrated that the environmental strategies chosen by corporate managers are significantly influenced by those managers' cognitive interpretations of environmental issues as either threats or opportunities. Cordano and Frieze (2000) found that both managerial attitudes toward pollution prevention and managerial interpretations of norms related to environmental regulation affect organizational decisions regarding the implementation of source-reduction activities such as materials reduction and materials substitution. Egri and Herman (2000) found that managers in organizations that provide environmentally related products and services tend to have more ecologically centered personal-value systems than their counterparts in other types of organizations. And Bansal and Roth (2000) found that personal values of managers influence organizational interpretations of environmental responsibilities, and these interpretations in turn influence the nature of organizations' environmental initiatives. Bansal and Roth go on to say that strong personal values for ecological responsibility can influence the ecological responses of firms in three ways: First, they serve as effective cognitive screening mechanisms that allow managers to determine which environmental signals are important to a firm's ecological responsiveness and which ones are not. Second, they often lead to the emergence of organizational members who champion ecological responsibility within the firm. "Third, a firm's top management team and other powerful organizational members are more receptive to changes in the organizational agenda, products, and processes if these fit with their own personal values" (Bansal and Roth 2000, 731).

Strategic Leadership: Human Energy for Sustainable Organizational Management

Taken together, the above research makes it clear that adopting the capabilities necessary for sustainable organizational management requires that firms channel their immense human energy into continuously creating, implementing, and changing organizational capabilities in ways that contribute to successful organizational adaptation in the economic, social, and ecological arenas. Channeling human energy is one of the most fundamental definitions of leadership (Nahavandi 2009). Thus, effective leadership is critical if organizations are to continuously adapt their sustainable organizational management capabilities to the rapidly changing sustainability demands in the business environment.

Effective leadership in the drive for sustainable organizational management is especially critical from the strategic, top-management level of the organization—that is, leadership from chief executive officers, chief operating officers, chief financial officers, top-management teams, and boards of directors. This is generally referred to as "strategic leadership" (Finkelstein and Hambrick 1996). Strategic leaders generally have broad responsibilities for the long-term direction of their firms, and their performance has traditionally been based primarily on the economic success of their firms. Of course, introducing sustainable organizational management adds social and ecological dimensions to the traditional economic responsibilities of strategic leaders. Thus, it is within this group that changes in thinking about the relationships between economic, social, and environmental protection are most critical.

Business organizations are now at the nexus of a world movement toward sustainability. They can be the difference-makers in the search for a sustainable balance among the Earth's ecological, social, and economic systems if they will collectively choose to contribute their considerable wealth, power, minds, and talents to this movement. Peter Senge (2007) outlines three fundamental principles of global strategic leadership, which he says are critical for successful organizational efforts to make such a difference. The first principle states that strategic leaders should use their considerable communication channels to publicly declare their organizations' commitments to dealing with crucial sustainability issues, and they should back up these public declarations with corporate actions designed to make their words a reality. He cites the example of John Browne, CEO of BP, who declared his firm's commitment to sustainability in a speech at Stanford University in 1997 and then followed up those words with increased investments in renewable energy, cleaner production, and other sustainability measures.

The second principle states that strategic leaders should develop partnerships with other organizations designed to actually shift the capabilities of the environment toward sustainability. Senge gives the example of how Unilever Dutch executives publicly established clean water, sustainable agriculture, and sustainable fishing as strategic priorities of the firm, and then followed up that declaration by partnering with other organizations to form the Marine Stewardship Council, which has established an independent certification program for sustainable fisheries.

Senge's (2007, 26) third principle states that strategic leaders must ultimately prepare their organizations to "undertake radical changes in their established ways of operating, including creating alternative products, processes and business models." He again gives Unilever as an example, discussing how it partnered with Oxfam and the W.K. Kellogg Foundation to establish the Global Sustainable Food Lab, a coalition of over 40 corporations that is working to bring sustainability to the global food system by promoting such ideas as fair trade coffee and local organic agriculture.

Implementing principles such as those outlined by Senge that allow organizations to become effective change agents in the global sustainability movement requires strategic leaders that are capable of guiding organizations along new, often uncharted pathways. For the remainder of this chapter, we will present an in-depth discussion of several strategic leadership roles and responsibilities that are critical for the executive-level managers in business organizations who are responsible for channeling the human energy of their organizations toward a sustainable future.

Serving as Transformational Leaders

We have established that adapting to the rapidly evolving capabilities of sustainable organizational management will require that organizations have processes in place for continuous transformational change. According to Doppelt (2003), organizations transforming to sustainable organizational management will require processes for: adopting sustainability as the dominant organizational mindset; creating sustainability-based visions and principles; implementing sustainability-based strategic initiatives; creating sustainability-based structures, goals, policies, and procedures; establishing sustainability-based information and communication channels; and establishing sustainability-based employee motivation and learning systems.

Succeeding in establishing and maintaining these processes is going to require a type of strategic leadership that differs significantly from the patriarchal, autocratic leadership models of the past (Doppelt 2003; Nahavandi 2009; Schumacher 1973; Senge 1990). Rather, managing the transformational changes necessary for sustainable organizational management will require transformational strategic leadership, which Nahavandi (2009, 206) defines as "leadership that inspires followers and enables them to enact revolutionary change." Jim Post (2007, 16–17) says, "Leadership is . . . the essential determinant of whether the future of the corporation will be one of transition, transformation, or revolution."

Leadership theory is one of the perpetual centerpieces of organizational behavior. According to Nahavandi (2009), leadership theory has passed through three eras: the trait era from the late 1800s to the mid 1940s, which says that effective leadership is determined by the personal intellectual, social, moral, and/or physical traits possessed by a leader; the behavioral era from the mid 1940s to the early 1970s, which says that effective leadership is determined by the types of task behaviors and relationship behaviors exhibited by a leader; and the contingency era from the early 1960s to the present, which says that effective leadership is determined by a leader's ability to match his/her behavior to the situation at hand.

Nahavandi (2009) says that taken together the theories of these three eras comprise transactional leadership theory, which focuses on the leader-follower exchange relationships that occur when leaders provide resources and rewards contingent on motivated, productive work by their followers. He says that, while understanding these transactional relationships is important for effective day-to-day leadership, they will not by themselves give leaders what they need to manage long-term transformational change. He says (Nahavandi 2009, 206), "Transactional contracts do not inspire followers to aim for excellence; rather, they focus on short-term, immediate outcomes. Long-term inspiration requires transformational leadership."

Nahavandi (2009) describes transformational leadership as the interaction of three factors: charisma and inspiration, intellectual stimulation, and individual consideration. Charismatic, inspirational leaders establish strong emotional relationships with followers that pierce organizational resistance to change, instilling a can-do organizational spirit in the face of great challenges. Inspirational leaders are self-confident, have strong convictions, are enthusiastic, have high energy, communicate well, and are good role models. Their followers show them genuine respect, loyalty, devotion, affection, and obedience, and they set high performance expectations for themselves. Intellectual stimulation involves empowering followers to create new ideas and innovations that challenge the current values and assumptions of the organization. It is the search for not only new answers but also new questions, and it requires open-dialogue processes that stimulate discussion and debate. Empowering followers improves their sense of self-confidence in their abilities and capabilities to be innovative and to accomplish change. Individual consideration is the motivational component of the transformational leadership formula. Showing genuine, equitable attention and encouragement to followers makes them feel special, improves their attitudes toward their jobs, and leads to higher levels of follower performance.

Senge (1990) says that effective transformational leaders must serve as designers, stewards, and teachers. To design means to mentally and visually conceive an idea, to have a goal or purpose, to make and execute plans. Thus, via their designer role transformational leaders reflect their organizations' most basic intentions, aspirations, and hopes. Senge points out that design work is seldom visible, is performed behind the scenes, focuses on the future, and involves integrating organizational visions, values, policies, strategies, structures, and systems. Stewards are people who keep something in trust for others. The key to understanding the stewardship role of transformational leaders is to recognize that stewards commit themselves to the long-term survival of something larger and more important than themselves. Stewards don't use, waste, and discard for short-term gain; rather they nurture, preserve, and save for long-term survival and success. As such, stewards are servant leaders who serve from the bottom rather than ruling from the top. Their role is to stand in service of the organizational vision, values, and stakeholders. The purpose of a teacher is to facilitate learning. As teachers, transformational leaders guide organizational members through processes that will allow them to clearly define the current realities of the environment, examine current organizational practices, processes, values, and assumptions, and make changes in these organizational elements so that they better match current reality. Among the key responsibilities of teachers are creating structures and processes in which learning can take place and providing for continuous open, accurate, honest dialogue (discussed later in the chapter) among organizational members.

Serving as Spiritual Leaders

Guiding organizations through transformational change processes requires spiritual leadership as well. Spirituality refers to peoples' search for meaning and purpose in life. Spiritual fulfillment is typically described as a sense of peace, love, joy, happiness, enlightenment, satisfaction, achievement, self-control, and/or creative expression. Although religion—devotion to an ultimate reality and/or deity—serves many humans as a valuable pathway to spiritual fulfillment, it is important to note here that spiritual leadership does not require bringing religion into the firm. As the discussion below will make clear, there are numerous pathways open to managers for providing greater meaning and purpose in the workplace.

Adding spiritual concerns to strategic leadership means recognizing that organizational members and stakeholders have an inner life that is important to nurture. Spiritual leaders focus on stimulating not only the minds and bodies but also the hearts and spirits of those that they serve. Spiritual leadership reflects values such as honesty, integrity, love, hope, humility, and faith. These values are not only deeply rooted in the culture of the organization, they are also important for making a difference in the greater community in which it exists. According to research, spiritual leadership has a positive impact on leader effectiveness both in terms of relationships with employees and relationships with stakeholders outside the organization (Nahavandi 2009).

E.F. Schumacher (1977) described human behavior as a higher-level phenomenon that separates humans from other species. He used the progression of Earth's inhabitants—from minerals to plants to animals to humans—to demonstrate this. He said that the difference between the lower-level minerals and higher-level plants is life, the difference between plants and higher-level animals is consciousness, and the difference between animals and higher-level humans is self-awareness. Developing ethically based behavioral systems that define right and wrong is only possible if self-awareness is present so that people can reflect on how their behavior affects themselves and others. Schumacher says that the progression from the lower mineral level to the higher human level is a progression from empirical to spiritual, from outer to inner, from mechanistic to organic, from control to understanding, and from the head to the heart. Schumacher said that invisible powers such as life, consciousness, and self-awareness can only be understood by moving away from lower-level quantifiable analysis to a higher level of analysis that seeks knowledge and understanding. He says that human happiness can only be achieved by developing people's higher human-level faculties. He says that when humans function at the lower animal level, they become deeply destructive and unhappy.

During the early part of the twentieth century, psychologists developed tests for measuring rational intelligence, which became known as intelligence quotient (IQ). According to the theory, a high IQ reflects a high ability to solve logical problems. During the mid 1990s, it was proposed that emotional intelligence (EQ) is as important as IQ in understanding human intelligence (Goleman 1996). EQ is a measure of people's awareness of their own feelings and the feelings of others. As such it is a measure of human compassion, empathy, and motivation. Recently, a third type of intelligence known as spiritual intelligence (SQ) has garnered attention (Zohar and Marshall 2000). SQ reflects humans' longing to feel part of a larger purpose, something toward which they can aspire. Thus SQ helps humans put their behaviors and lives within a larger context, adding meaning and value to what they do and experience.

Pruzan and Mikkelsen (2007) refer to spiritually based strategic leadership as "leading from wisdom." They interviewed 31 spiritually driven executives to determine how they define spirituality and how they use it as a basis for their leadership. These executives described spiritual leadership as arising from their true core, reflecting the essence of their being, allowing them to have deeper connections with divinity, and reflecting social, ecological, and religious principles. They essentially said that without spiritual leadership, organizational dialogues on ethics, responsibility, and sustainability are incomplete and not likely to lead to transformational change. Pruzan and Mikkelsen (2007) found that the spiritually motivated strategic leaders they interviewed were guided by principles that were fundamentally different from those found in both the corporate and academic worlds. These executives were motivated by three types of principles: those that stressed harmony among organizational ethics, economics, and ecology; those that stressed not harming anyone and caring for others; and those that stressed conscience over profit and success.

Seven broad themes ran through Pruzan and Mikkelsen's (2007) interviews with the 31 spiritual leaders. The first theme they identified is "love." The executives reflecting this theme in their interviews discussed the role of tough love in helping employees to improve and grow personally, and they discussed the important links between unconditional love, caring for others, and trust. The second theme they identified is "looking and listening within." Executives expressing this theme discussed the importance of clear conscience and the need to know and understand their own motives before they act, the inner peace that comes with acting from humility, the need to trust intuition, and the desire to connect to the source of one's being. The third theme they found is "live it and serve!." Pruzan and Mikkelsen (2007, 96) describe this theme as follows: "These spiritual-based leaders ... are really doers, people who appear to be fearless and unattached to the fruits of their deeds. Yet they are also characterized by their deep concern for contributing to society in general and, in particular, to serving those who are affected by their leadership." Their fourth theme is "compassion." Executives they interviewed who expressed this theme spoke of always having empathy and showing love for their neighbors in their business dealings, and they spoke of allowing people to learn from their mistakes. They also expressed the desire to be responsible to the Earth and its human and non-human inhabitants, to give out of the goodness of their hearts, and to care for people less fortunate than them.

Pruzan and Mikkelsen's (2007) fifth spiritual leadership theme revealed by the executives they interviewed is "divinity." Executives expressing this theme spoke of the difficulties they have had turning over control of their lives to the divine power they know exists, and they spoke of their employees and stakeholders as divine beings. The sixth theme they found is "purpose." It expresses the executives' beliefs that they should give of their talents without counting their rewards, they should help all of their employees to reach their full potential, and they should share their spiritual journeys with their stakeholders and business associates. Finally, Pruzan and Mikkelsen present the theme of "balance and grace." To support this theme, they discuss only one executive interview, which was with Amber Chand. She was co-founder and VP of Vision of Eziba, an Internet-based business that sold artisan crafts from around the world, and later she founded The Amber Chand Collection. She says that her companies are an expression of her love and her desire to serve others, and they are a platform for her spiritual practice. Being able to serve others and live her spirituality through her companies provides her with the balance she is seeking in her life. She says (Pruzan and Mikkelsen 2007, 269), "One can indeed create successful businesses that are spiritually inspired."

Establishing Adaptive, Self-Renewing Organizational Structures

We discussed in depth in Chapter 5 that the coevolutionary processes of organizational adaptation and selection inevitably lead to more self-renewing organizational structures. Recall that such structures should be developed around three principles: establishing internal rates of change that are calibrated to external rates of change, optimizing self-organization processes that stress self-responsibility and self-control, and balancing organizational exploitation and exploration efforts (Volberda and A. Lewin 2003). It is the role of strategic leaders to establish and maintain these self-renewing transformational structures.

There is general agreement among management scholars that organizational structures exist along a continuum ranging from highly formal, rigid, hierarchical, authority-based structures designed for stable environments to highly informal, flexible, team-based, knowledge-driven structures designed for turbulent environments. This idea took shape in the 1960s and 1970s. Burns and Stalker (1961) found in their case studies of 20 Scottish engineering firms that organizations operating in stable environments require rigid, formal, "mechanistic structures" that support standardization, while organizations operating in turbulent, unpredictable environments require flexible, informal "organic structures" that support innovation and change. Lawrence and Lorsch (1967) found in their study of the U.S. container, food, and plastics industries that the key structural processes of differentiation and integration vary widely with the dynamics of the business environment in terms of both their formality and the organizational level at which they occur. Mintzberg (1979) identified four organizational structures for large-scale organizations, ranging from highly mechanistic "machine bureaucracies" to less mechanistic "professional bureaucracies" to more organic "divisional structures" to highly organic "adhocracies." As should be clear from these descriptions, as structures progress from the mechanistic end of the continuum to the organic end of the continuum they become more adaptive and more self-renewing.

In their classic book, *In Search of Excellence,* Tom Peters and Robert Waterman (1982) chronicled the management practices of over 40 "excellent companies" that had survived and thrived in their industries for 25 years or longer. According to Peters and Waterman, the strategic leaders they interviewed in these excellent firms collectively identified eight structural characteristics they believed were critical for their organizations' ability to adapt and survive over the years. The first characteristic they identified was "a bias for action," which involves the creation of open communication channels that allow for the free flow of information and ideas necessary for organizations to be more flexible and change-oriented. The second structural characteristic was "close to the customer," which places customers and the employees responsible for directly serving them at the pinnacle of organizational concerns. The third was "autonomy and entrepreneurship," which involves creating internal organizational environments where innovation and a free flow of new ideas can flourish. Fourth was, "productivity through people," which recognizes both the economic value and moral responsibility of treating all employees with dignity and respect. The fifth characteristic they identified was "hands on, value driven," which says that strategic leaders are above all else responsible for clearly expressing, living, and preserving the core values of their organizations. Sixth was "stick to the knitting," which involves balancing organizational efforts to enhance current capabilities with their efforts to explore new ones. The seventh structural characteristic was "simple form, lean staff," which involves creating structures with as few administrative and executive levels as possible. Eighth was "simultaneous loose-tight properties," which means using the core values of the organization rather than rigid external authority systems as the primary organizational control mechanism, allowing employees the freedom to function as they see fit within the bounds of the firm's core values (Peters and Waterman 1982).

The structural characteristics outlined by Peters and Waterman (1982) are designed to meet the three principles of self-renewing structures established by Volberda and A. Lewin (2003). All eight are explicitly related to identifying, understanding, and creating effective organizational innovation and change processes that allow firms to continuously adapt to the rates and types of environmental changes that exist in their organizational fields. Five of the characteristics—close to the customer, productivity through people, hands on, value driven, simple form, lean staff, and simultaneous loose-tight properties—encourage the development and maintenance of processes that encourage self-organization, self-responsibility, and self-control; and stick to the knitting expressly states the need to balance the exploitation of established competencies with the exploration for new ones.

We mentioned in Chapter 5 that E.F. Schumacher's (1973) theory of large-scale organization provided what were likely the earliest sustainability-based structural principles explicitly designed to help large corporations manage in sustainable ways. Schumacher believed that large global corporations inhibit human freedom, creativity, and dignity, and he believed that they damage the ecosystem in the process. He also was a realist who understood that, despite his objections, large global corporations are going to dominate the business landscape for a long time to come, so he focused his attention on developing a theory for achieving "smallness within the large organization" (Schumacher 1973, 242).

Schumacher said that this theory of large-scale organization consists of five principles. The first says that large organizations should be divided into "quasi-firms," which are small, autonomous teams designed to foster high levels of entrepreneurial spirit. The second principle says that accountability of the quasi-firms to higher management should be based on a few items related to organizational profitability and goals. Decisions are made at the quasi-firm level without undue interference from upper-level management. Third, the quasi-firms should maintain their own economic identity; they should be allowed to have their own names and keep their own records. Their financial performance should not be merged with other units. Fourth, motivation for lower-level workers can be achieved only if jobs are intellectually and spiritually fulfilling with ample opportunities to participate in decisions (what Schumacher called "good work"). The fifth principle, which he called the principle of the middle axiom, says that top management can transcend the divergent problem of balancing the need for employee freedom with the need for organizational control by setting broad, strategic directions and allowing the quasi-firms to make their own decisions within these broad directions (Schumacher 1973). Schumacher (1979, 83) said that firms organized around these principles would be structured "like nature with little cells." He used the analogy of a helium balloon vendor with a large number of balloons for sale to demonstrate such structures. The vendor, who represents top management, holds the balloons from below rather than lording over them from above. Each balloon represents an autonomous quasi-firm that shifts and sways on its own within the broad limits defined by the vendor.

As was the case with the structural characteristics outlined by Peters and Waterman (1982), Schumacher's theory of large-scale organization coincides on many levels with Volberda and A. Lewin's (2003) three principles of self-renewing organizations. The quasi-firm structure and the concern for peoples' minds, bodies, and spirits encourage an atmosphere of innovation and change. Also, by pushing decisions down to the lowest level possible and giving the quasi-firms the right and responsibility to make their own operational decisions, Schumacher's theory focuses on establishing a system of self-organization, self-control, and self-responsibility in which strategic leaders serve primarily as the stewards of organizational goals, values, and visions.

Peter Senge (1990) also explicitly points to social and ecological as well as economic environmental challenges as reasons why self-renewing structures, which he calls "learning organizations," are so critical for survival in today's business world. Senge defines learning organizations in coevolutionary terms, saying that they are organizations capable of creating and recreating themselves in order to influence their environments in ways that ensure their survival. He says that learning organizations are comprised of five interrelated "learning disciplines." The central discipline is systems thinking. Recall that systems thinking focuses on identifying reinforcing and/or balancing patterns of long-term, mutually causal interrelationships among key organizational variables. Thus, systems thinking provides organizations with a means to understand the long-term implications of potential actions they may take. The other four disciplines include personal mastery, shared vision, mental models, and team learning. Personal mastery involves allowing organizational employees to pursue their personal visions within the context of the organization. A shared vision is an image that reflects a "common caring" among organizational employees. Questioning mental models involves establishing double-loop learning processes designed to examine the basic values and assumptions that underlie organizational actions, and team-learning involves establishing dialogue processes that allow organizational members to continuously reflect, discuss, question, and advocate transformational change.

Learning organizations are designed to provide a framework for a more intrinsic, spiritual view of organizational work, organizational life, and organizational purpose. Peter Senge (1990) says that learning organizations allow employees the opportunity to be creative and self-directed in the pursuit of their personal visions, which he calls the "spiritual foundation" of learning organizations. That is, learning organizations bring a holistic, spiritual dimension into the psyche of organizations; they help create processes that allow for increased meaningful employee participation in strategic decisions; and by doing so, they enhance the value of the human capital of the firm.

Thus, as with the other structural frameworks discussed in this section, learning organizations are designed to meet Volberda and A. Lewin's (2003) three characteristics. They are designed specifically for changing in concert with the environment, and their learning-team based structures are ideal for creating high levels of innovation, self-organization, self-responsibility, and self-control. Also, as mentioned in Chapter 5, the single- and double-loop learning processes established in learning organizations are ideal for both exploiting established capabilities and exploring new capabilities. In addition to meeting these three criteria, learning organizations as described by Senge (1990) are specifically designed to integrate sustainability into their values and visions, and they are effective structures for facilitating the translation of these sustainability-based values and visions into actions that are in concert with the economic success of the firm and the viability of the greater social system and ecological system.

Instilling Sustainability-Based Organizational Visions

One of the critical roles of strategic leaders is to establish and nurture the vision of the organization. Organizational visions are shared images that portray the ideal future of the firm. Authentic organizational visions: reflect the core values, beliefs, and aspirations of the firm; are simple, positive, and intrinsic; account for the personal visions of organizational employees; come from the heart; are perceived as achievable via hard work and dedication; are exhilarating, inspiring, and challenging; are motivational during hard times for the firm; serve as foundations for developing organizational missions, goals, objectives, and strategies; and serve as a basis for determining what information organizations consider important and how they measure success (Parker 1990; Senge 1990). Thus, powerful, well-crafted organizational visions act as mirrors that reflect the appropriateness of organizational actions.

Organizational visioning begins with a discovery process that determines what the organization stands for, how it views itself, and what factors hold it together. Key to an effective discovery process is creating a clear image of the current reality of the firm, including any hard truths that must be faced. Next comes crafting the vision. True visions (as opposed to slogans) emerge from creative processes that combine an organization's core values and core purposes (its core ideology) into an image of the future complete with challenging goals that require thinking beyond current capabilities (a stretch) and a vivid description of what it would be like to achieve these goals (a dream). This process involves creating pictures and phrases that reflect the passions, emotions, and convictions that drive the human energy of the organization. Fulfilling the visioning role allows strategic leaders to manage the synergy between stability and change by focusing their leadership efforts on preserving their firms' core ideology while at the same time encouraging continuous examination and changes in organizational practices, systems, processes, goals, and strategies (Collins 2001; Collins and Porras 1994; Parker 1990; Senge 1990).

Marjorie Parker (1990) provided an excellent narrative of an actual vision-building process at a large plant belonging to Hydro Aluminum, Europe's largest aluminum manufacturer. The process began with a literal imaging process in which managing director Tormod Bjørk and his team of strategic leaders worked with a professional artist to create a picture that could serve as a metaphor for their vision for the firm. The basic image they settled on was a garden. Parker (1990, 18) explains the selection of the garden metaphor this way: "Flowers growing near one another in the garden are collectively unique. The common soil, the bedrock and the underground water system influence each flower and plant in the garden and simultaneously they influence the whole garden." As the strategic leaders contemplated the garden, they saw how the types, colors, and arrangements of its flowers—which represented the firm's core values, its products and processes, and its employees and stakeholders—had changed and evolved over the years. Bjørk and his top-management team found the image-creation process to be both inspiring and empowering. Once they settled on the garden metaphor, the garden became the center-piece of the firm's strategic leadership processes. The top-management team held "garden seminars" with all employees of the firm. During the seminars, employees were asked to personalize the vision by verbaliz-ing the garden in ways that made it meaningful for them, and then they were asked to develop action plans to implement what they verbalized. The firm also created "garden project teams" and used the garden as the foundation of their leadership development program.

Instilling a Sustainability-Based Ethical System

The research findings of Bansal and Roth (2000) and Egri and Herman (2000) suggest that strategic leaders imbued with deep values for pro-tecting the greater society and ecosystem have the ethical foundations necessary for effective sustainable organizational management. These findings support one of the primary themes running through our entire discussion of strategic leadership roles and responsibilities: The real work strategic leaders do to channel the human energy of the firm toward sustainable organizational management happens at the fundamental levels of the organization's culture where the underlying values that compose its ethical system are found. Thus, adopting and maintaining sustainable organizational management requires leadership processes capable of instilling a network of values that collectively comprise a sustainability-based ethical system.

As we discussed in Chapter 1, core values represent the central themes of ethical systems. Recall we suggested that sustainability is an appropriate core value for organizations pursuing sustainable organizational management because it transcends the wide variety of divergent dilemmas facing humankind as it attempts to balance economic activity with social-system and ecosystem viability. Unfortunately, core values cannot stand alone as effective ethical systems because the guidance they provide, while inspirational, gives little insight into how to implement them. Thus, in addition to a core value, ethical systems must include a set of "instrumental values" that support the core value. Instrumental values generally define the behaviors and means for implementing and/or living up to core values. Unlike core values, instrumental values are typically varied and numerous and they can be more readily questioned and changed than core values. Below we discuss eight instrumental values that we believe are beneficial for organizations seeking to implement a core value of sustainability. As we present these values, it is important for readers to understand that our list is neither exhaustive nor exclusive. There are numerous other sustainability supporting instrumental values that organizations can implement.

Quality is a key instrumental value supporting sustainability. Since the quality revolution of the 1980s, improvements in the efficiency and effectiveness of firms' processes, products, and services have been determined through continuous interactions among managers, operational employees, customers, and suppliers. A value of quality will best support sustainability if it includes three basic dimensions—quality of products and services, quality of work, and quality of life. Quality products and services improve customer loyalty and increase efficiency and they also support sustainability because they last longer, are worth repairing, and can be exchanged more readily in second-hand markets. Attaining the sustainability promised by focusing on quality products and services is not possible unless organizations also value quality of work over quantity of work. Quality products and services are simply not possible without quality work from well-trained and motivated employees. Structuring jobs that satisfy human needs as well as organizational needs can no doubt improve the quality of products and services. Finally, valuing quality of life is important for achieving sustainability via quality. This encourages strategic leaders to recognize that all of their stakeholders have rights of physical wellbeing, long-lasting happiness, personal fulfillment, and a hopeful future. Valuing quality of life brings a wide variety of economic, social, and environmental issues to the attention of organizations that include job design, organizational reward systems, employee health and safety, shareholder wealth, community economic development, pollution, waste control, economic justice, social justice, and environmental justice.

Another instrumental value that supports a core value for sustainability is wholeness. Conceptually, wholeness is about interconnectedness, relatedness, balance, and mutual causality. A value for wholeness helps strategic managers recognize that all of the Earth's living subsystems are parts of a supranational ecological system. Wholeness helps strategic managers remember that organizational survival depends on successfully interacting with the other living subsystems on the planet, since the whole cannot survive if its parts are destroyed. Thus, valuing wholeness provides a much clearer understanding of the coevolutionary relationships between organizations and their economic, social, and ecological environments.

Another key instrumental value supporting sustainability is posterity. Valuing posterity means believing that the future generations of humans and other species should be considered in firms' strategic choices. Valuing posterity will encourage strategic leaders to consider clean water, clean air, abundant resources, biodiversity, natural beauty, economic justice, human rights, and employee rights as the birthrights of all generations, meaning that their decisions will better reflect a concern for the Earth and its people. The leaders of the Iroquois Nation with their seven-generation planning horizon tried to predict the effects of their decisions for the next seven generations to follow. This type of planning horizon for business organizations would tremendously enhance the prospects of achieving sustainability.

Community is also an important instrumental value that supports sustainability. The belief that individuals, organizations, and economies are parts of a larger community better equips strategic leaders to be more aware of the interconnections between their decisions and the quality of life in the communities where they operate. When this value is prominent in the organizational culture, strategic managers are better able to recognize that their organizations can prosper over the long run only if these communities can maintain a balance among a healthy natural environment, provide ample opportunities for human development and fulfillment, and sustain a healthy system of economic activity. Accordingly, organizations that value community will likely benefit from numerous economic advantages such as customer loyalty, a positive public image, and employee commitment, while making positive contributions to society and the natural environment. They are also more likely to become involved in the community-based decision-making structures that many believe are critical for protecting the commons.

Smallness is another key instrumental value for organizations pursuing sustainability. As noted numerous times, achieving sustainability is a matter of reducing the footprint of human economic activity. A value of smallness encourages organizations to reduce their footprints by reducing the scale of their operations. Basic to achieving smallness is reducing the amount of energy and resources transformed from their natural state into outputs, including wastes. Thus, a value for smallness will help managers more accurately account for the scarce natural capital they use. Organizations applying a value of smallness focus their attention on searching for ways to save energy, reduce materials, eliminate toxic substances, and use more renewable energy sources in the production and delivery of their products and services.

Diversity is another important instrumental value in a sustainability-based ethical system. Research has shown that diversity is critical for maintaining the ecosystems that support life, for providing the necessary linkages for social and cultural survival, and for maintaining successful organizations in today's global economy (Frederick 1995; Lovelock 1988; Moore 1996; Robinson and Dechant 1997; Wilson 1992). James Lovelock's Gaia hypothesis sprang from his discoveries that increased biodiversity improves the Earth's conditions for supporting life. Cultural diversity has also proven to be a major force in the survival of social systems; societies open to new people and ideas survive much longer than those that close themselves off to any ideas and persons that contradict their established dogma. Of course, in today's global economy, diversity is especially critical to the success of business organizations. Not only can promoting diversity help organizations avoid negative outcomes like increased turnover and legal problems, it can also help them improve their talent pools. Further, it can contribute significantly to improved competitiveness via better market understanding, higher-quality problem-solving, improved leadership, and more effective global relationships. Thus diversity contributes ecologically, socially, and economically to sustainability.

Effective dialogue is another instrumental value that supports sustainability. The term "dialogue" refers to the Socratic process of exploring issues and ideas until their underlying assumptions, values, and principles are revealed, exposed, and if necessary changed. Via dialogue, organizations are capable of creating interaction patterns that allow underlying assumptions and values to be openly surfaced and questioned. Using dialogue as the basis for interaction with both internal and external stakeholders puts organizations in positions to realistically assess their perceptions concerning their employees, their community, and the planet on which they do business. Thus, via dialogue organizations can establish the kinds of communication processes with their stakeholders that can be very instrumental in sustaining a healthy balance among the ecosystem, social system, and economic system. Valuing dialogue encourages firms to establish mechanisms that allow open discussion with all stakeholder groups, and it encourages firms to participate in established community organizations and processes designed to benefit the community and protect the planet around them.

The final instrumental value we will present that supports sustainability is spiritual fulfillment. As discussed earlier in the chapter, many scholars have said that organizations need to focus more clearly on their roles in improving the quality of life in the larger community, and they need to create structures, processes, and outputs designed to fulfill the spiritual as well as economic needs of the humans whose lives they touch (employees, customers, etc.; Covey 1990; Halal 1986; Handy 1989; Maslow 1962; Nahavandi 2009; Pruzan and Mikkelsen 2007; Schumacher 1973, 1977; Senge 1990). Valuing spiritual fulfillment allows organizations to put economic success, social responsibility, and ecological protection in their proper perspectives as avenues toward the realization of a higher quality of human life. As an instrumental value for sustainability, spiritual fulfillment can provide the mental pathways that lead individuals and organizations beyond material consumption and wealth to a higher level of satisfaction and purpose. This is essential if humankind is to ever truly accept a critical tenet of sustainability: finding joy in doing more with less.

Note that the interrelationships between the eight instrumental val-

Figure 6.1   **Sustainability-Based Value System**

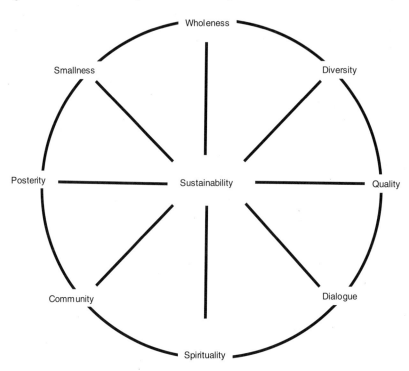

ues presented above and a core value for sustainability are mutually causal. That is, valuing sustainability will lead naturally to instrumental values such as those discussed above, and holding instrumental values such as these will strengthen a core value for sustainability. Further, numerous mutually causal interrelationships exist among the eight instrumental values themselves. Wholeness and posterity, wholeness and spirituality, quality and smallness, dialogue and community, dialogue and diversity, dialogue and quality, and posterity and community are just a few examples of such circular relationships. In other words, the interrelationships between a core value for sustainability and the eight instrumental values discussed above are coevolutionary in nature, each with the potential to strengthen the others. Thus, the sustainability-based ethical system presented here depicts a dynamic coevolutionary ethical process rather than simply a staid list of moral imperatives (see Figure 6.1).

Standing for Sustainability

Enterprise strategy provides strategic leaders with an excellent framework for crafting shared visions, developing strategies, and creating processes for sustainable organizational management. Recall from our discussion of stakeholder theory in Chapter 5 that enterprise strategy is a framework that explicitly articulates the ethical core of an organization as it relates to the firm's stakeholders and the issues it faces. As such, enterprise strategy is an overarching framework that allows a firm to apply its core values directly to the development of its strategies. Thus, a firm's enterprise strategy is designed to answer the question, "What do we stand for?" (Freeman 1984, 90). The true strength of enterprise strategy is that it explicitly addresses the value systems of managers and stakeholders in concrete terms, focusing attention on what the firm "should do."

Understanding a firm's enterprise strategy requires analyzing three interacting components. The first is values analysis, designed to uncover the core and instrumental values that compose the firm's ethical system. The second component is issues analysis, which allows the firm to develop a clearer understanding of its social and environmental context. The third component is stakeholder analysis, which helps the firm to identify its various stakeholders and their issues in order to understand what their stakes are and what powers they have to influence the firm (Ansoff 1979; Freeman 1984; Freeman and Gilbert 1988; Hosmer 1994; Stead and Stead 2000).

From an enterprise strategy perspective, strategic leaders guiding their firms toward sustainable organizational management facilitate the development of organizational value systems based on a core value of sustainability, providing them with an understanding of the social and environmental issues related to their firms' activities and allowing them to account for the social and environmental concerns of their stakeholders. Such an understanding better prepares strategic leaders to guide their organizations toward shared visions that communicate to employees, external stakeholders, and society that their organizations "stand for sustainability" (see Figure 6.2). Such a vision provides the foundation for making decisions that support a new definition of long-term organizational prosperity, one that integrates the need to earn a profit with responsibility to foster social welfare and environmental protection. Like sailing crafts in a relay race around the world, firms participating in the global economy can see that the key to their long-term success

Figure 6.2 **Standing for Sustainability**

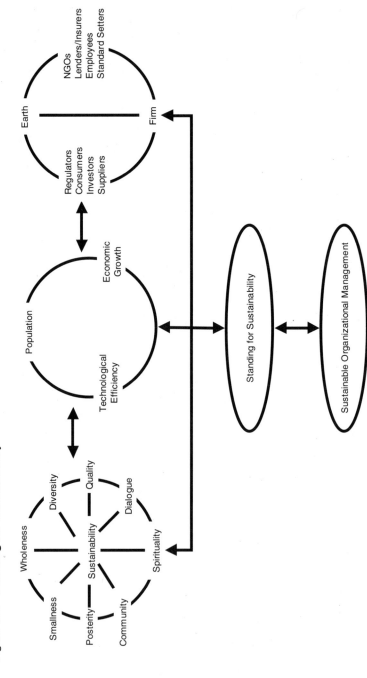

Source: Adapted from Stead and Stead 2000.

is the efficient and effective use of renewable resources and energy, the ability to be stable and yet light and maneuverable, the ability to contribute positively to the common good, and the ability to leave no trace of operations in their wakes.

Conclusions

Effective sustainability-based leadership is critical at all levels of an organization seeking to implement sustainable organizational management. However, effective sustainability-based strategic leadership is most important. One reason for this is that when strategic leaders demonstrate sustainability-based leadership values and behaviors, they are serving as clear role models for lower-level managers in their organizations. Also, strategic leaders are by definition the ones who make most of the decisions regarding the long-term direction of their organizations. This gives them the power to set their organizations on a course toward sustainable organizational management. Another reason effective sustainability-based leadership is crucial is that strategic leaders serve as the keepers of organizational visions and values. Organizations that see themselves as sustainable entities contributing to the greater economic, social, and ecological good do so because such visions and values are both espoused and lived by their strategic leaders. However, maybe the most important reason why effective strategic leadership is so critical for sustainable organizational management is because top-level executives are the most visible, most powerful external representatives of their organizations. Thus, strategic leaders are the managers most capable of making their organizations an integral part of the global movement toward sustainability.

— 7 —

Creating Sustainable Stakeholder Value

E.F. Schumacher described the Arab oil embargo of 1973 as the watershed economic event of the twentieth century. "Things will never be the same again," Schumacher (1979, 5) said, and they haven't. The embargo provided the small crack that many organizations (e.g., Japanese auto manufacturers) needed to get a stronger foothold in the international market, and the global economic race was on. With the world's two most populous countries, China and India, now in the race, the demand for oil and other natural resources is rising and will continue to rise for the foreseeable future. A key point exposed by the 1973 embargo is that the causes and effects of environmental turbulence go beyond the boundaries of economic activity, spilling into the arenas of politics, social welfare, and ecological concerns. Incredible advances in technology have paralleled the explosion of global economic activity since the embargo. Modern information technology has transformed almost every product and every process in every industry. Further, there have been increasing social and environmental demands from citizens worldwide leading to unprecedented levels of consumer advocacy, social activism, and legislation aimed at changing the way organizations do business. These complex, interrelated economic, geopolitical, technological, social, and ecological demands define the twenty-first century business environment that organizations must be capable of adapting to if they want to survive and thrive.

Forty years ago, Ansoff (1979) noted that there are four factors that make the modern business environment different from the past. First of all, as previously discussed in Chapter 3, the market scope for business is growing on a global scale. Further, the marketplace is becoming increasingly more fragmented due to inequities in economic, social, and ecological justice. Hart (2005) envisions today's global business environment as resulting from the merging of three highly differentiated economies: the money economy of developed and developing markets; the traditional, village-based economy of undeveloped markets; and the economy of the natural world in which the other two are embedded. Whereas these economies were at one time separate and distinct from one another, they are now in a common global arena where they are coevolving with one another. For example, purses handmade by indigenous South American villagers from recycled aluminum pull-tabs are available in chic boutiques across the United States. Examples such as this demonstrate that products and wealth are being transferred between the money economy and the traditional economy, and more aluminum from the natural economy is being reused in the process. Over time coevolutionary processes like this will lead to more consumer satisfaction in the money economy, more wealth and more meaningful work in the village economy, and less wastes and damage for the natural environment. Clearly, the coevolutionary nature of these markets will provide both business opportunities and challenges for twenty-first century organizations.

Ansoff's second factor was that the number and complexity of critical factors necessary for organizational success are increasing significantly. Today managers must not only focus on putting the right products and/ or services in the right markets, they must also focus on myriad nonmarket stakeholder concerns such as human rights, global poverty, climate change, complex regulatory frameworks, technological change, and resource constraints. More often than ever, business organizations are being called upon to close the gap between the needs and increasing demands of civil society and the solutions offered by the public sector (Laszlo 2008). As mentioned in Chapter 5, increasing stakeholder pressures for more social and environmental responsibility have manifested into what Esty and Winston (2008) refer to as the "green wave" of stakeholder concerns, issues, and regulations.

Ansoff's third factor was that today's business environment is characterized by high-speed change, and the fourth was that change in the current business environment is novel and discontinuous rather than linear. Taken together, the speed and discontinuity of change mean that predicting the future based on the past is very difficult, even impossible at times. For example, the Internet almost instantaneously transformed the business world by creating an unprecedented level of transparency. Now stakeholders have the ability to self organize via the Internet around particular issues that target corporations (Laszlo 2008). Stories criticizing companies such as Wal-Mart and Coca-Cola over such issues as unfair labor practices and the overconsumption of water now easily move from the Internet blogosphere to Wall Street. Esty and Winston (2008, 16) say that "full accountability is the emerging norm" because of this rising transparency. This type of discontinuous change makes it clear that it is more important than ever for organizations to develop double-loop learning processes that encourage questioning and changing the mental frameworks they use in their current decision-making processes.

Thus, the competitive landscape for global businesses today is complex, discontinuous, rapidly changing, and comprised of coevolving developed, developing, and undeveloped markets, all of which are embedded in the natural environment. There are now multiple, increasingly powerful stakeholders representing social, environmental, as well as economic interests in global corporations. Organizations that can realign their value chains to account for the needs of these increasingly influential sustainability-oriented stakeholders will have business opportunities now and into the future. Taking advantage of these opportunities will require that organizations develop capabilities to formulate strategies that create stakeholder value as a source of competitive advantage in the turbulent business environment.

The Coevolutionary Competitive Environment

Before strategies that create sustainability value for a firm's network of stakeholders can be formulated, the current narrow stakeholder perspective of industry analysis needs broadening. Traditional industry analysis is characterized by a strategic focus on increasing market share within defined industry boundaries that include only competitors that directly compete in individual product and/or service categories. Cooperative relationships are typically limited to those with direct suppliers and buyers. The capabilities to create value are typically viewed as residing in a single firm, and organizational performance is primarily measured in terms of how well the firm is managed with respect to its economic sustainability. This suggests that managers need only scan the product market segments in which their firm competes for opportunities and threats without much regard for the firm's broader social and ecological context. Doing so means engaging primarily in single-loop learning within well-defined industry segments, leaving managers with a narrow picture of current and future reality (Moore 1996; Stead and Stead 2004).

Creating sustainability value for the numerous stakeholders in a firm's stakeholder network requires a much broader framework that reflects the symbiotic coevolutionary relationships between the firm and the greater society and ecosystem. Stakeholder relationships in such coevolutionary industry analysis are generally seen as network-based because firms' stakeholders generally exhibit many direct and indirect interdependencies that result in simultaneous stakeholder influences across the value chain. Further, whereas traditional industry analysis is a narrow linear process in which the structure of the environment influences the conduct of the firm which influences the performance of the firm, coevolutionary industry analysis treats these three factors as circular and interactive. Therefore, the structure of the environment both influences and is influenced by the conduct and performance of the firm (Moore 1996; Senge 1990; Stead and Stead 2004).

In coevolutionary industry analysis, industry boundaries are blurred and the industries in which the firm competes are to a certain extent a matter of choice. The industry is viewed as a cluster of coevolving firms that have coalesced around some form of innovation, such as the microchip or the Internet. These firms are both competitors and alliance partners in a reinforcing system of symbiotic relationships. Just like predator/prey interactions, these organizations develop strategies to compete (to eat) and to cooperate (to avoid being eaten). For example, Cisco partners with leading firms in its own industry to develop cutting-edge technology. Their partners include Nokia, IBM, Intel, HP, Microsoft, EMC, and Fujitsu. Thus, in coevolutionary industry analysis, the competitive environment is seen as a set of intricate competition-cooperation inter-relationships occurring within clusters of firms sharing both competitive and complementary products and/or services, similar processes, and similar approaches to the marketplace (Moore 1996).

Industrial ecologies are special types of industry clusters in which all the firms in the network are committed to the core value of sustainability. Industrial ecologies involve a set of interorganizational arrangements where two or more organizations attempt to recycle material and energy byproducts to one another. Whereas these industrial ecologies typically begin as waste-exchange arrangements for the purposes of pollution prevention and cost reduction, coevolutionary industry analysis would suggest that these networks will likely expand to address resource depletion, overconsumption, biodiversity, community health, and human rights issues (Starik and Rands 1995).

Stakeholder Value-Creation Processes

Thus, from a coevolutionary perspective, the competitive environment for organizations today is composed of clusters of competitors, stakeholders, and industrial-ecology networks that both compete and cooperate with one another in a swirl of coevolving developed, developing, and undeveloped markets embedded in nature. To survive and prosper in such environments, organizations need to develop sustainable organizational management capabilities that create value for their multiple economic, social, and ecological stakeholders. Research indicates that proactively responding to environmental stakeholder concerns significantly improves an organization's capabilities for stakeholder integration, higher-order learning, and continuous innovation (Sharma and Vredenburg 1998), and logic says that the same is true for firms that effectively respond to the social concerns of stakeholders. Further, the ability to create value for the variety of stakeholders in a firm's stakeholder network depends on the organization's ability "to creatively destroy its current capabilities in favor of the innovations of tomorrow" (Hart 2005, 61). This requires applying double-loop learning processes that allow organizational decisionmakers to expand their traditional industry boundaries into the greater social and environmental domains. Below we discuss some important processes for creating stakeholder value in organizations pursuing sustainable organizational management.

Strategy Formulation Processes

Formulating strategies for sustainable organizational management requires that strategic managers encourage systems thinking throughout their organizations. A dialogue-based, open systems model of strategy formulation requiring the involvement of managers, suppliers, customers, and other important stakeholders along the firm's value chain is necessary. For example, "appreciative inquiry" has been successfully used by companies to create sustainable value for their networks of stakeholders. Appreciative inquiry "allows participants to discover the best of their shared experiences and tap into the larger system's capacity for cooperation" (Laszlo 2008, 154). Such a process opens paths of discovery via dialogue between stakeholders and the organization, and it provides managers the benefit of having the collective wisdom of the firm's stakeholders.

Incorporating stakeholders in strategy-formulation processes facilitates the development of double-loop organizational learning capabilities because having the perspectives of a wide variety of stakeholders encourages continuous questioning of fundamental assumptions and values related to why and how the firm is doing business. Formulation processes like these expand the organization's ability to create its own future by questioning the underlying assumptions and values upon which the firm's strategies are based. Thus, these double-loop formulation processes allow organizations pursuing sustainable organizational management to rewrite industry rules and to think beyond existing industry boundaries.

Environmental Forecasting Processes

Forecasts are critical because they shape managers' views of their future. As previously discussed the novel, discontinuous, nonlinear, change-oriented business environment makes predicting the future based on the past very difficult. This renders traditional forecasting techniques much less effective for predicting future trends unless they are combined with forecasting techniques that are not based on using the past as the sole predictor of the future. Thus, managers should be very cautious about limiting their forecasts to a single quantitative point estimate as the only possible future outcome in today's turbulent environment.

"Multiple scenario analysis" is a forecasting technique that creates a climate that fosters more double-loop, out-of-the-box thinking within the organization. The use of multiple scenario analysis was originally developed at Royal Dutch Shell during the late 1960s to prepare managers to think more clearly about the future (Swartz 1991; Wack 1985a, 1985b). Multiple scenario analysis has evolved over the past decades into a forecasting tool that allows managers the flexibility to develop several paths to the future. The use of scenario analysis reflects the explicit recognition by managers that the future is unpredictable. A scenario is a flowing narrative (rather than a quantitative point estimate) that depicts a possible path to the future. Each scenario in multiple scenario analysis is a story based on a particular mental model of the future. Thus, taken together, the multiple scenarios developed during the analysis provide a picture of the general direction of change an organization will face in the future. Scenarios for sustainable organizational management must include stakeholder impacts and anticipated stakeholder expectations that will help organizations be prepared for dynamic, coevolving sustainability-based issues such as climate change (Laszlo 2008; Marcus 2009). For example General Electric's ecomagination strategy is based on a scenario of a carbon-constrained world that the firm views as a major business opportunity.

Stakeholder Engagement Processes

Creating stakeholder value requires processes that engage the organization's stakeholders in dialogue concerning the economic, ecological, and social impacts of the firm in the greater global community. Techniques are available to firms that facilitate listening to stakeholders up and down the value chain, assisting firms in evaluating their organizational impacts (Esty and Winston 2008; Laszlo 2008). These techniques allow firms to internalize social and ecological stakeholder impacts that once were perceived as external to the firm, and this gives them the capability to create additional stakeholder value. Laszlo (2008) recommends that firms regularly engage in a process he calls "stakeholder discovery" to listen to the diverse views of their stakeholders regarding their environmental and social impacts in the communities where they operate. Also, engaging stakeholders such as the poor that were once considered fringe in strategy formulation and implementation can facilitate innovations that create sustainability value for firms (Carroll 2004; Hart and Sharma 2004).

Closing the Value Chain

Popularized by Michael Porter (1980), traditional value-chain analysis disaggregates the firm's capabilities according to their value-creating potential allowing relevant capabilities to be analyzed for their contributions to the firm's cost-reduction or product/service-differentiation competitive strategies. The traditional value chain includes primary activities, which are those directly related to creating, manufacturing, and marketing products and services, and support activities, such as human resource management, information systems, and auditing that provide inputs into the firm's primary value-creation processes.

From a sustainable organizational management perspective, the application of Porter's model is limited for three reasons: First, the stakeholder relationships implied in Porter's model are too narrow, consisting solely of the relationships between the firm, its suppliers, and its customers. This narrow perspective excludes the stakeholder networks necessary for value creation (Freeman and Liedtka 1997; Mahon and McGowan 1998). It does not account for the value of resources in nature and the value of wastes after consumption. It also fails to account for the social capital embedded in the greater society, the human capital within the firm, and the stakeholder and industrial-ecology networks that managers must simultaneously manage. Second, the support activities in the traditional value chain are not generally structured to support sustainable organizational management. For example, human resource policies that will enhance the value of human capital, full cost accounting systems that can account for natural and social capital over time, and design processes based on sustainability are all necessary for sustainable organizational management.

Third, the traditional value chain is depicted as a straight line; sustainable organizational management will require that the chain be viewed as a closed cycle. The traditional linear depiction (see Figure 7.1) of the value chain certainly supports the old type I industrial ecosystems (discussed in Chapter 3) that convert virgin materials into products that are in turn discarded as wastes with little or no regard for the ecological impacts of this process, and it reinforces the narrow conceptualization that the firm's stakeholders consist primarily of suppliers and customers. In this straight-line depiction, the stakes of employees are assumed to be accounted for simply by the fact that they work for the firm; they are simply labor, a factor of production.

In Figure 7.2, resources and wastes are added to the traditional linear value chain discussed above. This supports today's emerging type II industrial ecosystems that focus on improved ecological efficiency via resource reduction, process redesign, recycling, and reuse—often referred to as "eco-efficiency" (McDonough and Braungart 2002). As with any good strategy, eco-efficiency creates value by enhancing the firm's cost-and-differentiation competitive advantages. Even though this model accounts for high-entropy wastes and low-entropy resources, its linear depiction of the value chain operates under the idea of "cradle to grave"—resources from the cradle, wastes to the grave. These type II systems do less ecological harm than their type I counterparts, but they cause harm nonetheless.

Figure 7.1   **Type I Linear Value Chain**

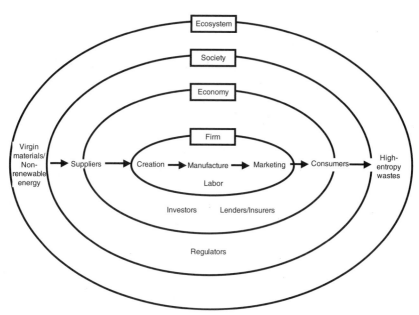

Source: Stead and Stead 2004.

In addition to opening the value chain to its ultimate resources and wastes, this model (Figure 7.2) also opens the value chain to the stakeholder influence of employees and the community, both of which have symbiotic, coevolutionary relationships with the firm. The human capital of the firm in this model is considered an important instrumental asset in the value-creation process. The development of human capital via innovative human resource practices that focus on the long-term capabilities of the workforce is encouraged because it leads to higher levels of performance in organizations, increasing the value added at each stage of the value chain. Jobs in this model are designed to be economically, intellectually, and socially fulfilling, enhancing both the personal development of the human capital and the economic sustainability of the firm. This model also extends the value chain to community stakeholders—governments, activists, interest groups, and others—that can influence the firm's economic sustainability. Being a good corporate citizen in the communities in which the firm operates helps to build social capital and contributes to the long-run

Figure 7.2   **Type II Linear Value Chain**

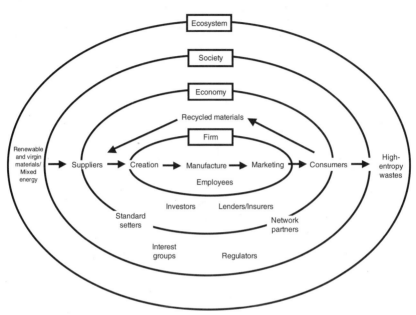

Source: Stead and Stead 2004.

profitability of the firm. The ability to enhance both the social capital of the community and the human capital of the firm while contributing to the organization's economic sustainability is referred to as "socio-efficiency" (Dyllick and Hockerts 2002; Figge and Hahn 2004, 2005, 2006; Hockerts 1999).

Socio-efficiency and eco-efficiency improve the state of the planet's natural and social capital as well as contributing to the firm's economic sustainability because managers calculate the relative social and eco-logical costs and benefits before making decisions. Strategies based on eco- and socio-efficiency, often called "greening" strategies, are important steps on the path toward sustainability. However, ultimately achieving sustainability will require going "beyond greening" (Hart 2005). It will mean closing the value chain, transforming it from a straight line to a circle, and in doing so creating a mental model that encourages managers to recognize the importance of granting stakeholder status to the greater society and ecosystem.

Closing the value chain into a cycle changes its orientation from cradle to grave to "cradle to cradle," making it appropriate for the shift to a type III industrial ecosystem where renewable energy and resources are transformed into products whose wastes in turn serve as inputs for other biological and/or industrial cycles—referred to as "eco-effectiveness." McDonough and M. Braungart (2002) say that the key to making the shift from cradle to grave to cradle to cradle lies in redesigning industrial systems in ways that mimic natural metabolic processes, which are not so much efficient as effective. Many of nature's processes have built in inefficiencies, but whatever wastes are generated are always absorbed and reused in the natural environment. No wastes are left as wastes. To accomplish this, they suggest that products be designed to include only two types of materials: "biological nutrients," materials that biodegrade and can be returned to the biological cycle, and "technical nutrients," materials that do not biodegrade but can be circulated continuously through the industrial cycle.

Closing the value chain also requires accounting for the responsibility of organizations to develop and sustain a just and equitable workplace and society. This is often referred to as "socio-effectiveness" (Benn and Probert 2006; Dyllick and Hockerts 2002; Hockerts 1999). Socio-effectiveness means that employees, the human capital of the firm, are no longer viewed as merely instrumental in value creation. They are considered to have intrinsic value in and of themselves. They become ends rather than means to ends (Freeman and Liedtka 1997). It also means that fringe stakeholders such as the poor, weak, and disenfranchised are accounted for in the organization's stakeholder network (Carroll 2004; Hart and Sharma 2004). Via socio-effectiveness global corporations can be part of the solution to many of the world's problems such as child labor, human rights, economic justice, the exploding human population, disease, poverty, overconsumption, and preservation of indigenous cultures, and in doing so they are adding to stakeholder value by making positive contributions to a sustainable society for posterity. Figure 7.3 represents the closed-loop value chain as described above.

Footprint Analysis

Closed-loop value-chain analysis provides a framework for assessing the organization's ecological and social footprints as well as its economic performance, which is critical for creating value for stakeholders in all

Figure 7.3   **Type III Closed Loop Value Chain**

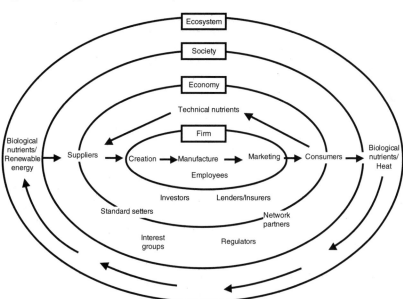

Source: Stead and Stead 2004.

three sustainability arenas. During the years, several tools have evolved to assist managers in assessing their organizations' footprints. Life-cycle analysis (LCA) is one such tool. LCA is a total systems approach that provides an appraisal of the ecological impacts of the firm's products and processes all along its closed-loop value chain (Svoboda 2008), making it "one of the most useful tools for measuring the footprint" (Esty and Winston 2008, 169). LCA involves analyzing resources, emissions, energy, and environmental impacts of each and every value-chain activity. LCA-based tools such as eco-tracking, which utilizes relative and absolute metrics that capture data at multiple organizational levels across the full spectrum of the value chain, have been instrumental for firms such as GE, Dow, DuPont, IBM, and Bayer in their efforts to respond proactively to the rising ecological consciousness across the globe (Esty and Winston 2008). LCA is a tool that can give organizations solid data on how to improve their environmental performance and reduce resource intensity, and it can help them to extend the life of their products, making them more competitive in the marketplace (Ciambrone 1997; Thompson 2002). Thus, LCA is designed to help firms improve their eco-efficiency.

Of course, a complete organizational footprint analysis must go beyond the limited ecological scope of LCA. It must also account for organizational impacts on social and human capital (Laszlo 2008).

In the first stage of footprint analysis, the types and amounts of raw materials and energy needed by the firm are determined, and the ecological and social impacts of acquiring and using these raw materials and energy are analyzed. In the second stage, the ecological and social impacts of the manufacturing process are assessed. This includes examining the materials and energy used in component-manufacturing processes, final-product manufacturing processes, and product-assembly processes; it includes examining the impact of the firm's operations on the communities in which it operates; and it includes examining the firm's impact on the human capital of the firm, including such issues as child labor and human rights. Third, the transportation and distribution systems related to delivering the product to market are analyzed in terms of distribution modes, distances, energy consumption, carbon emissions, and impacts on social and human capital. Fourth, the environmental and social consequences of how the product is used are analyzed, including assessments of product durability, energy requirements, polluting potential, and impacts on the health and safety of consumers. Fifth, the product's potential for reuse and/or recyclability are analyzed. The sixth stage of footprint analysis is to examine the product's ultimate disposal in terms of its toxicity, volume, biodegradability, and impacts on community health and safety (Laszlo 2008).

It is important to understand that footprint analysis is an extremely complex, newly evolving concept that is difficult to implement. Outcomes are easily skewed by the assumptions of those doing the analysis, and it seldom provides clear-cut answers concerning the environmental and social benefits and challenges of products and processes. Footprint analysis can also be very information intensive due to the required stakeholder engagement and dialogue processes and, therefore, cost intensive depending on how many factors are assessed and the extent of upstream or downstream activities within its scope (Allenby 1994; Richards, Allenby, and Frosch 1994). Nonetheless, footprint analysis is essential if the laws of thermodynamics and the absolute limits of social and human capital are to be effectively included in product and process design and development. Thus, even though footprint analysis is a complex, imperfect process that cannot currently give organizations all the answers they need concerning the impacts of their products and services on society and the planet, forging ahead with its development and improvement is absolutely essential for building eco- and socio-efficient capabilities for firms.

Adding Stakeholder Value Via Eco- and Socio-efficiency

As discussed in Chapter 5, core capabilities of firms exist within their functional levels. Functional-level strategies in such areas as marketing and operations are designed to exploit these core capabilities in order to create sustained cost- and differentiation-based competitive advantages that add value for organizational stakeholders. In sustainable organizational management, developing and exploiting core capabilities for eco- and socio-efficiency is critical for successful functional-level strategies that provide value for the plethora of economic, social, and ecological stakeholders. Thus, functional-level strategies based on eco- and socio-efficiency can afford firms cost- and differentiation-based competitive advantages that create economic value through environmental and social value added (Figge and Hahn 2004, 2005, 2006).

Measuring social and environmental value added requires calculating the organization's social and environmental stakeholder impacts and aggregating them into an organizational footprint (as previously discussed). Once complete, the firm can compare its current footprint with past efforts, government standards, and industry standards. Industry standards, such as those established by the Global Environmental Management Initiative (GEMI), the Sustainable Forestry Initiative (SFI), and the Responsible Care Program of the chemical industry have become particularly popular as benchmarks in this process. Other external indicators, including the Global Reporting Initiative (GRI), the UN Global Compact, metrics developed by socially responsible investment (SRI) rating agencies (such as Innovest, IW Financial, and Vigeo), and the Dow Jones Sustainability Index (DJSI), are also used extensively as sustainability performance benchmarks (Laszlo 2008; Rosinski 2006). Thus, by carefully benchmarking the organization's current footprint in relation to established standards for stakeholder wellbeing, firms can better determine their effectiveness regarding their ability to create eco- and socio-stakeholder value. This type of analysis provides a shift from a cost-based to a value-based assessment of environmental and social performance (Figge and Hahn 2004, 2005, 2006).

Socio-efficiency and Stakeholder Value Added

Using a stakeholder perspective, social performance can be defined as the social impacts the firm has on its stakeholders: The fewer the negative social impacts and the more the positive social impacts, the better the firm's social performance (Spirig 2006). The Global Reporting Initiative (GRI) categorizes social performance into four categories: labor practices, working conditions, human rights, and product responsibility. Socio-efficiency involves creating stakeholder value by connecting the investments in social and human capital to the firm's core business strategy (Holliday, Schmidheiny, and Watts 2002; Marcus and Kaiser 2006). Managers are familiar with the role of physical and economic capital in creating value, but the concept of social capital as a means of economic value creation is relatively new in managerial thinking. "Whereas economic capital is in people's bank accounts and human capital is inside their heads, social capital inheres in the structure of their relationships" (Portes 1998, 7).

Social capital refers to connections among individuals—social networks, the norms established by reciprocal relationships, and the trustworthiness that arises from them (Putnam 2000). According to the World Bank (1998) "Social capital refers to the institutions, relationships, and norms that shape the quality and quantity of a society's social interactions . . . Social capital is not just the sum of the institutions which underpin a society—it is the glue that holds them together." In other words, relationships and social networks are valuable assets, thus social capital comprises both the network and the assets that may be mobilized through that network. Interestingly, a society of isolated individuals such as the United States (see Chapter 3) is not likely to be as rich in social capital as a more integrative society. In fact during the last three decades of the twentieth century, social capital within the United States declined as citizen self-isolation increased (Putnam 2000).

Social capital is a multidimensional concept that works through a variety of channels, including information flows, norms of reciprocity, and collective action. These interactions knit the community's social fabric by enabling people to build communities and to commit to one another (Smith 2000). The social networks embedded in social capital help translate the "I" mentality to the "we" mentality, which as discussed in Chapter 3, is so necessary in moving toward sustainability. Indicators of social capital include measures of community life, such as percentage of the population who are participating in local organizations, measures of engagement in public affairs—such as the turnout in elections—measures of community volunteerism, measures of informal sociability, and measures of social trust (Putnam 2000).

Governments, nongovernment organizations (NGOs), business organizations, and others create social capital, either in isolation or in concert with one another. Research demonstrates that enhancing social capital can improve community sustainability through increased knowledge and information flows, increased cooperation among the citizenry, less resource degradation and depletion, more investment in common lands and water systems, and improvements in monitoring and enforcement (Smith 2000). High levels of social capital increase the potential for collective action to address local concerns. There is also mounting evidence of the benefits of social capital including increased child development, higher educational achievement, cleaner, friendlier public spaces, lower crime rates, increased economic development, and better human health. In fact, "As a rule of thumb, if you belong to no groups, but decide to join one, you will cut your risk of dying over the next year in half. . . . Civic connections rival marriage and affluence as predictors of happiness" (Putnam 2000, 333).

The human capital-creation process within organizations involves investing in developing human potential in the workplace by focusing on increasing the knowledge, training, and skills of employees. Human capital investment can be both socially responsible and economically profitable for the firm (Benn and Probert 2006; Holliday, Schmidheiny, and Watts 2002; Spirig 2006; Willard 2002). Research by McKinsey & Company indicates that the most important corporate resource over the next 20 years will be talented employees who are smart, technologically skilled, globally astute, and operationally agile. The consultants found that the battle for talented employees is dramatically intensifying, and they concluded that attracting and retaining talent is a business imperative for economic survival. Firms with progressive human resource policies and strategies based on an inspiring vision like sustainability have been shown to have a competitive edge in attracting and retaining high-quality employees. As previously discussed, the vision of sustainability engages employees' desires to feel like they are part of a larger purpose, thus retaining the talented, visionary employees. Managers that invest in the human capital of their organizations do so because they believe their investment is a means to greater productivity and profitability as well as a means of fulfilling their social responsibilities.

More managers are recognizing the importance of social and human capital in creating economic value for their firms, and thus they are incorporating the concept of socio-efficiency as a cornerstone in many of their competitive strategies. Because many global business leaders are beginning to understand that their firms can "do well by doing good" (Laszlo 2008), it is becoming easier for managers to make the business case for investing in social capital. For example, Lafarge, a $23 billion global industry leader in building materials with a workforce of 80,000, has a large presence in developing markets. Thus, it faces numerous social challenges in its markets such as poverty, illiteracy, and HIV/AIDS. Lafarge's governing principles and values are based on creating stakeholder value by "being the preferred partner for our communities . . ." (Laszlo 2008, 102). Many of its business decisions have resulted in social improvements in communities where it operates in the developing markets. For example, the firm paid to build an entire village for 72 families in India when it relocated a cement plant closer to its resource base. In the new village, Lafarge provided not only new housing but also a new school and healthcare facility for the community, neither of which existed in the old village. In Morocco, where Lafarge had to close an outdated plant and lay off 195 people, the firm redeployed some workers to another company, gave those over the age of 55 early retirement benefits, and gave grants up to 80 percent of the start-up costs for employees starting their own businesses. Ultimately 266 new jobs were created via 111 new microenterprises, and the firm has stronger partnerships with the government, unions, customers, and suppliers. The firm also has developed a HIV/AIDS prevention program in Zambia in partnership with a local organization; the program has led to improved knowledge about the risk of HIV/AIDS, reduction in high-risk behavior, and the reduced incidence of the disease and its effects on the community. In turn, Lafarge has experienced lower operational costs due to a decrease in absenteeism, higher productivity, and less turnover in its Zambian operations—all for an investment of only $48,000 (Laszlo 2008).

Eco-efficiency and Stakeholder Value Added

Eco-efficiency involves developing both cost and differentiation competitive advantages by eliminating or reducing resource depletion, materials use, energy consumption, emissions, and effluents. There are at least four processes common to eco-efficiency efforts in organizations: (1) dematerialization—designing products that use fewer and safer materials; (2) closing production loops—creating minimal/zero wastes in manufacturing processes, (3) service extension—customizing responses to customer demand and offering customers the choice of either leasing or buying goods; and (4) functional extension—products that are smarter with enhanced functionality and durability (Holliday, Schmidheiny, and Watts 2002).

Eco-efficiency techniques often include: redesigning pollution- and waste-control systems, redesigning production processes to be more environmentally sensitive, using recycled materials from production processes and/or outside sources, using renewable energy sources, and increasing the durability and service intensity of goods and services. Environmental value-added is created because eco-efficiency techniques provide the capabilities for firms to enhance their economic and environmental performance. Innovation is the strategic driver in improving eco-efficiency, and there are now significant data that demonstrate a direct relationship between eco-efficiency, competitiveness, and financial performance (Esty and Winston 2008; Laszlo 2008; Stanwick and Stanwick 2005).

Developing eco-efficient core capabilities in operations and logistics are the keys to creating the cost advantages afforded by eco-efficiency. In the biophysical sense, it is via their operations and logistics systems that organizations transform low-entropy natural resources into high-entropy goods and services; thus, these systems offer organizations the best opportunities to slow down their entropic processes. So the greatest financial, physical, and human capital expenditures that organizations generally must make in eco-efficiency are in new and improved operations and logistics systems. In today's business environment of unpredictable energy and materials costs, worldwide pressures to reduce greenhouse gas emissions, and the ever-incessant pressures from competitors and customers to improve efficiency, organizations are showing a willingness to make significant investments in eco-efficiency. Production facilities in most industries are being built or redesigned to use minimal energy and to generate minimal emissions and wastes. Products are being designed and packaged in ways that reduce materials and weight and allow for recycling and reuse. More efficient supply chains are being developed, with shorter distances and more efficient, less polluting modes of transportation.

From a coevolutionary perspective, eco-efficient capabilities are rapidly transforming from unique competitive advantages for a few cutting-edge organizations into environmental capabilities required for organizational survival. Eco-efficiency is now demanded by multiple organizational stakeholders including shareholders, customers, financial institutions, insurers, communities, governments, NGOs, industry associations, and numerous others. This emergence as a critical environmental capability means that eco-efficiency is now an important organizational-selection criteria. Organizations that can adapt by developing core eco-efficiency capabilities and successfully aligning them with these new selection criteria will survive and evolve in both form and function; organizations that do not will eventually give in to inertia and be selected out of the environment.

Developing Eco- and Socio-efficient Capabilities

Central to the development of organizational capabilities that create stakeholder value via eco- and socio-efficiency is the concept of product stewardship. Product stewardship refers to creating both cost and differentiation competitive advantages via the integration of eco- and socio-efficiency into every stage of the organization's closed-loop value chain (Hart 1995, 1997). This focus on the complete life-cycle impacts of the organization's products, services, and processes is designed to create safe, socially responsible products and services that use less materials and energy and generate less non-recyclable, non-biodegradable wastes. Thus, via product stewardship, product/service differentiation is achieved by attending to both internal process and external market factors. Product stewardship efforts are generally more effective if all of the firm's stakeholders—employees, suppliers, consumers, NGOs, regulators, the community, and others—are involved in the firm's product/service-development processes from the beginning. Also, continuous innovation is essential for creating and maintaining the competitive advantages gained from product stewardship because as soon as competitors can imitate a firm's environmentally and socially sensitive offerings, competitive differentiation is lost (Hart 2005; Reinhardt 2008).

   Creating and sustaining effective product stewardship efforts in organizations requires integrating eco- and socio-efficient capabilities into the organization's functional-level activities such as research and development, product/service-design processes, procurement, operations, and marketing. In this section, we will discuss the development of eco- and socio-efficient capabilities within these functional-level activities.

Readers may note from the discussion below that the integration of eco-efficient capabilities in organizations currently seems to be more highly developed and more prominent in firms than the development of socio-efficient capabilities. The primary reason for this discrepancy is that the economic value created by eco-efficiency is much more easily and precisely measured than that created by socio-efficiency (Esty and Winston 2008).

Research and Development

If much of human existence and progress can be said to be the result of ideas, organizational research and development should be considered the brains of sustainable organizational management. Here products and services are initiated, nurtured, manipulated, and tested. In addition to overall effectiveness, cost, and other typical product or service characteristics related to research and development activities, sustainable organizational management also focuses on characteristics such as dematerialization, resource intensity, recycled content, nontoxic components, ease and safety of use, durability, aesthetics, and social impacts.

The key to research and development in sustainable organizational management is to use nature as a model for the research and development system. Systems that mimic nature are effective systems that consider waste as lost profit and create economic, social, and/or ecological value by design. Nature uses feedback loops that trigger adaptations that lessen the physical constraints on species. Research and development efforts structured around a model of nature provide for the same sort of systems thinking processes in organizations, and they also provide an opportunity for organizations to view the ecological and social limits to economic growth as opportunities for new product development, innovation, and entrepreneurial learning (Hawken 2007; Kiuchi and Shireman 2002). Research and development tools have emerged that can aid managers in developing systems that mimic nature, including LCA and footprint analysis discussed previously.

Design for Environment

The idea behind design for environment (DFE) is to identify the relevant and ascertainable environmental considerations and constraints that are integrated into a firm's product design processes. The goal of DFE is to implement environmentally sound production processes and to produce environmentally sound products while remaining competitive in terms of product performance and price. There are a wide range of dimensions which encompass DFE including: design for disassembly, refurbishment, component recyclability, materials recyclability, material substitution, source reduction, waste reduction, product-life extension, remanufacturing, and energy and materials recovery (Allenby 1994). Implementing DFE requires that organizations engage in an array of comprehensive cross-functional endeavors utilizing the data from the firm's LCA. Analyzing upstream wastes—wastes generated by suppliers—and downstream wastes—wastes generated by customers—is an important part of this process. Analyzing wastes from their source allows organizations to "learn from waste" (King 1994). Data from these analyses are carefully translated for use by design teams (Allenby 1994; Richards, Allenby, and Frosch 1994). Both Hewlett-Packard and Apple have been pioneers in DFE efforts. Hewlett-Packard began its DFE program in 1992, and it currently operates under three DFE priorities: energy efficiency, materials innovation, and design for recyclability. Apple's DFE principles include controlling for quantity and types of raw materials used, energy consumption for both manufacturing and product use, and ease of recyclability (Anonymous 2008a; Anonymous 2008b).

DFE encourages managers to embrace the view that all products and services are part of nature. This means recognizing that two discrete metabolic processes influence organizational operations: the biophysical cycles of nature and the technical cycles of industry. As discussed above, if products are designed and manufactured based on biological and technical nutrients, product wastes would either biodegrade, providing nutrients for biological cycles, or remain in a closed-production loop where they perpetually circulate as valuable materials for industry. Designing products that contain technical and/or biological nutrients allows them to perpetuate their usefulness in the closed-loop value chain rather than being discarded as unusable wastes. Thus, products and services designed using biological and/or technical nutrients can safely feed both the biological and technical metabolisms, continuously providing nourishment for something new (McDonough and Braungart 2002).

One of the more promising current trends in DFE is the emergence of "green chemistry," which involves the search for and development of environmentally benign chemical synthesis and processing. Whereas DFE efforts traditionally focus on the mechanical design of products and processes, green chemistry provides a more fundamental focus on materials at the molecular level. At this level, there is a greater chance of identifying major product and process breakthroughs that can lead to radical fundamental solutions to DFE problems. Green chemistry has the potential for improving separation and extraction methods, providing more environmentally safe catalysis methods, increasing the use of renewable resources, improving product biodegradability, and improving feedstock regeneration from waste byproducts (Fiksel 2001). Since the introduction of its environmental program in 1990, many of Apple's DFE efforts have involved finding ways to eliminate harmful chemicals from its products and production processes. For example, just since 2007, Apple has introduced bromine-free circuit boards, mercury-free LED monitors, and arsenic-free LCD monitors (Anonymous 2008a).

Sustainable Procurement

Effective sustainable organizational management requires that social and environmental criteria be designed into organizational procurement systems. Simply stated, achieving sustainability-based competitive advantages requires that firms sell socially and environmentally sensitive products and services, and socially and environmentally sensitive products and services can only be produced with socially and environmentally sensitive inputs. This means that sustainability-based supplier relationships are critical for sustainable organizational management. Organizational purchasing strategies need to have as their overriding goal to minimize the ecological, economic, and social costs of the firm's resource acquisition. Raw materials, semi-finished goods, products ready for assembly or packaging, and the full range of contracted services are all potential areas covered by sustainable procurement systems. Within these systems, the content, manufacturing, and delivery of procured products and services should be assessed for desirable sustainability characteristics (Greeno 1994; Shrivastava 1996). Such an assessment should address several questions (Thompson 2002): Is the procured input necessary for the firm's products and/or services? Does the procured input meet the organization's environmental and social criteria? If so, which environmental and social standards are being met? What is the potential for reducing, reusing, or recycling the procured input? Are the most efficient modes of transportation being used? Is there potential for a long-term, firm-supplier sustainability partnership?

An innovative acquisition strategy that is getting significant attention involves purchasing services rather than physical products and materials. For example, rather than simply purchasing a certain amount of a chemical for a certain price per unit, a firm purchases the services related to the chemicals they need that includes production services, storage services, transportation services, and a per-unit price for the chemicals themselves. Such a procurement system places the organization and the supplier in a partnership that encourages both to reduce the amount of chemicals produced, transported, and consumed, and it encourages both parties to cooperate in reducing any other environmental and social costs related to the contracted services as well. Such cost reductions lead to lower costs for both the firm and the supplier, which will in turn provide competitive advantages to both by reducing total, average, and marginal use of energy and/ or materials. Clearly such a process is a whole new way of thinking about procurement. Thus, firms that can make the transition from thinking in terms of goods to thinking in terms of services are making the kind of fundamental paradigm shifts required for sustainable organizational management.

At the heart of developing effective environmentally and socially based supplier relationships is conducting regular audits of suppliers' environmental and social performance. Many firms require suppliers to secure ISO 14001 certification and to adopt pollution prevention policies. In addition to requiring ISO 14001 certification, Toyota also requires its suppliers to eliminate toxic substances from their manufacturing processes. Other firms, such as Royal Dutch Shell, use audits to monitor the child-labor practices of their suppliers. The apparel and textile manufacturers in the United States have developed a set of standards for working conditions, wages, and other terms of employment for their suppliers in undeveloped and developing markets. These standards can be used by organizations in the industry to benchmark their social performance and calculate their social value added.

However, just purchasing sustainable inputs is not enough to make sure that a firm's procurement system is sustainable. It is also important to use the supplies procured by the organization in sustainable ways (Nattrass and Altomare 2002). The rate of consumption of supplies within the organization has a great deal to do with employees' understanding of and commitment to sustainability. Thus, educating employees about sustainability can help to reduce the consumption of supplies. Employees make daily decisions involving resource flows into and out of the organization ranging from small decisions regarding the use of electricity, paper, and water to larger decisions regarding transportation, manufacturing, and purchasing. In other words, employees are resource gatekeepers whose willingness and ability to translate the organization's vision of sustainability into daily practices and decisions is critical for sustainable organizational management. For example, paper entails a considerable cost to businesses. Organizations engaged in sustainable organizational management may decide to purchase only 100 percent recycled content paper, and/or paper that is chlorine-free, and/or paper that is derived from non-tree materials. However, once these sustainable paper products flow into the organization, then employees must integrate sustainable consumption patterns into their daily paper utilization. Thus, sustainable procurement not only entails developing sustainability-based supplier relationships and input flows; it also requires developing a sustainable consumption culture within the organization to minimize material and energy flows into and out of the organization.

Energy Efficiencies

Energy efficiency and the substitution of renewable energy sources for traditional ones are important components of sustainable organizational management (Holliday, Schmidheiny, and Watts 2002; Willard 2002). More efficient motors, use of insulating materials, and right-sizing pipes and wires are being employed in operations systems to improve energy efficiency. Further, organizations now have more opportunities to purchase or produce renewable energy sources and other energy services that do not involve fossil fuels or nuclear energy. Large manufacturers often have the opportunity to use waste heat from their production processes to produce steam for electricity (called "cogeneration"). This captured heat is potentially useful to organizations themselves, their industrial ecology partners, or to other utility customers. Firms can also use renewable energy, especially wind and solar photovoltaic cells. One of the more ambitious examples of renewable energy use by a global corporation is BP's installation of solar photovoltaic panels on hundreds of its retail service stations worldwide. BP's efforts have made it a major customer of its own subsidiary, BP Solar, one of the world's largest developers and producers of photovoltaic cells. BP Solar recently began supplying solar panels to Home Depot for large-scale direct retail sale to the public (Randazzo 2008).

Substituting Information for Energy and Materials

The substitution of information for energy and materials is another technique that can be utilized to help develop functional-level, eco-efficient capabilities. Remember that physical resources are entropic in nature; the more you use, the less you have. On the other hand, information resources are regenerative in nature; the more you use, the more you have. Thus, as in nature, information beats scarcity. The advantage that information has over natural resources is that the more it is used, the less likely it will be to run out (Kiuchi and Shireman 2002; Nattrass and Altomare 2002). For example modern computer-based climate control systems and GPS systems provide direct energy-saving information. The advent of electronic-information systems including computers, telecommunication networks, and micro-electromechanical devices, provide organizations with virtually unlimited opportunities with regard to substituting information for energy and materials. These advanced information systems, through their hypersensing and real-time transmission capabilities, can provide organizations information about their products, services, and related activities that can help to minimize the amount of energy and materials necessary for their production, consumption, and distribution.

Among the numerous sustainability-related information technologies being developed and implemented are programmable (timed) building HVAC thermostats that reduce heating and cooling use, sound-and-motion lighting detection systems that turn off room lights when rooms are empty, and computer-assisted design and manufacturing systems with virtually zero tolerances that allow for significant reductions in raw material wastes. With these technologies, information is being automatically collected, processed, and disseminated to the appropriate decision sources so that energy and materials consumption are minimized. For example, Wal-Mart uses electronic light sensors to adjust the lighting in its stores to the amount of daylight flowing through the skylights in the roof. Computer control for these light sensors, as well as for all of the firm's heating and air-conditioning systems, is centralized at its headquarters in Bentonville, Arkansas (Anonymous 2005a).

Total Quality Environmental Management

Total quality environmental management (TQEM) is a tool that allows managers to integrate ecological dimensions via a system that links research and development, operations, and marketing in order to improve environmental performance. TQEM is an approach for continuously improving the environmental quality of processes and products through the participation of all levels and functions in an organization (Ahmed 2001; Nash et al. 1994; North 1997). TQEM has emerged as one of the most useful and widely implemented frameworks for achieving eco-efficient capabilities because it provides firms with a framework for accounting for the ecological impacts of products and processes all along the closed-loop value chain. By incorporating nature into the total-quality-management formula, firms are able to achieve high levels of top-management commitment and employee involvement in pollution prevention, materials reduction, materials substitution, and waste reduction. Though there are many approaches to TQEM, most attempt to incorporate the sustainability values and perspectives of all decision makers, to use as much qualitative and quantitative information as is available throughout the network, to measure and make adjustments for increasing levels of environmental effectiveness, and to attempt to continuously improve the firm's environmental profile.

One difficulty firms have in implementing TQEM at every stage of the closed-loop value chain is that most TQEM efforts have limited their scope to internal throughput processes. To overcome this limitation, firms need to practice "TQEM alliancing" with other environmentally linked firms (O'Dea and Pratt 2006). Essentially, TQEM alliancing involves using TQEM as a framework for forming industrial ecologies with other firms. Another difficulty that firms have in implementing TQEM is calculating the true costs of its implementation. Currently tools like LCA are helpful, but some believe that more traditional methods of calculating costs in total-quality-management efforts, such as Joseph Juran's "cost of quality analysis," would bring more precision to the TQEM cost measurement process (Curkovic, Sroufe, and Landeros 2008).

Sustainability Marketing

Environmental marketing first emerged during the 1990s with a focus on the ecological dimension of sustainability. It refers to activities that put the organization's product stewardship commitment at the center of its marketing efforts. Environmental marketing has two important objectives: to develop environmentally friendly products that effectively balance performance, price, convenience, and environmental compatibility; and to project an image to consumers that these products are both high quality and environmentally sensitive (Fuller 1999; Ottman 1998). Kirchgeorg and Winn (2006) call for expanding the scope of environmental marketing to include social concerns as well, which they call sustainability marketing. They contend that doing so is an essential prerequisite for transforming the consumer society into a sustainable society (Kirchgeorg and Winn 2006).

There are several challenges for sustainability marketing. The first is to identify the sustainability characteristics and potential of the firm's products and services. The second challenge is to find ways to convince consumers to make lifestyle changes that emphasize the need for more ecologically and socially sensitive products and services. Third, sustainability marketing is challenged to focus on educating consumers about the true nature of environmental and social problems and how they relate to the firm's products and services. Fourth, sustainability marketers must find legitimate, non-misleading ways to communicate the environmental and social features and benefits of products. The fifth challenge for sustainability marketing is to gain credibility for the idea that business interests do not necessarily conflict with environmental and social performance (Ottman 1998).

The degree of stakeholder value added via sustainable marketing depends on the interaction between the price and/or opportunity costs of the product and the environmental and/or social benefits of the product. If a product provides environmental and social benefits at a lower price and/or opportunity cost to consumers, then the added stakeholder value occurs because the product offers the firm both traditional competitive advantages and environmental and social advantages. If, however, a sustainable product is recognized by the consumer to be environmentally and socially beneficial, but the product is more expensive, harder to find, or both, then the stakeholder value added is achieved only through the product's sustainability. If the sustainability of a product is not perceived to be at least marginally environmentally and socially beneficial to the consumer and the product's price/opportunity costs exceed those of competing non-sustainable products, then stakeholder value added can only be achieved by changing consumer attitudes or providing regulatory structures to support the sustainable product (Ottman 1998). In fact, 66 percent of U.S. consumers say they don't buy sustainable products because they cost too much, and 44 percent say the lack of availability influences their purchasing decision of such products. Thus, although 80 percent of U.S. consumers consider themselves to be green to some degree, there is a wide gap between actual sales of sustainable products and consumers who want to buy them. This offers numerous unmet market opportunities (Hanas 2007).

Recall from our discussion of sustainable procurement that firms are now thinking in terms of marketing services as replacements for, or adjuncts to, material products. Ottman has identified four different groups of services that have the potential to substitute for products: First are product-life extension services, which are designed to extend the life of the product via technical assistance, maintenance, and disposal service. Second are product-use services, which entail such efforts as sharing products, such as cars, without the need to pay the full purchase price. Third are intangible services, which are designed to substitute products for labor-based services such as automated bill paying or voicemail. Fourth are result services, which are aimed at reducing the need for material products, such as using pedestrian access or mass transit instead of relying on individual cars. Selling services has the potential to lock in customers and increase repeat business as well as to reduce the organization's footprint (Ottman 1998).

Another technique for moving toward sustainable marketing systems is to engage in what is called "reverse distribution," which involves taking back products from end users when they have finished with them. This approach is gaining significant popularity, especially among some consumer groups, and the need for such programs is currently high. As noted in Chapter 2, e-wastes in the electronics industry are staggering. Sony has been one of the reverse distribution leaders in the electronics industry, having established a program to recycle Sony batteries in the early 1990s and expanding this effort to other Sony products in the late 1990s.

In sum, the key to building eco- and socio-efficient capabilities within the firm is to incorporate ecological and social performance into the value-creating functions of the firm and to formulate functional-level strategies based on eco- and socio-efficiency. These strategies are important in incrementally moving the firm toward sustainability.

Conclusions

In this chapter, we have examined some of the key functional eco- and socio-efficient core capabilities that organizations practicing sustainable organizational management need to develop. We discussed several stakeholder value-creation processes including strategy formulation, environmental forecasting, stakeholder engagement processes, closed-loop value chain analysis, and footprint analysis. These provide the processes and data necessary for formulating effective functional-level strategies that exploit opportunities to add socio- and eco-efficient value added thus building eco- and socio-efficient capabilities across the closed-loop value chain. The functional-level strategies necessary to develop eco- and socio-efficient capabilities include research and development, sustainable procurement systems, DFE, TQEM, energy efficiencies, information substitution, and sustainability marketing. All of the tools discussed in this chapter provide the means to help organizations design and market products and services that mimic nature. They help to reduce the environmental impacts, social impacts, and resource intensity of firms' products and services, and by doing so, they help organizations create competitive cost and differentiation competitive advantages in the marketplace.

— 8 —

Sustainable Strategic Management

We emphasized in Chapter 6 the critical role of strategic leadership in transforming global corporations into agents of positive change toward a sustainable world that supports a healthy human habitat. Ultimately, the success of strategic managers in leading their firms toward sustainable organizational management depends on their ability to design and implement strategic management processes capable of integrating the firm's economic, social, and ecological responsibilities. Collectively these processes are referred to as sustainable strategic management (SSM) (Stead and Stead 2008). SSM is a recent outgrowth of strategic management, which itself emerged out of the concepts of business policy and strategic planning in the 1980s in response to an increasingly complex and turbulent business environment. Via strategic management corporations can continuously adapt their organizational capabilities to environmental turbulence and change. Whereas, traditional strategic management is based on the perception that the economy is a closed system, SSM is based on the perception that the economy is an open subsystem of the larger social and ecological systems in which it is embedded. Thus, SSM encourages the development and implementation of strategic visions in organizations that reveal how firms can perpetuate themselves by contributing to the preservation of a sustainable world. Thus, SSM constitutes a complete mental shift regarding the role of corporations on today's small planet Earth.

The SSM Corporate Portfolio

Corporate strategy refers to the overall plan for a diversified organization. Generally, the focus of corporate strategy is on managing the mix, scope, and emphasis of a firm's portfolio of strategic business units (SBUs), exploiting the synergies among its lines of businesses, and deploying its resources accordingly. Via corporate strategy, a corporation seeks to create value through the configuration of its SBUs and the coordination of its multi-market activities. Thus, effective corporate level strategies are designed so that a firm's portfolio of SBUs can be integrated to create more value than each SBU standing alone.

A SSM corporate strategy portfolio includes strategic processes designed to manage a firm's portfolio of SBUs in ways that create synergy among the firm's economic, social, and ecological performance. Such strategic processes are based on the vision of a sustainable world and the firm's role as a change agent in achieving such a vision. In other words, the portfolio is based on eco- and socio-effectiveness where the firm makes positive contributions to both natural and social capital (Hamschmidt and Dyllick 2006). Thus, a SSM corporate portfolio is a set of corporate-level capabilities that integrate the SSM strategies of the firm's various SBUs. Because the open-system view of managers leading their organizations along pathways toward SSM differs so much from the closed-system view of traditional strategic management, developing a SSM-based corporate portfolio requires double-loop learning, dialogue, and transformational change processes that allow firms to think differently about how they can make positive contributions to the sustainability of social and natural capital while creating long-term economic sustainability for themselves. These capabilities provide the vehicles for strategic managers to question the underlying assumptions of their corporate portfolios and to develop innovative approaches for sustainable product and service introductions. Thus, a SSM corporate portfolio can provide corporations with avenues for progress toward sustainability not available to SBUs operating independently of one another.

In developing and implementing corporate SSM portfolios, it is important for strategic managers to build multi-stakeholder networks. These enable organizations to make positive contributions toward sustainability across the economic, social, and ecological sectors of the business environment. Such multi-stakeholder, multi-sector networks allow for effective dialogue that provides a vehicle for all voices to be heard and for collective stakeholder wisdom to be tapped. These networks provide a neutral space for safe discussion and partnering in order to solve global issues such as climate change and poverty. Thus, they allow strategic managers to integrate the complex issues of how to care for future generations, how to care for their organizations, and how to care for Earth's stakeholders.

The Global Sustainable Food Lab and the Unilever-Oxfam-Kellogg Foundation partnership mentioned in Chapter 6 are examples of such networks. Another example is the United Nation's Global Compact Cities Program, which is a multi-stakeholder partnership designed to obtain the collective wisdom of those affected by social problems such as urbanization (Fort 2007). Another example is the U.S. Climate Action Partnership, which brings together some of America's largest corporations and environmental groups to advocate for more progressive public policy on climate change. Accountability coalitions are an emerging type of multi-stakeholder network. These industry led coalitions focus on improving social and/or environmental accountability where there are market failures or governance gaps. For example, the Alliance for a Healthier Generation in the United States brought together the American Heart Association, the Clinton Foundation, Coca-Cola, PepsiCo, and Cadbury Schweppes to jointly implement guidelines for selling soft drinks in schools. Another type of network, the resource mobilization coalition, brings together governments, businesses and foundations to mobilize resources to address specific social or ecological needs. Examples include the Global Alliance for Improved Nutrition and the Global Fund Against HIV, TB and Malaria (Nelson 2007). Global action networks such as these that combine the resources and efforts of business, government, and civil society provide alliances that can affect transformational change toward sustainability across the globe. Such alliances may even represent an emerging form of global governance (Waddell 2007).

It is also important for strategic managers building SSM corporate portfolios to embrace the development of disruptive technologies, which are innovative technologies that create dramatic technological paradigm shifts that can transform entire industries, economies, societies, and/or ecosystems. They are the technologies that economist Joseph Schumpeter said fuel "creative destruction," which is economic disequilibrium caused by major technological shifts. Strategies based on effective eco- and socio-efficiency are valuable for creating continuous incremental changes in current products and services designed to serve current customers and markets. However, strategies based on creative destruction with its resulting change hold the promise of providing both socio- and eco-effective means for developing products and services that can make positive contributions to economic, social, and natural capital (Hart and Milstein 1999; Holliday, Schmidheiny, and Watts 2002). Cell phone and satellite technologies are examples of disruptive technologies. They have changed the global telecommunications industry, and they now provide nations without the resources to build expensive landline based telecommunications systems with the opportunity to build much less expensive cell and satellite based networks that connect them with the entire globe. Ecologically, disruptive clean-energy and zero-pollution technologies are critical for achieving global sustainability. Thus, developing and implementing these clean technologies offers organizations numerous SSM portfolio opportunities now and in the foreseeable future (Hart 2008).

Defining the Corporate SSM Mission

Strategic managers define the corporate mission of the firm by analyzing its purpose, scope, and the balance of cash flow within its portfolio of SBUs. By applying SSM thought processes when defining their firm's mission, strategic managers are better able to define the purpose and scope of their organization in terms of the three dimensions of sustainability, and they are better able to balance the strategies in their firm's portfolio in order to achieve synergy among their economic, environmental, and social pursuits. Thus, the mission of a firm pursuing a SSM corporate strategy portfolio will reflect a commitment to making positive contributions to a sustainable world while ensuring that the organization's business units are balanced in ways that contribute to the long-term economic viability of the firm.

Purpose

The overarching purpose of a SSM corporate portfolio is to provide firms a way to tie their long-term success to making positive economic, social, and ecological contributions to a human-friendly habitat on Earth. Therefore, a SSM corporate portfolio provides a framework that allows strategic managers to continually examine and, if necessary, change organizational values, assumptions, and strategies in light of eco- and socio-effectiveness. Thus, a SSM corporate portfolio serves the purpose of contributing to both socio- and eco-effectiveness via the long-term preservation and enhancement of social and natural capital. Doing this requires that firms move beyond strategies for eco- and socio-efficiency that allow them to readily calculate the direct social and ecological costs and benefits of their strategies (Hamschmidt and Dyllick 2006). By contrast, because the shift to socio- and eco-effectiveness strategies requires a long-term intergenerational perspective, the links between social, ecological, and economic performance of such strategies are not as direct and easily calculated as they are for socio- and eco-efficiency strategies. Therefore, strategic leaders must be very diligent in continuously focusing organizational attention on the overarching purpose of contributing to the long-term sustainability of the planet.

Scope

To fulfill this purpose, strategic managers will have to expand the scope of their corporate strategic portfolios. First of all, firms will have to expand their planning horizons to include future generations; this means making investments with long-term as well as short-term paybacks. Another critical expansion in scope involves finding ways to include fringe stakeholders from undeveloped and developing markets, addressing such issues as poverty, disease, and population growth (Hart and Sharma 2004). Hart (2005) calls this expanded scope "fanning out" from a narrow focus on local community sustainability to the broader focus on global economic, social, and ecological justice. Another necessary scope expansion for SSM corporate strategic portfolios involves finding ways to address issues of over-consumption and waste in the developed and developing markets of the world.

Balance

Of course in developing their SSM corporate portfolios, firms must find ways to enhance their economic sustainability while they make positive contributions to social and natural capital. This requires balancing the corporate portfolio by balancing the cash flow among the firm's various lines of business. Balancing the SSM corporate portfolio refers to using the cash flow from economically successful core business lines to fund business units created to address the opportunities arising from the expanded social and ecological scope and purpose of the portfolio. For example, firms may use profits from core businesses to pursue new market opportunities in undeveloped markets (Hart 2005).

"Sustainability balanced scorecards" have emerged as a tool to assist strategic managers in balancing their portfolios of SBUs in light of their sustainability performance by better integrating the firm's social, environmental, and economic aspects of its SSM portfolio. The sustainability balanced scorecard approach is an integrative approach that addresses the market issues of the conventional balanced scorecard as well as the non-market issues related to the firm's social and environmental performance. After the sustainability-balanced scorecard is developed, the key challenge to strategic managers is to integrate its sustainability performance measurement system into the firm's conventional management information and reporting systems (Wagner and Schaltegger 2006).

In sum, the SSM portfolio is a vehicle that helps strategic managers move their organizations toward a vision that clearly depicts their firm's role in achieving a sustainable world. By developing an in-depth understanding of the purpose, scope, and balance of the firm's mission, firms can use the SSM portfolio to help them clarify the road to long-term triple-bottom-line performance.

Coevolving Global Markets

As discussed in the previous chapter, the turbulent global business environment has coevolved from three highly differentiated economies: the money economy of the developed and developing markets of the world; the traditional, village-based economy of the undeveloped world; and the economy of the natural world in which the other two are embedded (Hart 2005). As noted in Chapter 4, significant wealth and income inequities exist both within and between the markets of the world. Thus, a country such as China may have coevolving undeveloped, developing, and developed market segments functioning within its borders. Thus, although markets are often characterized by their geographical location (i.e., the undeveloped markets of Africa or the developing market of India), they are more accurately portrayed in terms of their specific demographics and varying socio-economic factors. The coevolving undeveloped, developing, and developed markets of the world offer major opportunities and challenges for businesses that have a SSM portfolio consisting of SBUs and strategies that address the needs of these unique markets. However, developing such strategies will require firms to engage in dialogue-based double-loop learning processes that allow them to think and act differently regarding these unique markets.

Undeveloped and Developing Markets

Undeveloped and developing markets provide unique opportunities and challenges for businesses to make positive contributions in moving toward a sustainable world. Approximately 85 percent of the world's population will be living in the undeveloped and developing markets of the world by 2025 (Schmidt 1999). As discussed in Chapter 4, approximately 4.6 billion humans live on less than $4 per day in the mainly rural areas of China, India, Africa, and Latin America. These markets are typically village-based, traditional economies where people live at a subsistence level, primarily off the land, with little involvement in the cash or money economy (Hart 2005). The traditional, undeveloped markets are characterized by rural poverty, isolation, disease, exponential population growth, and environmental degradation. This untapped market of the world's poor, which has been labeled "the bottom of the pyramid," potentially offers numerous win-win opportunities for businesses to earn a profit while helping to alleviate poverty (Prahalad and Hart 2002; Prahalad 2006; Hart 2005).

Industrialization has brought increasing consumer demand for goods and services in the developing economies. As Hart (2005) notes, developing markets represent the collision of the money economy with nature's economy, where meeting future consumer demands without exceeding the carrying capacity of the planet is the major challenge. The markets of India, China, and other developing nations consist of the rural, isolated poor, the urban slum dwellers, an increasing number of refugees, and the increasingly affluent, all of whom want to emulate the consumption-based western lifestyle. The coevolution of these once distinct markets results in myriad social issues (discussed in Chapter 4). Finding sustainable solutions to these issues provides numerous business opportunities for organizations, allowing them to contribute to the preservation of human, social, and natural capital while earning a reasonable profit for their efforts.

Developed Markets

The developed markets of the world currently house the richest 25 percent of the world's population and control 75 percent of the world's income and purchasing power (Milanovic 2002). These markets, which include the United States, Canada, the European Union, Japan, and others, are the world's largest producers and consumers of goods and services, and they have controlled the global marketplace for most of its history. As previously discussed in Chapter 2, the human footprint in the developed markets is very large. The footprints of corporations in many of the resource intensive industries such as chemicals and energy are extremely large, and these industries are typically based on older technologies that have limited environmental performance improvement potential (Hart 2005). Thus, the primary need in the developed markets of the world is to reduce corporate footprints while providing consumer value through sustainable, innovative products and services that, in turn, enable consumers to reduce their footprints.

Interestingly (as noted in Chapter 4), even with all of the wealth and purchasing power in highly developed countries, they often have income and wealth inequities that lead to pockets of undeveloped markets within their borders. For example, the inner cities within the United States have historically demonstrated many of the characteristics of undeveloped markets. This is largely due to insufficient retail penetration in these areas; they have significantly fewer supermarkets, department stores, and pharmacies per capita than their higher income counterparts. This lack of economic activity results in cycles of poverty and social problems such as domestic violence, drug abuse, and crime. Restoring economic and social health to these undeveloped market segments offers numerous opportunities for businesses to become profitable, serve the local community, and export their products and services to surrounding communities (Dean and McMullen 2005; Porter 1995).

SSM Strategies

SSM strategies are what organizations that "stand for sustainability" do (Stead and Stead 2000). It is through these strategies that the philosophies and ethics of sustainable organizational management become tangible because SSM strategies are designed as vehicles for operationally integrating the ecosystem and the greater society into strategic decision-making processes. These strategies are typically multi-market, multi-sector strategies requiring broad collaboration with stakeholders. Thus, SSM strategies provide valuable avenues for bringing the ecological, social, and economic dimensions of an organization's strategic vision of a sustainable world to life. The coevolutionary nature of SSM strategies is reflected in the progression of the strategies over time. As discussed in depth below, there has been an evolution from eco- and socio-efficiency strategies that provide relatively short-term economic gains for organizations to eco- and socio-effectiveness strategies designed to enable organizations to make positive contributions to a sustainable world that will pay off economically for them in the long-term (Stead and Stead 2008).

As we proceed with our discussion, it's important to understand that even when strategies have their intended positive impacts on social and/ or environmental capital, they may also have unintended social and/or environmental consequences that are negative. Waddock (2008, 251) calls this "the dark-side paradoxes of success." For example, Wal-Mart's core value of cost leadership has achieved its intended (and laudable) positive social outcome of providing people of all income levels with the lowest possible prices for the things they need to survive and be comfortable in the modern world. However, by its very nature, this core value has also had negative social and environmental consequences, such as bankrupting local businesses and increasing the number of consumer miles traveled to shop at Wal-Mart. CEO Lee Scott has recently declared that Wal-Mart is now moving toward environmental sustainability. To achieve this, Scott has stated some very ambitious eco-efficiency goals, such as operating on 100 percent renewable energy, creating zero wastes, and selling products that sustain resources and the environment. Of course success in meeting these goals will enhance Wal-Mart's cost leadership position, potentially placing even more pressure on local businesses and consumer driving patterns (Laszlo 2008). Thus, as Wal-Mart's situation demonstrates, achieving continuous positive performance across all three dimensions of sustainability is challenging. As Elkington (2008) notes, economic, social, and ecological performance are always in a state of flux. He says that the three dimensions of the triple bottom line are like the continental plates, which move both in concert with and independently of each other.

Pollution Prevention Strategies

SSM strategies that are designed to provide firms with cost advantages and risk reduction through improved eco-efficiency are generally referred to as pollution prevention strategies (Christmann 2000; Hart 1995; Hart 1997; Senge et al. 2008; Stead and Stead 1995). These strategies, which were the first win-win strategies to be based on eco-efficient capabilities, help to improve a firm's environmental performance across its value chain. Further, eco-efficient pollution prevention strategies provide firms with opportunities to establish social legitimacy in the greater community, which means that these strategies provide firms with socio-efficient as well as eco-efficient value added.

3M is generally given credit for being the leader in pollution prevention. The firm introduced its now famous Pollution Prevention Pays (3P) program in 1975, demonstrating that preventing pollution before it occurs can create greater economic and ecological value added than cleaning it up after it has been generated. Since the inception of the 3P program, 3M has had about 5000 eco-efficient projects. These projects have been responsible for eliminating 2.2 billion pounds of pollutants from the firm's processes and products while providing about $1 billion in first-year project savings. Numerous other firms have also realized significant cost reductions via pollution prevention strategies. For example, Staples saved $6 million over a two-year period with centralized controls for heating, cooling, and lighting at its 1,500 stores, and furniture manufacturer Herman Miller saved over $1 million per year over the past 15 years by reducing its annual landfill wastes from 41 million pounds to 5 million pounds (Esty and Winston 2008).

Product Stewardship Strategies

Strategies designed to provide a firm with competitive advantages by allowing it to ecologically and socially differentiate its products and services from its competitors in the marketplace are referred to as product stewardship strategies (Hart 1995; Hart 1997; Reinhardt 1999; Stead and Stead 1995). These strategies can lead to increased revenue, market share, and profits via improvements in the firm's reputation, perceived legitimacy, brand value, and brand equity. Ecologically and socially, product stewardship strategies reflect the idea of minimizing environmental hazards, negative social impacts, and life-cycle costs of products or services. Doing so requires firms to focus on the complete life-cycle impacts of their products and processes.

Baxter International, a global healthcare company, is one example of a firm that practices product stewardship all across its product life cycles.

It has designed ecological responsibility into research and development, energy and materials, manufacturing and transportation, product promotion, product refurbishment, and waste/byproduct recycling (Anonymous, 2008d). Another example is Proctor and Gamble who discovered through life-cycle analysis that the greatest environmental impact of its Tide laundry detergent was the energy used to heat the wash water. This discovery led to the development of Tide Coldwater, which does not need hot water to clean laundry effectively (Ottman 2008).

Eco labeling is one tool that can enhance the environmental market differentiation of a firm's products (Holliday, Schmidheiny, and Watts 2002). Eco labeling is currently being used worldwide to inform consumers about the ecological impacts of products ranging from construction materials and household appliances to food and paper products. Germany's Blue Angel eco label, which began in the 1970s, is the grandfather of eco-labeling initiatives. The Blue Angel labels have penetrated many of the markets within the European Union (Reinhardt 2008). The Marine Stewardship Council (MSC) also has established an eco-labeling initiative to certify fish as sustainably harvested; Wal-Mart now requires MSC certification for all of the fish it sells in its North American stores. Another eco-labeling initiative entails using the standards established by the Forestry Stewardship Council (FSC) to evaluate the performance of wood products against a set of environmental, social, and economic standards. Over 600 companies, including IKEA and Home Depot, have joined trade networks committed to buying FSC certified wood.

Social labeling has also emerged as a means for firms to achieve differentiation in their product stewardship efforts. Social labeling provides consumers with assurance about the social and ethical impacts of an organization's processes and products. The Ethical Trade Initiative, the Fair Trade Foundation, and the Clean Clothes Campaign all aim to assure consumers that the conditions within a firm meet basic standards for human safety, health, comfort, and dignity, and do not utilize child labor, bonded labor, or sweatshops in the production of their products. Social-labeling criteria are usually based on the conventions of the International Labour Organization. For example, Reebok (now owned by Adidas) found that incorporating these internationally recognized human rights standards into its business practices leads to improved worker morale, a better working environment, and higher quality products. A number of companies, including BP and Shell, have incorporated elements of the United Nations Declaration of Human Rights into their competitive strategies. Regardless of the specific set of standards used, having corporate citizenship connected to the core of a firm's competitive strategy reaps benefits for employees, local communities, and shareholders (Holliday, Schmidheiny, and Watts 2002).

A key to successful social and environmental differentiation is to competitively position products and services into carefully segmented markets. Ottman (2008) concluded that consumer interest in sustainability jumped 50 percent from 2007 to 2008. She found that consumer interest was especially high regarding the impacts of climate change and water insecurity. Her data indicate that formulating and implementing product stewardship strategies to address these two issues may create first mover advantages for firms in today's market. As discussed in Chapter 7, continuous innovation is essential to maintaining such an advantage because as soon as competitors can imitate environmentally or socially sensitive offerings, competitive differentiation is lost. For example, eco labeling and social labeling may provide preemptive, first mover advantages, but these can be easily lost if and when competitors follow suit (Reinhardt 2008).

Developed Market Strategies

As previously discussed, the developed markets of the world provide unique opportunities for organizations to create innovative sustainability-based solutions to the issues of over-consumption and production. The strategies of pollution prevention and product stewardship discussed above originated in these developed markets where their win-win nature could be immediately seen in terms of reduced environmental/social impacts for the planet and short-run profits for the firm. Because of this short-run profitability, implementing such strategies is often referred to as "picking the low-hanging fruit." However, achieving global sustainability will require that organizations engage in innovative developed-market strategies that go beyond picking the low-hanging fruit (Senge et al. 2008). Such strategies will need to deliver long-term consumer value in ways that enhance the planet's ecological and social systems. They will need to contribute to planetary reductions in carbon emissions to levels that are in balance with a human-friendly carbon cycle, and they will need to encourage sustainable consumption patterns that are in balance with the carrying capacity of the Earth. For example, Hoffman and Woody (2008) have proposed a three-step process for organizations to develop effective strategies to address the complex issue of climate change.

Encouraging sustainable consumption is a rather complex issue. Although consumption is critical for economic success, over consumption is an addictive pattern that can only be changed by a radical shift in the consumption-oriented, throwaway thinking that dominates the cultures of today's developed markets (Ehrenfeld 2008). Thus, sustainable consumption is about more than just consuming less; it is about changing underlying consumption patterns (Ehrenfeld 2008; Holliday, Schmidheiny, and Watts 2002). These new patterns will need to reverse the throwaway mentality that currently exists. Planned obsolescence will have to be replaced with the idea that products should be as durable and long lasting as possible, and firms will need to establish processes such as automatic product take backs that reduce their waste streams.

New patterns like this represent a shift in thinking from producing products, increasing throughput, and making energy- and capital-intensive investments, to bundling services, selling end-use value, and ensuring cradle-to-cradle product stewardship. Through such innovative strategies, firms can create value for consumers while minimizing the environmental and social impacts resulting from the production and consumption of goods. Hawken, Lovins, and Lovins (1999, 146) say, "In the new model, value is delivered [to consumers] as a flow of services—providing illumination, for example, rather than selling light bulbs." Firms currently following this philosophy include United Technologies' Carrier Division, the world's largest manufacturer of air conditioners, which has changed its mission from selling air conditioners to leasing comfort, and elevator manufacturer Schindler, which now sells vertical transportation services rather than elevators (Willard 2002).

Ottman says that in developed markets a firm's strategy must promote "responsible consumption," which she defines as, "encouraging consumers not to buy more of your products than they actually need . . . [and] developing products that last longer and have higher consumer value" (Ottman 2008, 5). This allows firms to build long-term relationships with customers. Responsible consumption entails encouraging consumers to conserve resources when consuming the product, "like encouraging consumers not to just buy [compact fluorescent light bulbs], but to turn them off when they're not in use" (Ottman 2008, 4). Other examples include not only encouraging consumers to buy water-efficient front-loading washing machines, but also encouraging them to only wash full loads. Responsible consumption can be promoted through product design, such as Toyota's Prius, with a dashboard that helps drivers monitor their energy efficiency. Innovation, technology, and imagination are also essential in promoting responsible consumption. For example, the development of the Wattson, a device that monitors how much electricity is being used in homes at anytime during the day so the consumer can see the energy impacts of turning off lights or using appliances, is reflective of the role of technology in responsible consumption. In fact, Ottman (2008, 4) contends that the future is in eco innovation, a double-loop learning process that entails "inventing new products, new materials and new technologies, rather than simply making incremental improvements to existing ones." Theses processes are critical if organizations are to move from picking the low-hanging fruit—such as Tide Coldwater, to new strategic possibilities, such as Tide Waterless (Ottman 2008).

Undeveloped Market Strategies

There are two types of generic market strategies for addressing the needs of the poor in the undeveloped markets of the world. One involves the reduction of poverty through the use of market strategies that focus on the poor as a market of consumers for global corporations (Boyle and Boguslaw 2007; Kirchgeorg and Winn 2006). The needs of these poor at "the bottom of the pyramid" (BOP) provide an untapped market that potentially offers win-win opportunities for businesses to make economic profits while reducing poverty and improving lives (Prahalad and Hart 2002; Prahalad 2006; Hart 2005). The premise of these strategies is that corporations relate the idea of disruptive technology to their current products and services, thus creating innovative sustainable products and services to meet the needs of undeveloped markets (Hart and Christensen 2002). These strategies are designed to provide low-cost products and services that address the basic needs of the poor, such as poverty reduction, disease, sanitation, and clean water (Boyle and Boguslaw 2007).

As pointed out earlier in the chapter, disruptive technologies can help undeveloped markets to leapfrog into the future, allowing them to reverse their poverty trends and increase both the longevity and quality of life of their people. For example, undeveloped markets can today forego developing traditional electric generation plants and distribution systems in favor of adopting decentralized solar photovoltaic electricity systems and, as mentioned above, undeveloped markets can leapfrog expensive hardwired communications systems in favor of cellular- and satellite-based wireless technology. Water scarcity and sanitation also provide opportunities in undeveloped markets. For example, there is currently exploding demand for water purification systems in undeveloped markets, and ITT and GE have already positioned themselves in this niche. The demand for water-efficient processes and products is also expected to experience significant growth, thus providing unique opportunities for sustainable entrepreneurship in undeveloped markets (Dean and McMullen 2005).

There are issues, however, associated with these types of BOP strategies. One issue is that these strategies are often not well designed to serve the needs of those at the bottom of the pyramid; rather they are designed to merely sell an organization's standard products at lower prices to the masses or to generate rapid sales without regard to environmental sustainability. Another issue is that these strategies are considered by some to be a new form of corporate imperialism (Hart 2008). Avoiding these issues requires developing and implementing these strategies via partnerships and alliances with BOP stakeholders designed to co-create "entirely new businesses that generate mutual value" (Hart 2008, xi). These partnerships and alliances serve as mechanisms for "deep dialogue" with BOP stakeholders, leading to the development of capabilities and strategies that truly serve the needs of the world's poor (Hart 2008). Successfully developing these partnerships and alliances allows firms to socially embed their BOP strategies into the chosen undeveloped markets (Hart 2005; Sánchez, Ricart, and Rodríguez 2005; Kirchgeorg and Winn 2006). In order to more effectively do this, Hart (2008) has developed a BOP Protocol, which he says is a "co-venturing process that . . . creatively marr[ies] companies' and communities' resources, capabilities, and energies [in order to] bring life to new business ideas and models that exceed what either partner could imagine or create on their own" (Hart 2008, xi).

The second type of generic strategy for undeveloped markets is to focus on developing producers of goods and services. This means developing entrepreneurs and wealth asset builders among the poor themselves. By enabling them to build "sustainable livelihood businesses" (Kirchgeorg and Winn 2006, 172), the poor become co-producers in the value chain, helping to reduce production and distribution costs while generating income and creating local enterprises. The real advantage of these strategies is that the poor are not just consumers; they are full economic partners who create value while helping their communities to meet their basic needs (Boyle and Boguslaw 2007; Kirchgeorg and Winn 2006).

Urban slums and inner cities are undeveloped markets that offer opportunities to build competitive advantages by providing local entrepreneurs with low cost land and labor and close proximity to suppliers and
transportation networks. Thus, competitive advantages can be achieved
by creating a home-based cluster of supporting firms within inner cities
(Dean and McMullen 2005; Porter 1995). According to Porter (1995),
the inner cities of the United States offer the advantages of strategic
location, local market demand, integration with regional clusters, and
human resources. Using Boston's food processing cluster as an example,
he demonstrates how location in the inner city can be a strategic advantage. The company, Be Our Guest, was founded in 1984 and is located
in the inner city area of Roxbury. It rents linens, party equipment, and
other hard goods associated with the catering business. The firm's close,
easy access to downtown Boston enables it to provide a higher level of
customer service than its suburban competitors while it creates economic
and social capital for its urban community. Examples like this demonstrate
how local inner-city entrepreneurs can provide critical avenues to the
creation of sustainable local economies within urban areas.

   The rural poor represent another critical component of undeveloped
markets. Rural entrepreneurship is an important vehicle for alleviating
poverty, increasing economic development, and providing sustainable
livelihoods. Stimulating rural entrepreneurship is important in moving
toward more sustainable local economies because it reduces the human
ecological footprint, generates more economic impact by increasing
the local economic multiplier, and builds both social and human capital
within communities. Co-creating stakeholder value by building alliances
along the value chain is a key for success in rural entrepreneurship. For
example, the Jubilee Project, a United Methodist Mission located in rural
Hancock County, Tennessee—the second poorest county in the state and
one of the 100 poorest counties in the United States—is dedicated to
improving the lives of the rural poor in the county who primarily live off
the land. Led by Steve Hodges, a visionary strategic leader, the Jubilee
Project has partnered with local farmers and small businesses to provide
a community kitchen for production of value added agricultural products
offered for sale through the Appalachian Springs Cooperative. The cooperative is a member-owned association of farmers and entrepreneurs
that create locally produced specialty food and self-care products for
sale in local and regional communities via their website and local store.
Thus, the Jubilee Project has developed alliances and networks along

the value chain to co-produce and market local products that generate economic benefits for the local community.

Micro financing has had a revolutionary impact on how market solutions are utilized for poverty reduction. It has played a critical role in the creation of microenterprises that provide access to credit and increase the earning potential of the poor. Muhammad Yunus, the winner of the 2006 Nobel Peace Prize and father of micro financing, founded Grameen Bank over 25 years ago to make micro loans to the poor in rural Bangladesh. The bank is founded on Yunus' principle that access to credit is a fundamental human right (Yunus 2003). By effectively addressing the issues related to extending credit to the lowest income consumers, such as high credit risk and lack of collateral, the poor are able to break the cycle of poverty by building small businesses that provide them with a sustainable livelihood. Grameen Bank has loaned approximately $8 billion to four million poor in Bangladesh, 97 percent of whom are women. There are now hundreds of micro financing institutions across the globe using the Grameen methodology to serve both the urban and the rural poor. There is, however, a dark side to micro financing, and that is the possibility of lenders charging usurious interest rates. For example, in India SKS Microfinance (owned in part by Sequoia Capital, a U.S. firm), charges its customers interest rates ranging from 24 to 30 percent (Epstein and Smith 2007).

Developing Market Strategies

As discussed earlier in the chapter, developing countries such as China and India consist of numerous market segments, all with consumers desirous of western products and lifestyles. This brings with it issues such as disease, poverty, unemployment, sanitation, and pollution that provide opportunities to the business sector to make a positive contribution to social, natural, and economic capital in these developing markets. A balanced portfolio of strategies tailored to the unique needs of each of these market segments must be formulated, including pollution prevention, product stewardship, sustainable consumption, and undeveloped market strategies that focus on creating stakeholder value all along the value chain. As previously discussed, the portfolio of SSM strategies for developing markets must actually be tailored to the needs of developed, developing, and undeveloped market segments. However, the promotion of sustainable entrepreneurship is a key strategy for moving toward a sustainable world regardless of the segment.

Sustainable Management Systems

At the heart of implementing SSM in organizations is the development of integrated sustainable management systems (SMS). These systems have traditionally been referred to as environmental management systems (EMS) or environmental health and safety management systems (EHS). However, a shift from EMS to SMS is necessary to expand the scope beyond the traditional environmental focus to fully account for all three dimensions of sustainability. By including the full array of sustainability dimensions in the SMS, organizations naturally expand the scope of their strategic management processes to include long-term impacts on future generations (Oktem et al. 2007; Stead and Stead 2004).

Depending on the nature of the firm, SMSs may vary both in terms of what elements are included in them and the relative importance of each element. However, there is general agreement on some of the important elements necessary for an effective SMS. First, the design of the SMS should reflect strong top management commitment to sustainability. Second, clear sustainability goals along with specific objectives and targets to support these goals should be developed and communicated throughout the organization. Third, information and reporting systems should be established that provide critical information on sustainability performance. Fourth, measured sustainability performance should be compared to stated goals, past performance, and established external benchmarks in order to determine performance gaps and appropriate corrective actions to close these gaps. Fifth, human resource processes including training, performance appraisal systems, and reward systems must be brought into line with the firm's sustainability performance goals. Sixth, participative empowerment-based organizational structures should be established (as discussed in Chapter 5) that encourage all employees to take direct responsibility for sustainability improvements as basic parts of their jobs (McElhaney, Toffel, and Hill 2007; Oktem et al. 2007).

The Natural Step is a popular model used in designing and implementing SMSs. The Natural Step is an international educational organization with a mission to accelerate society's progression toward sustainability. The Natural Step model is built upon the idea of applying the fundamental principles of nature to business decisions. The principles of The Natural Step specify system conditions that represent the three components of sustainability. The Natural Step principles provide a framework for developing eco-effective and socio-effective strategies designed to make positive contributions to both natural and social capital, and they also provide a framework for firms to address the gaps and interactions between undeveloped, developing, and developed global markets (Kiuchi and Shireman 2002; Nattrass and Altomare 2002).

Clearly, there are numerous critical components to an effective SMS. Three of the most important are to establish full cost accounting systems, SSM reporting systems, and SSM auditing systems that can provide firms and their stakeholders with meaningful data for evaluating the firm's sustainability performance. Below we discuss these three important SMS components.

Full Cost Accounting

Having accurate, timely financial data that reflect the true economic, social, and environmental costs of producing, delivering, and consuming products and services is essential for effective SSM. Unfortunately, traditional accounting methods are inadequate for this task. At the heart of this inadequacy is that the discounting methods used in traditional financial accounting are virtually useless for providing the long-term financial perspectives necessary for SSM. Thus, traditional financial accounting is incapable of providing answers to numerous important SSM financial questions. For example: What is the economic value of a cubic meter of clean air? How much is the aesthetic beauty of the land worth? What monetary amount can be placed on the psychological costs of human displacement due to environmental or social upheaval? How much value can be assigned to future generations of human beings? How much value can be assigned to other species, now and in the future?

The inadequacy of traditional financial accounting methods for SSM has led to the development of "full cost accounting" systems, which are financial accounting systems capable of accounting for both the short-term and long-term economic, social, and environmental costs of doing business (Bebbington et al. 2001). These systems fully integrate economic, social, and environmental criteria, assign fundamental rather than secondary importance to social and environmental concerns, account for all internal and external costs now and in the future, and reflect long-term financial performance (Sherman, Steingard, and Fitzgibbons 2002). For example, from the perspective of full cost accounting, the costs of an automobile would include all of the traditional costs associated with designing the car, acquiring the materials, producing and transporting the parts to the manufacturer, assembling the car, and delivering it to the customer, but they would also include the costs of potential CO_2 emissions, public health, resource depletion, congestion, injury, and death (Beaumont, Pedersen, and Whitaker 1993; Elkins, Hillman, and Hutchinson 1992; Todd 1994).

One group committed to both research and development of full cost accounting is the Association of Chartered Certified Accountants (ACCA) (Bebbington et al. 2001). The ACCA is an association of professional accountants in the United Kingdom that has been a proponent of sustainability accounting and reporting for over two decades. According to its former CEO, "Business as usual is no longer an option. We all have our part to play to progress towards sustainable development, and the accountancy profession has a pivotal role within this" (Association of Chartered Certified Accountants 2008, 1). Recently the ACCA released its first social and environmental policy statement highlighting the importance of the accountancy profession in achieving sustainability. Among other things, the new policy expands the commitment of the ACCA to help organizations integrate sustainability into their core business strategies, to develop measurement protocols for carbon and greenhouse emissions, to develop a portfolio of social and environmental accounting techniques that more accurately account for negative sustainability impacts in the short-term and long-term, and to develop sustainability reporting tools designed to increase firm transparency and credibility (discussed further below). The ACCA is also working to use full cost accounting to improve the accuracy and usefulness of individual firm footprint analysis (Chambers and Lewis 2001).

More and more firms are working to develop full cost accounting systems, including Dow Chemical and Baxter International. In Baxter's system, the firm calculates and reports its monetary positive and negative environmental impacts as subsets of more traditional accounts, breaking out those sustainability items that can be identified and reported to users. Further, in recent years Baxter has expanded the bounds of its benchmark environmental accounting system by combining it with its information technology system to create an integrated data system that can more fully account for the firm's environmental, health, and safety performance (Koehler 2001).

SSM Reporting

Accurately and fully reporting a firm's social and environmental performance to its stakeholders is critical for effectively engaging stakeholders and contributing to the firm's legitimacy within society. Sustainability reports should meet several criteria: They should cover the information in ways that are readily comprehensible. They should respond to stakeholder inquiries and concerns. They should ensure both continuity and comparability of data over time. They should fully describe all activities, products, processes, policies, programs, and performance targets related to implementing the firm's SSM strategies. They should report on both normal operations and unusual events or incidents (Association of Chartered Certified Accountants 2001).

Some reports are mandatory, such as the U.S. EPA's Toxic Release Inventory (TRI) report that gives the public access to vast amounts of environmental performance data. However, many corporations today are taking a more proactive approach to reporting their SSM activities and results. In addition to the traditional shareholder reports that focus on the economic performance of firms, organizations are now creating detailed social and environmental performance reports. These reports are generally distributed widely to employees, shareholders, financial institutions, customers, local communities, interest groups, the media, regulators, and often to the public at large. A common practice (and in some cases a requirement) is to use external sustainability indices, such as those discussed in Chapter 7, as the basis for these reports. For example, many corporations use SRI investment firm criteria, the Dow Jones Sustainability Index, the chemical industry's Responsible Care Guidelines, or the U.N. Global Compact as indices for benchmarking their sustainability performance and determining performance gaps in their SSM strategies.

One very extensive sustainability reporting effort is the Global Reporting Initiative (GRI). Started by CERES (the Coalition for Environmentally Responsible Economies) in 1997, GRI became independent in 2002. The focus of the GRI is to develop environmental, social, and economic reporting guidelines that help advance global comprehensiveness and consistency in SSM reporting. GRI released its third generation guidelines (G3) in 2006. The G3 guidelines provide principles for defining content and quality as well as for establishing the boundaries of the report. They include 79 "core" and "additional performance" indicators, covering economic, labor practices, human rights, decent work, environment, society, and product responsibility (Fox, Littlehales, and Kennan 2008). The GRI guidelines not only include separate criteria for environmental, social, and economic performance data; they also ask organizations to report on the interactions among these three. For example, under GRI guidelines firms may want to report how they measure their environmental justice efforts and outcomes in order to ensure that their environmental activities do not have a disproportionately negative impact on low-income or minority communities (Association of Chartered Certified Accountants 2001; Waddock 2007).

One of the most important current trends in SSM reporting is to ensure that sustainability reports (and other corporate reports) are produced and delivered in sustainable ways to shareholders and other stakeholders. Thus, sustainability reports are now regularly being provided on the Internet (Holliday, Schmidheiny, Watts 2002). Using electronic media to produce and transmit reports has a number of economic, social, and environmental advantages. It saves on production and transmission costs, allows for more in-depth information to be distributed to more people from more cultures and social strata across the globe, and saves both paper and energy. Another reason why Internet-based sustainability reporting is one of the fastest growing trends is because of its value-added feature of using a variety of media (i.e., video and audio) to supplement and enhance the reports (Isenmann and Bey 2007).

Baxter International's sustainability report is an excellent example of an in-depth, Internet-based, globally available sustainability report. Baxter issued its first environmental report in 1992 and published its first sustainability report in 1999. The firm uses its report as a primary entry point to meaningful stakeholder engagement. According to the 2007 sustainability report, the primary purpose of sustainability reporting at Baxter is to inform its stakeholders of the firm's sustainability goals, priorities, initiatives, and performance. Baxter solicited feedback on its 2006 sustainability report from several external sustainability-oriented organizations (i.e., GRI). Based on feedback from these organizations as well as other stakeholders, Baxter determined that it had some performance gaps in its 2006 Sustainability Report, including the need for more transparency in political activities and contributions, the need for more transparency in the stakeholder engagement process, and the need for further information about Baxter's carbon footprint (Anonymous 2008d). Reporting systems like Baxter's can encourage stakeholder engagement and improve sustainability performance across a firm's value chain.

SSM Auditing

The purpose of SSM auditing is to regularly evaluate a firm's economic, social, and environmental performance all along its value chain, thus providing useful data for closing a firm's sustainability performance gaps. Social auditing began as a field in the 1970s, but it really began to gain attention in the late 1990s. Waddock (2000) now refers to it as "responsibility auditing," which she says involves using external benchmarks (such as the GRI guidelines) along with internal performance data to determine how organizational practices impact stakeholders. Responsibility audits are generally undertaken to improve sustainability performance. For example, a responsibility audit may assess employee practices, community relations, environmental performance, and quality performance. The performance in these areas is then compared to the firm's stated vision, values, and mission to determine the performance gaps where stakeholder value can be added (Waddock 2000, 2007). Thus, responsibility auditing is essential in evaluating and improving sustainability performance.

Conclusions

In sum, managing at the corporate level of an organization pursuing sustainable organizational management requires that strategic managers shift the organization's portfolio of SBUs to a sustainability focus. The resulting SSM portfolio will be characterized by strategies designed to make an absolute positive contribution to the social, natural, and economic capital of the undeveloped, developing, and developed markets that the organization serves. Many global corporations have begun to develop such portfolios, and they are realizing that the portfolios actually provide some potential solutions to some of the fundamental sustainability challenges faced by humankind.

For example, the Coca-Cola Company (Coke) has effectively used a multi-sector multi-stakeholder alliance with the World Wildlife Fund (WWF) to address the issue of water insecurity. The alliance came about after an incident in 2003 during a three-year drought in southern India. Although the company was using a deep aquifer that was technically unrelated to the surface water that the local farmers depended upon, the community perceived that Coke was taking its very scarce and very precious water. The incident tarnished Coke's reputation, and the company became a target for protestors on the Internet and college campuses. The strategic management team of Coke realized during the incident that the firm should have taken a more active role in helping the community to solve its water problems. In 2007, E. Neville Isdell, CEO and chairman of Coke, announced a new guiding principle the firm would follow in growing its business in the future, which was not to cause more water to be removed from a watershed than the firm can replenish. From this promise the alliance with the WWF was formed. Also, Coke embarked on internal transformation processes that utilized surveys, team meetings, and workshops to explore solutions to other water insecurity issues, and it expanded its partnership with WWF to provide more expertise on ecosystems and watersheds. Ultimately, the SSM alliance with Coke led the WWF to rethink its mission as well, moving from viewing the corporate sector as merely donors to viewing it as a source of partners in addressing sustainability concerns (Senge et al. 2008). Coevolutionary changes like this are at the heart of what SSM is all about.

— 9 —

Capabilities for Managing on a Small Planet: A Final Look

We want to remind managers of two central themes that run through this book: Change is necessary, and change is inevitable. Regarding the necessity of change, humankind can no longer afford to risk threatening its home. There are now multiple signals that fundamental changes in how organizations do business on the small planet Earth are required for the protection, improvement, and perpetuation of a human-friendly habitat. The climate is changing, clean water and fertile farmland are becoming scarce, the air is often not fit to breathe, the human population is rapidly growing, and serious economic, social, and environmental inequities abound throughout all of the world's markets.

Regarding the inevitability of change, the business environment today is rife with demands for greater social and ecological responsibility on the part of organizations. There is a rapidly growing global sustainability movement afoot that is putting real pressure on business organizations to function in sustainable ways. Organizations have a choice of how to respond to these changing sustainability-based environmental demands. They can choose to establish and enhance the sustainable organizational management capabilities that will allow them to integrate their economic, social, and ecological performance, or they can choose to forego such changes in favor of doing business in traditional ways that exclude serious concern for the social and ecological dimensions of the environment. According to coevolutionary management theory, organizations that choose to develop sustainable organizational management capabilities that meet the demands of today's business environment will enhance their potential to compete, survive, and thrive over the long term. On the other hand, organizations that eschew the development of such capabilities—choosing instead to do business without concern for the social and ecological consequences of their actions—risk losing their competitive edge in today's environment and disappearing from the business landscape.

Coevolving Sustainable Organizational Management Capabilities

Therefore as the environment increasingly demands that more attention be paid to the social and ecological aspects of doing business, firms are faced with the need to continuously develop and refine their sustainable organizational management capabilities in order to adapt to these changing demands. That is they must develop strategies, structures, resources, technologies, and processes that can help them adapt to the continuously growing social and environmental demands that they must incorporate into their pursuit of economic success. Below is a brief summary of some key sustainable organizational management capabilities gleaned from the previous eight chapters that we believe organizations will need to develop in order to succeed in the sustainability-rich business environment of the twenty-first century.

Organizations will need to develop environmental-scanning capabilities that can accurately reveal the social and ecological impacts of their current and future economic activities. Developing capabilities for uncovering how products, services, and operations affect (or may affect) society and the natural environment provides the critical data channels that organizations require in order to adapt and change in today's sustainability-rich business environment. One critical dimension of these environmental-scanning capabilities is establishing action-research processes in organizations that can effectively tie organizational actions to accurate data. Two data sources available to organizations implementing sustainable organizational management are their footprint analysis and their network of stakeholders. By monitoring the organization's footprint, managers can continuously improve their awareness and understanding of their organizations' social and ecological impacts. By gathering information from the firm's stakeholder network via dialogue with both traditional economic stakeholders—such as shareholders and customers—and fringe stakeholders—such as the poor and the disenfranchised—managers can have constant open communication with all of those who have an impact on and/or are impacted by what the organization does and how it does it. Although neither footprint analysis nor stakeholder dialogue alone is going to provide organizations with all of the accurate information they need, both the volume and accuracy of the data can be significantly enhanced by using both tools continuously and simultaneously and by benchmarking the data garnered from these tools against past results and established external standards from government and industry.

Organizations will need to develop the strategic capabilities to offer products and services that provide them with viable sustainability-based cost and/or differentiation competitive advantages for the long term. Developing such capabilities requires implementing sustainable-strategic-management processes that tie economic efficiency and effectiveness to socio- and eco-efficiency and effectiveness from the corporate level down through the functional level of the organization. At the corporate level, strategic managers must develop sustainability strategies that can synergize the sustainability efforts of the firm's portfolio of SBUs. At the functional level, managers must implement strategies designed to reduce the ecological and social costs and improve the ecological and social value of the firm's products, services, and processes. Pollution-prevention strategies, product stewardship strategies, BOP strategies, DFE, TQEM, sustainable procurement, substituting information for energy and materials, sustainability marketing, disruptive technology, full cost accounting, and sustainability reporting are some of the specific strategies, practices, and processes related to the development of these strategic capabilities. In the final analysis, such strategic capabilities provide organizations with their own unique pathways to doing well by doing good.

Organizations will need to develop the innovation capabilities to exploit their current sustainability-based opportunities and to explore new ones. This means developing effective single-loop learning processes that seek improved sustainability performance in present operations, and it means developing effective double-loop learning processes that seek new avenues to improved sustainability performance in the future. Effective single- and double-loop learning requires implementing dialogue processes designed to allow all stakeholders to be aware of, reflect on, inquire about, discuss, and make suggestions regarding an organization's sustainability performance. Dialogue provides the means for the organization to continuously examine two key questions regarding their efforts to implement and refine sustainable organizational management processes in their organizations: "What is?" and "What can be?"

Organizations will need to develop the structural capabilities to continuously adapt to the changing demands of today's sustainability-oriented business environment. Organizational structures have become more flexible and self-renewing as a natural part of the coevolutionary adaptation-selection cycles in the business environment over the years. Currently, the fundamental environmental shifts brought on by the sustainability revolution are making the need for more flexible, self-renewing structures even more acute. These structures must be calibrated to the volatility of the shifts taking place in the environment, function on the principles of self-responsibility and self-control, and balance the search for exploitative sustainability changes with the search for explorative sustainability changes. Burns and Stalker's (1961) organic structures, Mintzberg's (1979) ad hoc structures, Peters and Waterman's (1982) excellent organizations, Senge's (1990) learning organizations, and Schumacher's (1973) large-scale organizations are just a few of the available models that inform managers of ways to build these three structural characteristics into their sustainable organizational management efforts.

Organizations will need to develop the type III-industrial-ecosystem capabilities to produce and deliver products and services using renewable energy, biological and technical nutrients, and operating systems that mimic nature. These capabilities are at the heart of ecological sustainability in industrial organizations because they are specifically designed around the concept of the closed-loop value chain. Organizations operating alone have a very difficult time creating type III-industrial-ecosystem capabilities. Thus, building these capabilities generally requires that organizations join networks of firms that are linked together in ways that allow them to share materials and energy and to reduce byproducts and wastes.

Organizations will need to develop strategic-leadership capabilities to channel their immense human energy into continuously creating, refining, and strengthening their sustainability performance. Leadership capabilities are important at all levels of organizations, but they are particularly critical at the strategic level because top managers provide the most direct route to organizational participation in the sustainability revolution. Establishing these capabilities involves building an ethical system around a core value for sustainability, and it involves creating and shepherding an organizational vision that effectively connects the organization's sustainability-centered values with the societal issues it faces and the stakeholders it serves. Establishing these capabilities also involves providing all organizational stakeholders with the inspiration, intellectual stimulation, individual consideration, sense of purpose, and empowerment to act in the best interests of the organization, the society, and the natural environment.

Note that these capabilities are not separate and distinct. Rather, they are interrelated and coevolutionary with numerous complex, reciprocal, simultaneous interrelationships among them. For example, self-renewing structures are specifically designed to encourage innovation through dialogue, and they cannot function without effective environmental-scanning systems that provide relevant data regarding environmental changes. Also, well-designed product stewardship or BOP strategies are based on accurate information collected via effective environmental-scanning processes and implementing them requires continuous innovation of sustainability-based products and services that spring from disruptive technologies and organizational dialogue processes. In another example, building, improving, and maintaining type III-industrial-ecosystem capabilities requires accurate environmental data regarding the firm's ecological footprint, and it requires developing and implementing innovative eco- and socio-efficiency strategies. Further, none of the first five capabilities—scanning the environment, developing socio- and eco-efficient and effective strategies, creating innovative products, services, and processes, creating adaptive self-renewing structures, and creating type III-industrial-ecosystem technologies, processes, and networks—can be implemented without visionary strategic leaders who encourage self-responsibility and self-control, inspire new ways of thinking and acting, and shepherd their organizations toward super-ordinate goals that will contribute to the protection and perpetuation of the human habitat.

The Road to Sustainable Organizational Management

There is an overarching theme running through all of the capabilities enumerated above: Managers wishing to implement sustainable organizational management in their organizations will need to establish effective change-management strategies, structures, processes, and technologies that allow their organizations to effectively and efficiently adapt to the continuously coevolving sustainability demands of the twenty-first century business environment. We have presented throughout the book numerous changes that organizations can make in order to reduce their ecological and social footprints, build sustainability into their products and services, and contribute to humankind's quest for a high quality of life for all people forever. Many of these changes, such as pollution prevention, are already entrenched in the business environment; organizations without these capabilities are already behind the competitive curve. Others, such as BOP strategies, are not yet entrenched; organizations currently engaged in these are ahead of the curve. Further, many of these changes are surface-level, requiring organizations to do things differently; while numerous others are fundamental-level, requiring organizations to view things differently.

Managers can lead their organizations along either of two roads in their efforts to continuously identify, design, implement, and institutionalize the changes necessary to develop the sustainable organizational management capabilities their firms need to adapt in today's dynamic sustainability-rich environment. The first is the incremental road, and it is likely the most traveled of the two. On this road, managers instill the changes in an orderly linear fashion. Whereas incremental change processes are effective in helping organizations do things differently, they are less effective in helping organizations to view things differently. For that, organizations must take the second and least-traveled road: transformational change. Recall that transformational change is designed to lead organizations to entirely different qualitative states. It requires dialogue-based change processes that allow organizations to reveal and change the underlying core and instrumental values upon which their decisions and actions are rooted. Changing these core value systems constitutes a fundamental shift in how the organization thinks about the world and its role in it.

As we see it, an organization that chooses the incremental road may be capable of implementing the basic practices of sustainable organizational management, but developing such proficiencies will not necessarily lead it to a fundamental transformation to a value system based on a core value of sustainability. Thus, the organization may be quite capable of doing things in more sustainable ways, but they may still lack the capability to view things in more sustainable ways. Without a guiding sustainability-based value system in place, an organization is more likely to eventually lose its way in its search for improved sustainability performance, and this threatens its potential to continuously adapt to the increasing sustainability demands in the environment.

On the other hand, an organization that chooses the transformational road starts its environmental adaptation journey by examining and changing the fundamental values that guide what it does. This provides the organization with the underlying cognitive foundation necessary for thinking in terms of sustainability, and thinking in terms of sustainability makes acting in terms of sustainability a more natural, logical process. When this happens, the organization's road to sustainable organizational management becomes clearer and more navigable, and this increases its chances of successfully adapting to the changing sustainability-rich business environment. Thus, as we have said from the beginning of the book, we believe that the transformational change road—the road least traveled because the changes it brings are so fundamental—is the best route to the long-term adoption and implementation of sustainable organizational management.

Conclusions: Redefining Managerial Success

We believe that sustainable organizational management offers managers a way to make real contributions to improving and perpetuating humankind's habitat on the small planet Earth now and for posterity. It offers a new mental framework that will fundamentally transform the way that managers view the coevolutionary dance of organizational adaptation and selection that ultimately determines their success or failure. This new mental framework allows managers to broaden their views of the benefits and consequences of their organizations' actions to include the greater society and ecosystem in which they are embedded, and it allows them to extend their views of the benefits and consequences of their organizations' actions to include future generations of humans and other species.

This longer, broader view redefines the two most fundamental criteria of successful management: efficiency and effectiveness. From a traditional management perspective, managers are efficient and effective if their organizations are capable of using their resources in economically wise ways to create products and/or services demanded by consumers in the marketplace. However, in sustainable organizational management managerial success is defined not just economically but also socially and ecologically. Thus, in addition to economic efficiency and effectiveness, success of managers in sustainable organizational management is measured by their organizations' social and ecological efficiency and effectiveness. That is, from a sustainable organizational management perspective, managers are efficient and effective only if their organizations are capable of using their economic, social, and natural capital in wise ways to create products and/or services that provide both economic benefits to their firms and social and ecological benefits to the planet and its people.

Bibliography

Ahmed, N.U. 2001. "Incorporating Environmental Concerns into TQM." *Production and Inventory Management Journal,* First quarter, 25–30.

Allenby, Braden R. 1994. "Integrating Environment and Technology: Design for Environment." In *The Greening of Industrial Ecosystems,* ed. B.R. Allenby and D.J. Richards, 137–148. Washington, DC: National Academy Press.

Anonymous. 2002. "Cold Spelt End of Dinosaurs." BBC News World Edition, August 31. Available at http://news.bbc.co.uk/2/hi/science/nature/2225779.stm (accessed September 22, 2008).

Anonymous. 2005a. "Some Facts About Wal-Mart's Energy Conservation Measures." Wal-Mart Facts and News, January 7. Available at http://walmartstores.com/FactsNews/NewsRoom/5015.aspx (accessed September 1, 2008).

Anonymous. December 14, 2005b. "Coal, China, and India: A Deadly Combination for Air Pollution." Worldwatch Institute. Available at http://www.worldwatch.org/node/3862 (accessed March 19, 2008).

Anonymous. 2008a. "Apple and the Environment." Apple.com. Available at http://www.apple.com/environment/ (accessed September 1, 2008).

Anonymous. 2008b. "Design for Environment." HP Eco Solutions. Available at http://www.hp.com/hpinfo/globalcitizenship/environment/productdesign/design.html (accessed September 1, 2008).

Anonymous. 2008c. "Eat Locally, Ease Climate Change Globally." *Washington Post,* March 9, B8.

Anonymous. 2008d. "Sustainability Reporting." Baxter.com, October 18. Available at http://sustainability.baxter.com/sustainability_reporting/ (accessed November 10, 2008).

Ansoff, Igor. 1979. "The Changing Shape of the Strategic Problem." In *Strategic Management,* ed. D. Schendel and C. Hofer, 30–44. Boston, MA: Little Brown and Co.

Argyris, Chris, and Donald A. Schön. 1978. *Organizational Learning: A Theory of Action Perspective.* Reading, MA: Addison-Wesley.

Assadourian, Erik. 2007a. "Acknowledgments." *Vital Signs 2007–2008,* 104–105. New York: W.W. Norton and Company.

———. 2007b. "Sustainable Communities Become More Popular." *Vital Signs 2007–2008,* 9–11. New York: W.W. Norton and Company.

Association of Chartered Certified Accountants. 2001. *An Introduction to Environmental Reporting.* London: The Association of Chartered Certified Accountants.

———. 2008. "Sustainability Focus," September 9. Available at http://www.accaglobal.com/allnews/members/2008/NEWSQ3/Features/3136043 (accessed November 4, 2008).

Ayres, Richard. 1989. "Industrial Metabolism." In *Technology and Environment,* ed. J. Ausubel and H. Sladovich, 23–49. Washington, DC: National Academy Press.

———. 1994. "Industrial Metabolism: Theory and Policy." In *The Greening of Industrial Ecosystems,* ed. B. Allenby and D. Richards, 23–37. Washington, DC: National Academy Press.

Bansal, Pratima, and Kendall Roth. 2000. "Why Companies Go Green: A Model of Ecological Responsiveness." *Academy of Management Journal* 43, no. 4: 717–736.

Barney, Jay. 1991. "Firm Resources and Sustained Competitive Advantage." *Journal of Management* 17: 99–120.

———. 1995. "Looking Inside for Competitive Advantage." *Academy of Management Executive* 9: 49–61.

Bartunek, J., and M. Moch. 1987. "First-Order, Second-Order, and Third-Order Change and Organization Development Interventions: A Cognitive Approach." *Journal of Applied Behavioral Science* 23: 483–500.

Baum, Joel A.C., and Jitendra Singh. 1994. "Organization-Environment Coevolution." In *Evolutionary Dynamics in Organizations,* ed. J. Baum and J. Singh, 379–402. New York: Oxford University Press.

Beaumont, John R., Lene Pedersen, and Brian Whitaker. 1993. *Managing the Environment.* Oxford, UK: Butterworth Heinemann.

Bebbington, Jan, R. Gray, C. Hibbitt, and E. Kirk. 2001. *Full Cost Accounting: An Agenda for Action,* ACCA Research Report 73. London: The Association of Chartered Certified Accountants.

Beckhard, Richard, and Wendy Pritchard. 1992. *Changing the Essence: The Art of Creating and Leading Fundamental Change in Organizations.* San Francisco: Jossey-Bass.

Benn, Suzanne, and E. Jane Probert. 2006. "Incremental Change Towards Sustainability: Integrating Human and Ecological Factors for Efficiency." In *Managing the Business Case for Sustainability,* ed. Stefan Schaltegger and Marcus Wagner, 542–552. Sheffield, UK: Greenleaf Publishing Limited.

Boulding, Kenneth E. 1956. "General Systems Theory: The Skeleton of Science." *Management Science* 2, no. 3:197–208.

———. 1966. "The Economics of the Coming Spaceship Earth." In *Environmental Quality in a Growing Economy,* ed. H. Jarrett, 3–14. Baltimore, MD: Johns Hopkins University Press.

———. 1970. "Fun and Games with the Gross National Product: The Role of Misleading Indicators in Social Policy." In *The Environmental Crisis,* ed. H.W. Helfrich, 157–170. New Haven, CT: Yale University Press.

Boyle, Mary-Ellen, and Janet Boguslaw. 2007. "Business, Poverty and Corporate Citizenship: Naming the Issues and Framing the Solutions." *Journal of Corporate Citizenship* 26: 101–120.

Briggs, Helen. 2003. "Polar Bear 'Extinct Within 100 Years.'" *BBC News,* January 9. Available at http://news.bbc.co.uk/1/hi/sci/tech/26427773.stm (accessed April 16, 2008).

Brown, Lester R. 2008. *Plan B 3.0: Mobilizing to Save Civilization.* New York: W.W. Norton and Company.

Burns, Tom, and G.M. Stalker. 1961. *The Management of Innovation.* London: Tavistock Publications.

Butler, Rhett A. 2007. "Just How Bad Is the Biodiversity Extinction Crisis?" *Mongabay.com,* February 6. Available at http://news.mongabay.com/2007/0206-biodiversity.html (accessed December 30, 2007).

Capoor, Karan, and Philippe Ambrosi. 2006. *State and Trends of the Carbon Market 2006,* May. Washington, DC: World Bank. Available at http://carbonfinance.org/docs/StateoftheCarbonMarket2006.pdf (accessed May 27, 2008).

Capra, Fritjof. 1982. *The Turning Point.* New York: Bantam Books.

Carroll, Archie B. 1995. "Stakeholder Thinking in Three Models of Management Morality: A Perspective with Strategic Implications." In *Understanding Stakeholder Thinking,* ed. J. Nasi, 47–74. Helsinki, Finland: SR-Publications.

———. 2004. "Managing Ethically with Global Stakeholders: A Present and Future Challenge." *Academy of Management Executive* 18, no.2: 114–120.

Central Intelligence Agency. 2008. *The World Factbook.* Available at http://www.cia.gov/library/publications/the-world-factbook/geos/xx.html (accessed June 23, 2008).

Chafe, Zoë. 2007a. "Child Labor Harms Many Young Lives." *Vital Signs 2007–2008,* 112–113. New York: W.W. Norton and Company.

———. 2007b. "Weather-Related Disasters Climb." *Vital Signs 2007–2008,* 44–45. New York: W.W. Norton and Company.

Chambers, N., and K. Lewis. 2001. *Ecological Footprint Analysis: Towards a Sustainability Indicator for Business.* London, UK: The Association of Chartered Certified Accountants.

Chandler, Alfred D. 1962. *Strategy and Structure: Chapters in the History of American Industrial Enterprise.* Cambridge, MA: MIT Press.

Child, John. 1972. "Organization Structure, Environment and Performance. The Role of Strategic Choice." *Sociology* 6, no. 1: 1–22.

Chiras, Daniel. 1991. *Environmental Science: Action for a Sustainable Future.* Redwood City, CA: Benjamin Cummings.

Christmann, C. 2000. "Effects of Best Practices of Environmental Management on Cost Advantage: The Role of Complementary Assets." *Academy of Management Journal* 43, no. 4: 663–680.

Ciambrone, D. 1997. *Environmental Life Cycle Analysis.* Boca Raton, FL: Lewis Publishers.

Clarkson, Max B.E. 1995. "A Stakeholder Framework for Analyzing and Evaluating Corporate Social Performance." *Academy of Management Review* 20, no. 1: 92–117.

Collins, D., and J. Barkdull. 1995. "Capitalism, Environmentalism, and Mediating Structures: From Adam Smith to Stakeholder Panels." *Environmental Ethics* 17: 227–244.

Collins, Jim 2001. *Good to Great: Why Some Companies Make the Leap and Others Don't.* New York: HarperBusiness.

Collins, Jim., and Jerry I. Porras. 1994. *Built to Last: Successful Habits of Visionary Companies.* New York: HarperBusiness.

Cordano, Mark, and Irene Hanson Frieze. 2000. "Pollution Reduction Preferences for U.S. Environmental Managers: Applying Ajzen's Theory of Planned Behavior." *Academy of Management Journal* 43, no. 4: 627–641.

Costanza, Robert. 1989. "What Is Ecological Economics?" *Ecological Economics* 1, no. 1: 1–7.

Costanza, Robert, Herman E. Daly, and Joy A. Bartholomew. 1991. "Goals, Agenda, and Policy Recommendations for Ecological Economics." In *Ecological Economics: The Science and Management of Sustainability*, ed. R. Costanza, 1–20. New York: Columbia University Press.

Covey, Stephen. 1990. *The 7 Habits of Highly Effective People*. New York: Simon and Schuster.

Curkovic, Sime, Robert Sroufe, and Robert Landeros. 2008. "Measuring TQEM Returns from the Application of Quality Frameworks." *Business Strategy and the Environment* 17, no. 2: 93–106.

Cyert, Richard M., and James G. March. 1963. *A Behavioral Theory of the Firm*. Englewood Cliffs, NJ: Prentice-Hall.

Daly, Herman E. 1977. *Steady State Economics*. San Francisco: W.H. Freeman.

———. 1986. "Toward a New Economic Model." *Bulletin of the Atomic Scientists* 42, no. 4: 42–44.

———. 1991. "Elements of Environmental Macroeconomics." In *Ecological Economics: The Science and Management of Sustainability*, ed. R. Costanza, 32–46. New York: Columbia University Press.

———. 1993. "The Perils of Free Trade." *Scientific American* (November): 50–57.

Daly, Herman E., and John B. Cobb, Jr. 1989. *For the Common Good*. Boston, MA: Beacon Press.

Daly, Herman E., and Joshua Farley. 2004. *Ecological Economics: Principles and Applications*. Washington, DC: Island Press.

Davies, James B., Susanna Sandström, Anthony Shorrocks, and Edward N. Wolff. 2008. "The World Distribution of Household Wealth." Discussion Paper No. 2008/03 February presented at the United Nations University, World Institute for Development Economics Research.

Dean, Thomas J., and Jeffrey S. McMullen. 2005. "Toward a Theory of Sustainable Entrepreneurship: Reducing Environmental Degradation Through Entrepreneurial Action." *Journal of Business Venturing* 22, no. 1: 50–76.

Delgado, Alessandra. 2007. "Information Economy Thrives in Cities." *Vital Signs 2007–2008*, 114–115. New York: W.W. Norton and Company.

Dinnick, Wilf. 2008. "Ethiopian Children Dying Daily from Starvation." *CNN.Com/World*, May 20. Available at http://www.cnn.com/2008/WORLD/africa/05/20/ethiopia.children/index.html (accessed May 20, 2008).

Donaldson, Lex. 1995. *American Anti-Management Theories of Organization: A Critique of Paradigm Proliferation*. Cambridge, UK: Cambridge University Press.

———. 2003. "Organization Theory as a Positive Science." In *The Oxford Handbook of Organization Theory*, ed. Haridimos Tsoukas and Christian Knudsen, 39–62. New York: Oxford University Press.

Donaldson, Thomas, and Lee Preston. 1995. "The Stakeholder Theory of the Corporation: Concepts, Evidence, and Implications." *Academy of Management Review* 20, no. 1: 65–91.

Doppelt, Bob. 2003. *Leading Change Toward Sustainability: A Change-Management Guide for Business, Government, and Civil Society*. Sheffield, UK: Greenleaf Publishing Limited.

Drazin, Robert, and Andrew H. Van de Ven. 1985. "Alternative Forms of Fit in Contingency Theory." *Administrative Science Quarterly* 30: 514–539.

Drucker, Peter F. 1980. "Toward the Next Economics." Special issue, The Crisis in Economic Theory. *The Public Interest* (Spring): 4–18.

———. 1989. *The New Realities.* New York: Harper and Row.

Dunphy, Dexter, Andrew Griffiths, and Suzanne Benn. 2007. *Organizational Change for Corporate Sustainability,* 2nd ed. London: Routledge.

Dyllick, Thomas, and Kai Hockerts. 2002. "Beyond the Business Case for Corporate Sustainability." *Business Strategy and the Environment* 11, no. 2: 130–141.

Edwards, Anders R. 2005. *The Sustainability Revolution: Portrait of a Paradigm Shift.* Gabriola Island, BC: New Society Publishers.

Egri, Carolyn P., and Susan Herman. 2000. "Leadership in the North American Environmental Sector: Values, Leadership Styles, and Contexts of Environmental Leaders and Their Organizations." *Academy of Management Journal* 43, no. 4: 571–604.

Ehrenfeld, John R. 2008. *Sustainability by Design: A Subversive Strategy for Transforming Our Consumer Culture.* New Haven, CT: Yale University Press.

Ehrlich, Paul R. 1991. "Coevolution and Its Applicability to the Gaia Hypothesis." In *Scientists on Gaia,* ed. Stephen H. Schneider and Penelope J. Boston, 19–22. Cambridge MA: The MIT Press.

Ehrlich, Paul R., and Ann H. Ehrlich. 1990. *The Population Explosion.* New York: Simon and Schuster.

Ehrlich, Paul R., and Peter H. Raven. 1964. "Butterflies and Plants: A Study in Coevolution." *Evolution* 18: 586–608.

Elkington, John. 1997. *Cannibals with Forks.* Oxford, UK: Capstone Publishing Limited.

———. 2008. "The Triple Bottom Line: Sustainability's Accountants." In *Environmental Management: Readings and Cases,* 2nd ed., ed. Michael V. Russo, 49–66. Los Angeles, CA: Sage.

Elkins, Paul., M. Hillman, and R. Hutchinson. 1992. *Wealth Beyond Measure.* London: Gaia Press.

Emery, Fred E., and Eric L. Trist. 1965. "The Causal Texture of Organizational Environments." *Human Relations* 18: 21–32.

———. 1973. *Towards a Social Ecology: Contextual Appreciations of the Future in the Present.* New York: Plenum Publishing Co.

Epstein, Keith, and Geri Smith. 2007. "The Ugly Side of Micro-Lending." *Business Week,* December 24, 39–44.

Esty, Daniel C., and Andrew S. Winston. 2008. *Green to Gold: How Smart Companies Use Environmental Strategy to Innovate, Create Value, and Build Competitive Advantage.* New Haven, CT: Yale University Press.

Etzioni, Amitai. 1988. *The Moral Dimension: Toward a New Economics.* New York: The Free Press.

Figge, Frank, and Tobias Hahn. 2004. "Sustainable Value Added—Measuring Corporate Contributions to Sustainability Beyond Eco-Efficiency." *Ecological Economics* 48, no. 2: 173–187.

———. 2005. "The Cost of Sustainability Capital and the Creation of Sustainable Value by Companies." *Journal of Industrial Ecology* 9, no. 4: 47–58.

———. 2006. "Sustainable Value Added: A New Approach to Measuring Corporate Sustainable Performance." In *Managing the Business Case for Sustainability,* ed. Stefan Schaltegger and Marcus Wagner, 146–164. Sheffield, UK: Greenleaf Publishing Limited.

Fiksel, Joseph. 2001. "Emergence of a Sustainable Business Community." *Pure and Applied Chemistry* 73, no. 8: 1265–1268.

Finkelstein, Sydney, and Donald C. Hambrick. 1996. *Strategic Leadership: Top Executives and Their Effects on Organizations*. St. Paul, MN: West Publishing Company.

Flier, Bert, Frans A.J. Van Den Bosch, and Henk W. Volberda. 2003. "Co-evolution in Strategic Renewal Behaviour of British, Dutch and French Financial Incumbents: Institutional Effects and Managerial Intentionality." *Journal of Management Studies* 40, no. 8: 2163–2187.

Fort, Timothy L. 2007. "Introduction." *Journal of Corporate Citizenship* 26: 20–24.

Fox, Kellie, Beth Littlehales, and Ryan Kennan. 2008. "A Primer on the Global Reporting Initiative." In *Environmental Management: Readings and Cases,* 2nd ed., ed. Michael V. Russo, 243–261. Los Angeles, CA: Sage.

Frederick, William. 1995. *Values, Nature, and Culture in the American Corporation*. New York: Oxford University Press.

Freeman, R. Edward. 1984. *Strategic Management: A Stakeholder Approach*. Boston MA: Pitman/Ballinger.

Freeman, R. Edward, and Daniel R. Gilbert, Jr. 1988. *Corporate Strategy and the Search for Ethics*. Englewood Cliffs, NJ: Prentice-Hall.

Freeman, R. Edward, and Jean Liedtka. 1997. "Stakeholder Capitalism and the Value Chain," *European Management Journal* 15, no 3: 289–299.

Freeman, R. Edward, Jessica Pierce, and Richard H. Dodd. 2000. *Environmentalism and the New Logic of Business*. Oxford, UK: Oxford University Press.

Friedman, Thomas L. 1999. *The Lexus and the Olive Tree*. New York: Anchor.

———. 2004. *The World Is Flat: A Brief History of the Twenty-First Century*. New York: Farrar, Straus and Giroux.

Fuller, Donald A. 1999. *Sustainable Marketing*. Thousand Oaks, CA: Sage Publications.

Georgescu-Roegen, Nicholas. 1971. *The Entropy Law and the Economic Process*. Cambridge, MA: Harvard University Press.

Gladwin, Tom, James Kennelly, and T-S Krause. 1995. "Shifting Paradigms for Sustainable Development: Implications for Management Theory and Research." *Academy of Management Review* 20, no. 4: 874–907.

Goleman, Daniel. 1996. *Emotional Intelligence*. New York: Bantam Books.

Greeno, J.L. 1994. "Corporate Environmental Excellence and Stewardship." In *Environmental Strategies Handbook,* ed. Rao V. Kolluru, 43–64. New York: McGraw-Hill, 1994.

Gregory, Robin. 2000. "Using Stakeholder Values to Make Smarter Environmental Decisions." *Environment* 42, no. 5: 34–44.

Guillén, Mauro F., and Sandra L. Suárez. 2005. "Explaining the Global Digital Divide: Economic, Political and Sociological Drivers of Cross-National Internet Use." *Social Forces* 84, no. 2: 681–708.

Halal, William. 1986. *The New Capitalism*. New York: John Wiley and Sons.

Halweil, Brian. 2007a. "Grain Production Falls and Prices Surge." *Vital Signs 2007–2008,* 20–21. New York: W.W. Norton and Company.

Halweil, Brian. 2007b. "Ocean Pollution Worsens and Spreads." *Vital Signs 2007–2008,* 100–101. New York: W.W. Norton and Company.

Hamschmidt, Jost, and Thomas Dyllick. 2006. "ISO 14001: Profitable? Yes! But Is It Eco-Effective?" In *Managing the Business Case for Sustainability,* ed. Stefan Schaltegger and Marcus Wagner, 554–568. Sheffield, UK: Greenleaf Publishing Limited.

Hanas, Jim. 2007. "A World Gone Green." *AdvertisingAge,* June 8. Available at http://adage.com/ecomarketing/article?article_id=117113&search_phrase=A%20 World%20gone%20Green (accessed November 21, 2008).

Handy, Charles. 1989. *The Age of Unreason.* Boston, MA: Harvard Business School Press.

Hannan, Michael T., and John H. Freeman. 1977. "The Population Ecology of Organizations." *American Journal of Sociology* 82, no. 5: 929–964.

———. 1984. "Structural Inertia and Organizational Change." *American Sociological Review* 49: 149–164.

Hardin, Garrett. 1974. "Lifeboat Ethics: The Case Against Helping the Poor." *Psychology Today,* September. Available at http://www.garretthardinsociety. org/articles/art_lifeboat_ethics_case_against_helping_poor.html (accessed June 6 2008).

Hart, Stuart L. 1995. "A Natural Resource-Based View of the Firm." *Academy of Management Review* 20, no. 4: 986–1014.

———. 1997. "Beyond Greening: Strategies for a Sustainable World." *Harvard Business Review* 75, no. 1: 67–76.

———. 2005. *Capitalism at the Crossroads: The Unlimited Business Opportunities in Solving the World's Most Difficult Problems.* Upper Saddle River, NJ: Wharton School Publishing.

———. 2008. "Foreword." In *Sustainability Challenges and Solutions at the Base of the Pyramid: Business, Technology, and the Poor,* ed. Prabhu Kandachar and Minna Halme, ix–xi. Sheffield, UK: Greenleaf Publishing Limited.

Hart, Stuart L., and Clayton M. Christensen. 2002. "The Great Leap: Driving Innovation from the Base of the Pyramid." *MIT Sloan Management Review* 44, no. 1: 51–56.

Hart, Stuart L., and Mark Milstein. 1999. "Global Sustainability and the Creative Destruction of Industries." *Sloan Management Review* (Fall): 23–33.

Hart, Stuart L., and Sanjay Sharma. 2004. "Engaging Fringe Stakeholders for Competitive Imagination." *Academy of Management Executive* 18, no. 1: 17–18.

Hawken, Paul. 2007. *Blessed Unrest.* New York: Viking.

Hawken, Paul, Amory Lovins, and L. Hunter Lovins. 1999. "A Road Map for Natural Capitalism." *Harvard Business Review* 77, no. 3: 145–157.

Herro, Alana. 2007. "Literacy Improves Worldwide." *Vital Signs 2007–2008,* 110–111. New York: W.W. Norton and Company.

Hockerts, Kai. 1999. "SustainAbility Radar." *Greener Management International* 25: 25–35.

Hoffman, Andrew J. 1999. "Institutional Evolution and Change: Environmentalism and the U.S. Chemical Industry." *Academy of Management Journal* 42, no. 4: 351–371.

Hoffman, Andrew J., and John G. Woody. 2008. *Climate Change: What's Your Business Strategy?* Boston: Harvard Business Press.

Holliday, Charles O., Jr., Stephan Schmidheiny, and Philip Watts. 2002. *Walking the Talk: The Business Case for Sustainable Development.* Sheffield, UK: Greenleaf Publishing Limited.

Hosmer, L.T. 1994. "Strategic Planning as if Ethics Mattered." *Strategic Management Journal* 15: 17–34.

Isenmann, Ralf, and Christopher Bey. 2007. "Environmental Reporting on the Internet: From a Technical Tool to a Strategic Necessity." *Strategic Sustainability,* ed. Robert Sroufe and Joseph Sarkis,123–143. Sheffield, UK: Greenleaf Publishing Limited.

Jones, Thomas M. 1995. "Instrumental Stakeholder Theory: A Synthesis of Ethics and Economics." *Academy of Management Review* 20, no. 2: 404–437.

Jordan, Lindsay Hower. 2007. *Vital Signs 2007–2008,* 120–121. New York: W.W. Norton and Company.

King, Andrew A. 1994. "Improved Manufacturing Resulting from Learning-from-Waste: Causes, Importance and Enabling Conditions." Paper presented at the Academy of Management Annual Meeting, Dallas, Texas, August.

King, Andrew A. and Michael W. Toffel. forthcoming. "Self-Regulatory Institutions for Solving Environmental Problems: Perspectives and Contributions from the Management Literature." In *Governance for the Environment:New Perspectives,* eds. Magali A. Delmas and Oran R. Young. Cambridge, UK: Cambridge University Press.

Kirchgeorg, Manfred, and Monika Winn. 2006. "Sustainability Marketing for the Poorest of the Poor." *Business Strategy and the Environment* 15, no. 3: 171–184.

Kiuchi, Tachi, and Bill Shireman. 2002. *What We Learned in the Rainforest: Business Lessons from Nature.* San Francisco: Berrett-Koehler Publishers.

Koehler, Dinah A. 2001. "Developments in Health and Safety Accounting at Baxter International." *Eco-Management and Auditing* 8: 229–239.

Lampel, Joseph, and Jamal Shamsie. 2003. "Capabilities in Motion: New Organizational Forms and the Reshaping of the Hollywood Movie Industry." *Journal of Management Studies* 40, no. 8: 2190–2210.

Laszlo, Chris. 2008. *Sustainable Value: How the World's Leading Companies Are Doing Well by Doing Good.* Sheffield, UK: Greenleaf Publishing Limited.

Lawrence, Paul R., and Jay W. Lorsch. 1967. *Organization and Environment: Managing Integration and Differentiation.* Boston: Harvard Business School Press.

Lee, Kai N. with Lisa Mastny. 2007. "World Is Soon Half Urban." *Vital Signs 2007–2008,* 52–53. New York: W.W. Norton and Company.

Lewin, Arie Y., Chris P. Long, and Timothy N. Carroll. 1999. "Coevolution of New Organizational Forms." *Organization Science* 10, no. 5: 535–553.

Lewin, Arie Y., and Henk W. Volberda. 1999. "Prolegomena on Coevolution: A Framework for Research on Strategy and New Organizational Forms." *Organization Science* 10, no. 5: 519–534.

———. 2003a. "Beyond Adaptation and Selection Research: Organizing Self-Renewal in Co-evolving Environments." *Journal of Management Studies* 40, no. 8: 2109–2110.

———. 2003b. "The Future of Organization Studies: Beyond the Selection-Adaptation Debate." In *The Oxford Handbook of Organization Theory,* ed. Haridimos Tsoukas and Christian Knudsen, 568–595. New York: Oxford University Press.

Lewin, Kurt. 1946. "Action Research and Minority Problems." *Journal of Social Issues* 2, no. 4: 34–46.

————. 1947. "Group Decision and Social Change." In *Readings in Social Psychology*, ed. Theodore M. Newcomb and Eugene L. Hartley, 330–344. New York: Henry Holt and Company.

Lovelock, James. 1979. *Gaia: A New Look at Life on Earth.* London: Oxford University Press.

————. 1988. *The Ages of Gaia.* New York: Bantam Books.

Mahon, John, and Richard A. McGowan, 1998. "Modeling Industry Political Dynamics." *Business and Society* 37, no. 4: 390–413.

March, James G. 1991. "Exploration and Exploitation in Organizational Learning." *Organization Science* 2, no. 1: 71–87.

Marcus, Alfred. 2009. *Strategic Foresight: A New Look at Scenarios.* New York: Macmillan.

Marcus, Alfred and Sheryl Kaiser. 2006. *Managing Beyond Compliance: The Legal and Ethical Dimensions of Corporate Social Responsibility.* San Francisco: North Coast Publishing.

Margulis, L., and G. Hinkle. 1991. "The Biota and Gaia: 150 Years of Support for Environmental Sciences." In *Scientists on Gaia*, ed. Stephen H. Schneider and Penelope J. Boston, 11–18. Cambridge MA: The MIT Press.

Maslow, Abraham. 1962. *Toward a Psychology of Being.* Princeton, NJ: Van Nostrand Reinhold.

McDonough, William, and Michael Braungart. 2002. *Cradle to Cradle: Remaking the Way We Make Things.* New York: North Point Press.

McElhaney, Kellie A., Michael W. Toffel, and Natalie Hill. 2007. "Designing a Sustainability Management System at BMW Group." In *Strategic Sustainability,* ed. Robert Sroufe and Joseph Sarkis, 76–90. Sheffield, UK: Greenleaf Publishing Limited.

McKibben, Bill. 2007. *Deep Economy: The Wealth of Communities and the Durable Future.* New York: Times Books.

McKinley, William, and Mark A. Mone. 2003. "Micro and Macro Perspectives in Organization Theory: A Tale of Incommensurability." In *The Oxford Handbook of Organization Theory,* ed. Haridimos Tsoukas and Christian Knudsen, 345–372. New York: Oxford University Press.

Mellgren, Doug. Associated Press. 2008. "Norway Marks Seed Vault Opening." *National Geographic News,* February 26. Available at http://news.nationalgeographic.com/news/2008/02/080226-AP-norway-doom.html (accessed May 26, 2008).

Milanovic, B. 2002. "True World Income Distribution, 1988 and 1993: First Calculation Based on Household Surveys Alone." *The Economic Journal* 112, no. 476: 51–92.

Miles, Raymond E., and Charles C. Snow. 1978. *Organizational Strategy, Structure, and Process.* New York: McGraw-Hill.

Mintzberg, Henry. 1979. *The Structuring of Organizations.* Englewood Cliffs, NJ: Prentice-Hall.

Mitchell, Stacy. 2006. *Big-Box Swindle: The True Cost of Mega-Retailers and the Fight for America's Independent Businesses.* Boston, MA: Beacon Press.

Moore, James F. 1996. *The Death of Competition: Leadership and Strategy in the Age of Business Ecosystems.* New York: Harper Business.

Nahavandi, Afsaneh. 2009. *The Art and Science of Leadership,* 5th ed. Upper Saddle River, NJ: Pearson-Prentice Hall.

Nash, J., K. Nutt, J. Maxwell, and J. Ehrenfeld. 1994. "Polaroid's Environmental Accounting and Reporting System: Benefits and Limitations of a TQEM Measurement Tool." In *Environmental TQM,* ed. J. Willig, 217–234. New York: McGraw-Hill.

Nattrass, Brian, and Mary Altomare. 2002. *The Natural Step for Business: Wealth, Ecology and the Evolutionary Corporation.* Gabriola Island, BC: New Society Publishers.

Nelson, Jane. 2007. "New Networks for a Changing Corporation." Notes on an All Academy Symposium entitled "Corporations and the 21st Century: How Do Today's Corporations Need to Change to Meet Tomorrow's Needs," 13–15. Presented at the Academy of Management Annual Meeting, Philadelphia, Pennsylvania, August.

Nierenberg, Danielle. 2007. "Farm Animal Diversity: Forgotten in Interlaken?" Worldwatch Institute, September 11. Available at http://www.worldwatch.org/node/5343 (accessed March 19, 2008).

North, K. 1997. *Environmental Business Management.* Geneva, Switzerland: International Labour Office.

O'Dea, Katherine, and Katherine Pratt. 2006. "Achieving Environmental Excellence Through TQEM Strategic Alliances." *Environmental Quality Management* 4, no. 3: 93–108.

Odum, Howard T. 1983. *Systems Ecology: An Introduction.* New York: John Wiley and Sons.

Oktem, Ulku, Phil Lewis, Deborah Donovan, James R. Hagan, and Thomas Pace. 2007. "EMS and Sustainable Development: A Model and Comparative Studies of Integration." In *Strategic Sustainability,* ed. Robert Sroufe and Joseph Sarkis, 56–75. Sheffield, UK: Greenleaf Publishing Limited.

Ottman, Jacquelyn A. 1998. *Green Marketing: Opportunity for Innovation.* New York: NTC-McGraw-Hill.

———. 2008. "Sustainable Branding in the 21st Century." Keynote Address to Sustainable Brands '08 Conference, Monterey, California, June 3. Available at http://www.greenmarketing.com/index.php/articles/complete/jacquelyn-ottmans-keynote-at-sustainable-brands-08/ (accessed November 10, 2008).

Parker, Marjorie. 1990. *Creating Shared Vision: The Story of a Pioneering Approach to Organizational Revitalization.* Clarendon Hills, IL: Dialog International, Ltd.

Peters, Thomas J., and Robert H. Waterman Jr. 1982. *In Search of Excellence: Lessons from America's Best-Run Companies.* New York: Harper and Row.

Pfeffer, Jeffrey. 1993. "Barriers to the Advance of Organizational Science: Paradigm Development as a Dependent Variable." *Academy of Management Review* 18, no. 4: 599–620.

Pinkse, Jonatan and Ans Kolk. 2008. *International Business and Global Climate Change.* London: Routledge.

Porter, Michael E. 1980. *Competitive Strategy: Techniques for Analyzing Industries and Competitors.* New York: The Free Press.

———. 1985. *Competitive Advantage: Creating and Sustaining Superior Performance.* New York: The Free Press.

———. 1990. *The Competitive Advantage of Nations.* New York: The Free Press.

———. 1995. "The Competitive Advantage of the Inner City." *Harvard Business Review* 73, no. 3: 55–71.

————. 1998. "Clusters and the New Economics of Competition." *Harvard Business Review* 76, no. 6: 77–90.

Porter, Terry B. 2006. "Coevolution as a Research Framework for Organizations and the Natural Environment." *Organization and Environment* 19, no. 4: 1–26.

Portes, Alejandro. 1998. "Social Capital: Its Origins and Applications in Modern Sociology," *Annual Review of Sociology* 24: 1–24.

Post, James E. 1991. "Managing as if the Earth Mattered." *Business Horizons* (July/August): 32–38.

————. 2007. "Corporations and 21st Century Needs." Notes on an All Academy Symposium entitled "Corporations and the 21st Century: How Do Today's Corporations Need to Change to Meet Tomorrow's Needs," 16–20. Presented at the Academy of Management Annual Meeting, Philadelphia, Pennsylvania, August.

Post, James E., and Barbara Altman. 1992. "Models for Corporate Greening: How Corporate Social Policy and Organizational Learning Inform Leading-Edge Environmental Management." In *Research in Corporate Social Policy and Performance,* ed. James Post, 3–29. Greenwich, CT: JAI Press.

————. 1994. "Managing the Environmental Change Process: Barriers and Opportunities," *Journal of Organizational Change Management* 7, no. 4: 64–81.

Prahalad, C.K. 2006. *The Fortune at the Bottom of the Pyramid: Eradicating Poverty Through Profits.* Upper Saddle River, NJ: Wharton School Publishing.

Prahalad, C.K., and Stuart L. Hart. 2002. "The Fortune at the Bottom of the Pyramid." *Strategy+Business,* 26. Available at http://www.cs.berkeley.edu/~brewer/ict4b/Fortune-BoP.pdf (accessed November 5, 2008).

Pruzan, Peter, and Kirsten Pruzan Mikkelsen. 2007. *Leading with Wisdom: Spiritual-based Leadership in Business.* Sheffield, UK: Greenleaf Publishing Limited.

Putnam, Robert D. 2000. *Bowling Alone: The Collapse and Revival of American Community.* New York: Simon and Schuster.

Quah, Danny. 1997. "Empirical Growth and Distribution: Stratification, Polarization and Convergence Clubs." London School of Economics, Center for Economic Performance, Discussion Paper 324, 1–29.

Randazzo, Ryan. 2008. "Solar Power Systems Arrive in More Stores." *USA Today,* January 5. Available at http://www.usatoday.com/money/industries/energy/2008–01–05-solarpower_N.htm (accessed September 2, 2008).

Reinhardt, Forest L. 1999. "Bringing the Environment Down to Earth." *Harvard Business Review* 77, no. 4: 149–157.

————. 2008. "Environmental Product Differentiation: Implications for Corporate Strategy." In *Environmental Management: Readings and Cases,* 2nd ed., ed. Michael V. Russo, 205–227. Los Angeles, CA: Sage.

Renner, Michael. 2007. "Number of Violent Conflicts Steady." *Vital Signs 2007–2008,* 76–77. New York: W.W. Norton and Company.

Richard, Orlando C. 2000. "Racial Diversity, Business Strategy, and Firm Performance: A Resource-Based View." *Academy of Management Journal* 43, no. 2: 164–177.

Richards, Deanna J., Braden R. Allenby, and Robert Frosch. 1994. "The Greening of Industrial Ecosystems: Overview and Perspective," In *The Greening of Industrial Ecosystems,* ed. B. Allenby and D. Richards, 1–19. Washington, DC: National Academy Press.

Robinson, G., and K. Dechant. 1997. "Building a Business Case for Diversity." *Academy of Management Executive* 11, no. 3: 21–31.

Rodrigues, Suzana, and John Child. 2003. "Coevolution in an Institutionalized Environment." *Journal of Management Studies* 40, no. 8: 2137–2162.

Rosinski, Niki. 2006. "Benchmarking Competitiveness and Management Quality with the Dow Jones Sustainability Index: The Case of the Automotive Industry and Climate Change." In *Managing the Business Case for Sustainability,* ed. Stefan Schaltegger and Marcus Wagner, 242–254. Sheffield, UK: Greenleaf Publishing Limited.

Roudi-Fahimi, Farzaneh, Liz Creel, and Roger-Mark De Souza. 2002. "Finding the Balance: Population and Water Scarcity in the Middle East and North Africa." *Population Reference Bureau,* July. Available at http://www.prb.org/pdf/FindingTheBalance_Eng.pdf (accessed April 16, 2008).

Russo, Michael V., and Paul A. Fouts. 1997. "A Resource-Based Perspective on Corporate Environmental Performance and Profitability." *Academy of Management Journal* 40, no. 3: 534–559.

Sachs, Jeffrey. 2008. *Common Wealth: Economics for a Crowded Planet.* New York: The Penguin Press.

Sale, Kirkpatrick. 1985. *Dwellers in the Land.* San Francisco: Sierra Club Books.

Sánchez, Pablo, Joan Enric Ricart, and Miguel Angel Rodríguez. 2005. "Influential Factors in Becoming Socially Embedded in Low-Income Markets." *Greener Management International* 51: 19–38.

Schein, Edgar. 1985. *Organizational Culture and Leadership.* San Francisco: Jossey-Bass.

Schmidt, J. 1999. "Corporate Excellence in the New Millennium." *Journal of Business Strategy* (November/December): 39–43.

Schumacher, E.F. 1973. *Small Is Beautiful: Economics as if People Mattered.* New York: Harper and Row.

———. 1977. *A Guide for the Perplexed.* New York: Harper and Row.

———. 1979. *Good Work.* New York: Harper and Row.

Schumpeter, Joseph A. 1950. *Capitalism, Socialism, and Democracy.* New York: Harper and Brothers.

Schwenk, Charles R. 1988. *The Essence of Strategic Decision Making.* Lexington, MA: Lexington Books.

Scott, W.R. 1991. "Unpacking Institutional Arguments." In The *New Institutionalism in Organizational Analysis,* ed. W. Powell and P. DiMaggio, 164–182. Chicago: University of Chicago Press.

Senge, Peter M. 1990. *The Fifth Discipline: The Art and Practice of the Learning Organization.* New York: Doubleday/Currency.

———. 2007. "Waking the Sleeping Giant: Business as an Agent for Consumer Understanding and Responsible Choice." *Journal of Corporate Citizenship* 26: 25–27.

Senge, Peter, M., Bryan Smith, Nina Kruschwitz, Joe Laur, and Sara Schley. 2008. *The Necessary Revolution: How Individuals and Organizations Are Working Together to Create a Sustainable World.* New York: Doubleday.

Sharma, Sanjay. 2000. "Managerial Interpretations and Organizational Context as Predictors of Corporate Choice of Strategy." *Academy of Management Journal* 43, no. 4: 681–697.

Sharma, Sanjay, and Harrie Vredenburg. 1998. "Proactive Corporate Environmental Strategy and the Development of Competitively Valuable Organizational Capabilities." *Strategic Management Journal* 19: 729–753.

Sherman, W., D. Steingard, and D. Fitzgibbons. 2002. "Sustainable Stakeholder Accounting: Beyond Complementarity and Towards Integration in Environmental Accounting." In *Research in Corporate Sustainability: The Evolving Theory and Practice of Organizations in the Natural Environment,* ed. Sanjay Sharma and Mark Starik, 257–294. Northampton, MA: Edgar Elgar Publications.

Shuman, Michael H. 1998. *Going Local: Creating Self-Reliant Communities in a Global Age.* New York: The Free Press.

———. 2006. *The Small-Mart Revolution: How Local Businesses Are Beating the Competition.* New York: The Free Press.

Shrivastava, Paul. 1995. "Ecocentric Management in Industrial Ecosystems: Management Paradigm for a Risk Society." *Academy of Management Review* 20, no. 1: 118–137.

———. 1996. *Greening Business: Profiting the Corporation and the Environment.* Cincinnati, OH: Thompson Executive Press.

Smith, Mark K. 2000. "Social Capital." *The Encyclopedia of Informal Education.* Available at http://www.infed.org/biblio/social_capital.htm (accessed August 28, 2008).

Speth, James Gustave. 2008. *The Bridge at the Edge of the World.* New Haven, CT: Yale University Press.

Spirig, Kuno. 2006. "Social Performance and Competitiveness: A Socio-Competitive Framework." In *Managing the Business Case for Sustainability,* ed. Stefan Schaltegger and Marcus Wagner, 82–106. Sheffield, UK: Greenleaf Publishing Limited.

Stanwick, Peter A., and Sarah D. Stanwick. 2005. "The Relationship Between Environmental Sustainability, Environmental Violations and Financial Performance: An Empirical Study." In *New Horizons in Research on Sustainable Organizations,* ed. Mark Starik and Sanjay Sharma with Carolyn Egri and Rick Bunch, 79–98. Sheffield, UK: Greenleaf Publishing Limited.

Starik, Mark. 1995. "Should Trees Have Managerial Standing? Toward Stakeholder Status for Non-Human Nature." *Journal of Business Ethics* 14: 207–217.

Starik, Mark, and Gordon Rands. 1995. "Weaving an Integrated Web: Multilevel and Multisystem Perspectives of Ecologically Sustainable Organizations." *Academy of Management Review* 20, no. 4: 908–935.

Starmer, E., and M.D. Anderson. 2007. "Agribusinesses Consolidate Power." *Vital Signs 2007–2008,* 86–87. New York: W.W. Norton and Company.

Stead, Jean Garner, and W. Edward Stead. 2000. "Eco-Enterprise Strategy: Standing for Sustainability." *Journal of Business Ethics* 24, no. 4: 313–329.

———. 2008. "Sustainable Strategic Management: An Evolutionary Perspective." *International Journal of Sustainable Strategic Management* 1, no. 1: 62–81.

Stead, W. Edward, and Jean Garner Stead. 1994. "Can Humankind Change the Economic Myth? Paradigm Shifts Necessary for Ecologically Sustainable Business." *Journal of Organizational Change Management* 7, no. 4: 15–31.

———. 1995. "An Empirical Investigation of Sustainability Strategy Implementation in Industrial Organizations." In *Research in Corporate Performance and Policy, Supplement 1,* ed. J. Post, vol. eds. D. Collins and M. Starik, 43–66. Greenwich, CT: JAI.

———. 2004. *Sustainable Strategic Management.* Armonk, NY: M.E. Sharpe.

Stead, W. Edward, Jean Garner Stead, and Don Shemwell. 2003. "Community Sustainability in the Southern Appalachian Region of the USA: The Case of

Johnson County, Tennessee." In *Research in Corporate Sustainability,* ed. Sanjay Sharma and Mark Starik, 61–84. Northampton, MA: Edward Elgar Publishers.

Stern, Nicholas. 2006. *The Stern Review on the Economics of Climate Change.* London: HM Treasury.

Svoboda, Susan. 2008. "Notes on Life Cycle Analysis." In *Environmental Management: Readings and Cases,* 2nd ed., ed. Michael V. Russo, 385–394. Los Angeles, CA: Sage.

Swartz, Peter. 1991. *The Art of the Long View: Planning for the Future in an Uncertain World.* New York: Doubleday.

Thompson, Dixon. 2002. *Tools for Environmental Management.* Gabriola Island, BC: New Society Publishers.

Todd, Rebecca. 1994. "Zero-Loss Accounting Systems." In *The Greening of Industrial Ecosystems,* ed. B. Allenby and D. Richards, 191–200. Washington, DC: National Academy Press.

Tolle, Eckhart. 2005. *A New Earth: Awakening to Your Life's Purpose.* New York: Plume.

United Nations Development Programme. 2007. *Human Development Report 2007/2008.* New York: Palgrave Macmillan.

United Nations Environment Programme. 2007. *Global Environment Outlook.* Valletta, Malta.

U.S. Census Bureau. 2007. *International Data Base.* Available at http://www.census.gov/ipc/www/idb/worldpopinfo.htm (accessed May 26, 2008).

U.S. Department of Energy. 2007. *International Energy Outlook.* DOE/EIA-0484, May.

Volberda, Henk W., and Arie Y. Lewin. 2003. "Coevolutionary Dynamics Within and Between Firms: From Evolution to Coevolution." *Journal of Management Studies* 40, no. 8: 2111–2136.

Wack, P. 1985a. "Scenarios: Uncharted Waters." *Harvard Business Review* 63, no. 5: 73–89.

———. 1985b. "Scenarios: Shooting the Rapids." *Harvard Business Review* 63, no. 6: 139–150.

Waddell, Steve. 2007. "Realising Global Change: Developing the Tools; Building the Infrastructure." *Journal of Corporate Citizenship* 26: 69–84.

Waddock, Sandra. 2000. "The Multiple Bottom Lines of Corporate Citizenship: Social Investing, Reputation, and Responsibility Auditing." *Business and Society Review* 105, no. 3: 323–345.

———. 2007. "On Ceres, the GRI and Corporation 20/20: An Interview with Allen White." *Journal of Corporate Citizenship* 26: 38–42.

———. 2008. "Corporate Citizenship: The Dark-side Paradoxes of Success." In *Leadership and Business Ethics,* ed. Gabriel Flynn, 251–268. New York: Springer Science+Business Media.

Wagner, Marcus, and Stefan Schaltegger. 2006. "Mapping the Links of Corporate Sustainability: Sustainability Balanced Scorecards as a Tool for Sustainability Performance Measurement and Management." In *Managing the Business Case for Sustainability,* ed. Stefan Schaltegger and Marcus Wagner, 108–126. Sheffield, UK: Greenleaf Publishing Limited.

Weick, Karl E., and Robert E. Quinn. 1999. "Organizational Change and Development." *Annual Review of Psychology* 50: 361–386.

Willard, Bob. 2002. *The Sustainability Advantage: Seven Business Case Benefits of a Triple Bottom Line.* Gabriola Island, BC: New Society Publishers.

Wilson, Edward O. 1992. *The Diversity of Life.* New York: W.W. Norton.

Winerip, Michael. 2007. "In Gaps at School, Weighing Family Life." *New York Times,* December 9. Available at http://www.nytimes.com/2007/12/09/nyregion/ nyregionspecia12/09Rparenting.html?_r=1&oref=slogin (accessed June 23, 2008).

Winn, Monika L. and Linda C. Angell. 2000. "Toward a Process Model of Corporate Greening." *Organization Studies* 21, no. 6: 1119–1147.

Woodward, Joan. 1965. *Industrial Organization: Theory and Practice.* Oxford, UK: Oxford University Press.

World Bank. 1998. "What Is Social Capital." Social Capital Initiative Working Paper No. 1, April. Available at http://web.worldbank.org/WBSITE/EXTERNAL/ TOPICS/EXTSOCIALDEVELOPMENT/EXTTSOCIALCAPITAL/content MDK:20185164~menuPK:418217~pagePK:148956~piPK:216618~theSiteP K:401015,00.html (accessed August 28, 2008).

World Commission on Environment and Development. 1987. *Our Common Future.* Oxford, UK: Oxford University Press.

Wren, Daniel A. 1994. *The Evolution of Management Thought,* 4th ed. New York: John Wiley and Sons.

Yunus, Muhammad. 1999. *Banker to the Poor: Micro-Lending and the Battle Against World Poverty.* New York: PublicAffairs.

Zakaria, Fareed. 2008. *The Post-American World.* New York: W.W. Norton and Company.

Zohar, Danah, and Ian Marshall. 1999. *Spiritual Intelligence: The Ultimate Intelligence.* New York: Bloomsbury Publishing.

Index

207

About the Authors

Jean Garner Stead is a professor of management at East Tennessee State University. She earned her BS and MA in economics from Auburn University, her MBA from Western Illinois University, and her PhD in business administration from Louisiana State University in Baton Rouge. Prior to her appointment at ETSU in 1982, she served on the economics faculty of Western Illinois University. Jean has written extensively for more than a quarter of a century on business ethics, organizations and the natural environment, and social issues in management. Her works have been cited hundreds of times, and the first edition of her book, *Management for a Small Planet* (with W. Edward Stead), received a 1992 *Choice* Outstanding Academic Book award. In addition to her research, Jean was a founding member of the Organizations and the Natural Environment (ONE) Division of the Academy of Management, and she has held positions in both ONE and the Social Issues in Management (SIM) Division of the Academy of Management. In 1995, she received East Tennessee State University's Faculty Award for Outstanding Teaching. Jean has served as a strategic management consultant to numerous business organizations and community groups throughout her long career, most recently with the Powell Companies of Johnson City, Tennessee. She also serves on the boards of both Appalachian Sustainable Development and the Jubilee Project, and she is active in the homeless ministries of Munsey Memorial United Methodist Church.

W. Edward Stead is a professor of management at East Tennessee State University. He earned his BS in business administration and his MBA from Auburn University, and he earned his PhD in management from

Louisiana State University in Baton Rouge. Before coming to ETSU in 1982, he held faculty positions at Western Illinois University, Louisiana State University, and the University of Alabama at Birmingham. Ed has written extensively for more than a quarter of a century on business ethics, organizations and the natural environment, and social issues in management. His works are frequently cited, and the first edition of his book, *Management for a Small Planet* (with Jean Garner Stead), received a 1992 *Choice* Outstanding Academic Book award. In addition to his research, Ed was a founding member of the Organizations and the Natural Environment (ONE) Division of the Academy of Management, which he has served as program chair, chair-elect, and chair. He has also been an active member of the Social Issues in Management (SIM) Division of the Academy of Management. Ed has served as a strategic management, team-building, and community sustainability consultant to numerous business organizations, communities, and non-profit organizations throughout his long career, most recently with the Clinch River Chapter of the Nature Conservancy. He also serves on the boards of both Appalachian Sustainable Development and the Jubilee Project, and he is a member of the Creation Care Task Force of the Holston Conference of the United Methodist Church. In addition, Ed is a certified yoga instructor and active yoga practitioner and teacher.

DATE DUE